The Story of
Moody Bible Institute

MBI

The Story of Moody Bible Institute

Gene A. Getz

Revised and Updated by James M. Vincent

MOODY PRESS

CHICAGO

© 1969, 1986 by
THE MOODY BIBLE INSTITUTE
OF CHICAGO

Library of Congress Cataloging-in-Publication Data

Getz, Gene A.
    MBI, the story of Moody Bible Institute.

    Bibliography: p.
    1. Moody Bible Institute.   I. Vincent, James M.
II. Title.
BV4070.M76G4   1986   207'.77311   86-2422
ISBN 0-8024-8375-5

1 2 3 4 5 6 7 Printing/ RR /Year 90 89 88 87 86

Contents

Part 4 — LITERATURE MINISTRIES OF MOODY BIBLE INSTITUTE

Part 5 — PROCLAMATION THROUGH PREACHING AND ELECTRONIC MINISTRIES

Part 6 — PAST, PRESENT, AND FUTURE

Foreword

"I tell you what I want, and what I have on my heart. . . .Take men that have the gifts and train them for this work of reaching people. . . . I believe we have got to have gap-men—men to stand between the laity and the ministers.''

With these words Dwight Lyman Moody, addressing a gathering of like-minded men and women, laid the groundwork for what has become the Moody Bible Institute. The idea of a Bible institute was typical of Moody the innovator. He was a man of unique ability and vision, often ahead of his time. When he saw a need, he met it. If unable to find an appropriate method to accomplish his goal he would invent one. Many of his innovations have endured for more than a century.

Moody Bible Institute, following in the steps of its founder, has been on the cutting edge of evangelical Christianity. It has found a place of leadership that has been trusted and followed for decades. The principles and techniques developed at MBI have served as the model and base for others to build upon.

In my days as a student at Moody Bible Institute there existed no complete historical account of how the Institute began, nor of the influence it has exerted. The following twenty years produced popular accounts, but no comprehensive, scholarly chronicle. Fortunately, a young faculty member at the Institute chose as his doctoral dissertation "the study of the history of Moody Bible Institute and its contributions to evangelical education.'' Gene Getz discovered that to study the growth and development of MBI, one must also study the growth of secular movements. He recognized that various ministries of the Institute took shape parallel to or even prior to the development of the same concepts in the secular world. His work has provided an authoritative account of these innovative strides made in the name of Christ.

But an historical record, like a photograph, shows a picture of but one point in the annals of an organization. History does not stop with the recording of facts. During the past two decades since this work first appeared, twenty more years of history have been added to the Moody Bible Institute story. New endeavors have been undertaken, statistics have changed. It is therefore appropriate that, as part of our centennial celebration, we have undertaken to update this valuable resource.

Today there are more than 23,000 former students of the Moody Bible Institute serving the Lord in full-time Christian service. We are fulfilling the purpose for which we were founded, but our task still lies before us. Though its history has been updated, the Institute must not remain as portrayed in these pages. This work must serve as a launching pad from which we explore new and more effective means of "teaching the Word and reaching the world."

GEORGE SWEETING
President, Moody Bible Institute

Foreword to the First Edition

The Bible institute has a genius all its own. It is an undergraduate professional school. It trains for Christian service with a large emphasis on the practical so far as that training is concerned. By its very nature it attracts students who love the Lord, who want to serve Him and who have a seriousness of purpose. We do not mean that other types of Christian schools do not attract such students, only that by and large the very nature of the course and of the environment tends to bring students thus qualified. Moreover, since spiritual knowledge and life are the goals, the attempt has been made from the beginning to afford a climate in which this growth will be best accomplished. This is the reason emphasis is laid on testimony, on prayer, on hiding the Word of God in one's heart, on refraining from everything that dims one's spiritual sight, that diminishes one's ardor for holy things, or makes one ineffective as a witness for Christ.

In the latter part of the nineteenth century God moved men to provide such training—in the Word of God, in soul-winning, in missionary endeavor at home and abroad. In the Midwest it was D. L. Moody and his colleagues who responded first to the call. Moody, with great perceptiveness, was led of God to bring in Dr. Reuben Archer Torrey as the first superintendent of what was then called the Chicago Evangelization Society. So, under God, Dr. Torrey set the pattern that has been largely followed by Bible Institutes.

It is a story that needs larger telling than has been given it. References here and there in biographies of Moody and of Dr. James M. Gray, one of his successors, speak to the theme. Dr. S. A. Witmer of the Accrediting Association of Bible Colleges in his volume *Education with Dimension* speaks to the beginnings of Moody Bible Institute. Bernard R. DeRemer brought much material together in his worthy book *Moody Bible Institute, a Pictorial History*. Occasional articles in magazines supplement the available material. Some dissertations on the Bible institute-college movement as a whole have been written. But a comprehensive, firsthand study of Moody Bible Institute has not been available.

It is therefore a joy to write this prefatory word commending this volume, the first of its kind. Dealing largely with primary sources supplemented by hundreds of references elsewhere, plus personal interviews, the author has placed us in his debt. Dr. Gene Getz is a graduate of Moody. For thirteen years he taught at Moody, and for five of those years he also directed the Moody Evening School. He loves the Institute. He labored indefatigably to gather this material. It was submitted as partial requirement for the obtaining of his doctoral degree at New York University. I commend the work and the author.

WILLIAM CULBERTSON
President, Moody Bible Institute
(1947-1971)

Preface

Until you have had contact with one of the many ministries of Moody Bible Institute, it is easy to imagine a one-hundred-year-old school's being backward or old-fashioned. However, you have probably been affected by one of MBI's many ministries and know the innovative and progressive nature of the Institute. After all, its books, magazine, radio broadcasts, films, Bible conferences, and missionary alumni circle the nation and the globe.

This historical account attempts to paint crisp, genuine images of Moody Bible Institute. When the original edition appeared, MBI leaders lauded its accuracy and scope, while historians appreciated its scholarship. Dr. Getz had written the first comprehensive history of Moody Bible Institute. He had explored the trends and decisions that caused MBI to begin, expand, and thrive. This revised edition integrates the twenty years of development since the initial publication, and its release coincides with the school's centennial year.

The revised edition has been written especially for friends and alumni of the school. The book chronicles key events in the school's history and analyzes MBI's place in evangelical education. Readers will discover the successes, setbacks, and even confrontations of MBI leaders. Surprisingly D. L. Moody and Emma Dryer had their confrontations during the school's early years (see chapter 1). Their dispute is included to suggest the zeal and diversity of the school's leadership.

My deep thanks to Dr. Getz for his cooperation in producing the revised edition. His thorough work in the first edition has simplified my task; his keen scholarship will become evident to the reader. Writing twenty years of history is not as difficult as uncovering and reporting the first eighty, and that is what Dr. Getz accomplished in the first edition.

I am also grateful to many administrative leaders at MBI who granted extensive interviews, supplied important material, and reviewed portions of the manuscript. They include: Ray Tallman, Department of World Missions; Jay Fernlund, Department of Continuing Education; Robert Neff and Phoebe Millis, Division of Broadcasting; Howard Whaley, academic dean; Donald Hescott, executive vice-president; and George Sweeting, president.

Special thanks go to Kenneth Hanna, vice-president and dean of education, who provided free access to important records and reports by the educational branch. His personal encouragement and helpful suggestions have assured a thorough, accurate account of important academic changes during the past six years.

Finally my thanks to Ella Lindvall and Jill Wilson of Moody Press. Mrs. Lindvall, managing editor, believed I could handle this major project, and her confidence reassured me during the long summer days when monster statistics and details threatened to overwhelm. As trade editor, Jill Wilson provided focus to the project and practical suggestions.

As MBI celebrates one hundred years of service for Christ's kingdom, I consider the challenges and accomplishments of the school and agree with Getz's conclusion: "The success of MBI is due to the specific guidance and intervention by the sovereign . . . hand of God." The history demonstrates the results of man's plans and God's power joined together.

JAMES M. VINCENT

Acknowledgments to the First Edition

The author is deeply indebted to a number of individuals who have helped to make this volume a reality. Special appreciation is due Bernard DeRemer, who served faithfully as the Institute's historian prior to the time this historical study was begun. Without DeRemer's groundwork in gathering together and organizing the original sources that make up the Moodyana exhibit, the task of writing this comprehensive history would have been almost an impossibility.

The author is also indebted to the School of Education of New York University, where this treatise was begun and completed as a doctoral dissertation. Special appreciation is expressed to Dr. Norma Thompson, Dr. William P. Sears, and Dr. Roger P. Phelps who critically read the manuscript several times and made many valuable suggestions for improvement.

Special thanks is also due to many leaders in a number of departments at Moody Bible Institute who supplied much helpful information, both orally and in writing. A special word, however, is due those who reviewed the manuscript as it was being prepared for publication: Dr. William Culbertson, president of Moody Bible Institute; Robert Constable, executive vice-president; Dr. S. Maxwell Coder, vice-president and dean of education; and Will Mayfield, vice-president in charge of development.

Again, the author would like to express appreciation to President Culbertson, who not only read the manuscript and offered many helpful suggestions, but who also gave much personal encouragement during the six-year process of research and writing, and then graciously wrote the foreword.

The author would also like to gratefully acknowledge Dr. Wilbur M. Smith, who reviewed the manuscript, and offered many significant suggestions. . . . Dr. Smith's own personal interest in the history of Moody Bible Institute is reflected in his annotated bibliography of D. L. Moody and his biography of Will H. Houghton, former president of the Institute. In preparation for the sixtieth anniversary of Moody Bible Institute in 1946, Dr. Smith was also responsible for gathering many significant historical materials for display purposes. As Bernard DeRemer acknowledges in his book *Moody Bible Institute: A Pictorial History*, this groundwork was the beginning of the Moodyana exhibit.

A final word of appreciation is due three women who served in the Evening School office and who each had a share in typing various drafts of the manuscript: Mrs. Glenn Arnold, Mrs. Michael Matthews, and Miss Ruth Bringer.

GENE A. GETZ

Part 1

HISTORICAL PERSPECTIVES

1

How Moody Bible Institute Began

At age 17, Dwight Lyman Moody, restless and dissatisfied with farming and logging, left Northfield, Massachusetts, for Boston. Soon he became a storeboy doing odds and ends in his uncle's shoe store. Though he and his family were Unitarians, he began attending the Mount Vernon Congregational Church. A concerned Sunday school teacher came to the shoe store one day and talked to him about receiving Christ. Moody responded, and his conversion experience led him to immediately abandon Unitarianism for evangelical Christianity.

In September 1856, Moody went to Chicago where he soon became a successful businessman. His personal ambition was to become wealthy—he hoped to make $100,000 in his lifetime,[1] a princely sum in those days before inflation. He was well on his way to achieving that goal when, in 1860, he decided to give up his business plans and to devote his efforts entirely to Christian work.

Eventually D. L. Moody's evangelical fervor and straight-forward manner would make him one of the nineteenth century's outstanding evangelists and the driving force behind the oldest Bible institute in America—Moody Bible Institute.

Moody had been active as a Sunday school and mission worker almost from the time he arrived in Chicago. He had joined the Plymouth Congregational Church, "rented five pews and kept them filled with young men at every service. He also went out and hunted up boys and girls for the Sunday school."[2]

Next he started a mission school in an old shanty, formerly a saloon, on the north side of the Chicago River in a vice-ridden section called Little Hell. The growing school soon moved to a large hall over the North Market. Moody encouraged his converts to attend the church of their choice, but they in turn encouraged him to start his own. Consequently, the Illinois Street Church was built, and opened on February 28, 1864, with Moody as the pastor.

When the Chicago fire of 1871 destroyed that building, Moody rebuilt the church on the property now occupied by Houghton Hall, the women's dormitory of Moody Bible Institute. At first the church was called the North Side Tabernacle.

1. Arthur P. Fitt, *The Life of D. L. Moody*, p. 18.
2. John Wilbur Chapman, *The Life and Work of Dwight L. Moody*, p. 88, 91.

Eventually it was named the Chicago Avenue Church and, after Moody's death, it became the Moody Church, now located at LaSalle Street and North Avenue, approximately eight blocks north of the Institute.

Moody entered full-time religious work with the same zeal he displayed in business. He soon became a leading figure in the national Sunday school movement, and in 1865 he became president of the Chicago Young Men's Christian Association. After several visits to the British Isles in connection with his Sunday school and YMCA activities, Moody was invited to conduct evangelistic meetings in England. That was the beginning of a well-known, successful evangelistic career both in Great Britain and in America.

In the midst of his busy schedule in mass evangelism, Moody also became keenly interested in educational endeavors. As early as 1873 he took the preliminary steps that eventually resulted in the founding of Moody Bible Institute in Chicago. He served as the Institute's first president and held that position until his death from a heart ailment on December 22, 1899, at sixty-two. Since then, his school has became known around the world as the mother of the Bible institute movement, a movement that with the centennial celebration of Moody Bible Institute, is now one hundred years old.

Founding Date

The year that has come to be the accepted date of origin of the Moody Bible Institute is 1886. However, since the Institute came into being as a result of a process, the exact founding date has been challenged through the years.

The first reference to any beginning date seems to have appeared in a school calendar published in 1894. The date of origin is designated as September 26, 1889. This 1889 date continued to be used until 1905, at which time a published annual report stated that the Institute was "founded by D. L. Moody in 1886, under the name of the 'Chicago Evangelization Society.' "[3]

The confusion and discussion regarding what should be classified as the founding date continued. In a letter to A. F. Gaylord, the school's business manager, on August 21, 1929, employee A. G. Olson suggested that a special observance be held to celebrate the fortieth anniversary of the Institute, using the date of the "formal opening on September 26, 1889." The letter was passed on to James M. Gray, president of the Institute. Gray wrote back the following informal note:

> Mr. Gaylord:
>   I would not wish to reopen the old controversy as to the date of the founding of the Institute. We have always held it to be 1886, and although Mr. Olson is speaking of the date when it was "formally opened," yet it would be difficult to keep this distinction clear before the public.[4]

---

3. *Annual Report of the Moody Bible Institute for the Year Ending December, 1904*, p. 5.
4. Original letters in Moodyana files in the Moody Bible Institute library.

To understand more fully why this uncertainty resulted, it is necessary to trace the events prior to 1886 as well as those developments that took place during the several years following.

EVENTS LEADING TO THE FOUNDING OF MOODY BIBLE INSTITUTE

In order to reconstruct the events prior to 1886, we must rely heavily upon the testimony of two individuals who not only were eyewitnesses but also historical participants. Miss Emma Dryer played by far the most important part in those early days. Charles A. Blanchard also played an important, though secondary role, as he helped Miss Dryer while active in pulpit supply at the Chicago Avenue Church in 1883 and 1884.[5]

The story of Moody Bible Institute seems to have begun in the summer of 1870, when D. L. Moody first met Emma Dryer, a college graduate, who was principal and teacher of grammar and drawing at Illinois State Normal University. Though Moody had learned of Miss Dryer and had wished to meet her, he knew little about her. After meeting her through mutual friends, he became impressed with her educational background as well as her knowledge of the Bible.

One year later the great Chicago fire broke out. Miss Dryer had been visiting friends in Chicago on October 8, 1871; suddenly she found herself involved in various kinds of relief work. Of this experience she wrote:

> Churches, Sunday school, day schools, were scattered. The hungry were to be fed, the naked clothed, the sick cared for. I was accustomed to organize and conduct schools, and not all willing hearts and hands around me, could organize as quickly as I could do it. . . . I saw clearly, that I must remain for a time and learn much while teaching and helping others.[6]

Sensing the great need, Miss Dryer began three busy years of conducting mothers' meetings and children's industrial schools in Moody's Northside Tabernacle, which had been reconstructed at Ontario and Wells streets after the fire. Working alongside one another while helping the needy, Miss Dryer and D. L. Moody often talked about his special work in England, known as the Mildmay Institutions. The Mildmay Conference had been inaugurated in 1856 by the Reverend William Pennyfather, vicar of St. Jude's Mildmay Park at Bermet. Evangelistic and missionary enterprises thrived in a large conference hall. Closely connected with the conference hall was a deaconess house, where lady workers received training for home and foreign missionary work.

Moody was particularly interested in the training home for lady workers. He urged Miss Dryer not to return to the State University but to become active in this

---

5. Fortunately, both Miss Dryer and Blanchard, who served as second president of Wheaton College, Illinois, prepared two lengthy manuscripts in 1916 at the request of President James Gray, in which they describe their experiences and association with Moody in those early days. The original manuscripts are in the Moodyana files in the Moody Bible Institute library.
6. Unpublished manuscript written by Miss Emma Dryer (January 1916), p. 4.

type of religious work. He told her he was planning to go to England for ten months, but he was keenly interested in beginning something similar to the Mildmay work, even before he left. This he wanted Miss Dryer to do, and upon returning from England, he would build a home for the work and make it his primary concern.

Miss Dryer told Moody that she felt this proposed training school should be for young men as well as women. Moody, however, was hesitant to embark on this type of training program for fear of giving the impression he was trying to compete with seminaries. Eventually this problem resolved itself in his mind, but it was Miss Dryer who raised the idea of coeducational training at the Chicago school.

The ten months that Moody planned to be away from Chicago before he returned to promote this new work turned out to be more than ten years. His intentions were good, but his zeal for evangelistic work both at home and abroad dominated his schedule. Not until 1886 was he able to follow through on the plans he and Miss Dryer had talked about so enthusiastically in the winter of 1873.

Meanwhile, Miss Dryer worked hard to develop what she called the "Bible Work" in Chicago. Though absent most of the time, Moody kept in contact with her, encouraging her financially and providing personal motivation and enthusiasm.

The first Bible classes were conducted in the temporary Northside Tabernacle, later in the Relief and Aid Society building, and eventually in a room provided in the new YMCA building. The Bible work continued to expand and the staff of workers grew, being supported by a number of friends in Chicago. Among them were N. S. Bouton, Mrs. John V. Farwell, and the Cyrus McCormicks. Writing at that time Miss Dryer reported: "Our workers had their appointed districts, in which they held meetings, and visited from house to house, cooperating with near churches. Workers read their reports of daily work, weekly, in the Bible-Work Room, in the Y.M.C.A. building, 150 Madison Street, to which all contributors and friends of the work were invited."[7]

Moody remained pressed by his evangelistic efforts. Though unable to visit the Chicago work, Moody never lost his vision for the work, according to Miss Dryer. "It was still Mr. Moody's hope to fill Chicago with Christian workers, who should competently instruct, and who working from missions, and selected stations, by house to house visitation, distribution of the Bible, teaching in homes and missions, should do a continued work for Christ here, and also in foreign fields."[8]

In 1879 Emma Dryer's health broke, and Moody and other friends arranged for her to visit England to inspect the Mildmay work personally. She lived for many weeks in the deaconess house and testified later that this was a very educational experience. That opportunity, no doubt, spurred her on to develop the Chicago Bible Work to an even greater extent.

7. Dryer, p. 14.
8. Dryer, p. 19.

MAY INSTITUTES

In 1882 Miss Dryer met the Reverend W. G. Moorehead, then a professor at Xenia Theological Seminary in Ohio, and later president from 1899-1914. Impressed with his teaching ability, she considered him as a possible teacher for a "test" institute in May of 1883. Later she shared her idea with Charles A. Blanchard, who was serving as pastor of the Chicago Avenue Church. Blanchard liked the idea at once. When she told Blanchard the school would need $500 to begin, he replied, "Very well, you may calculate on having that amount of money and you may begin making your arrangements immediately."[9]

Moorehead agreed to come for this special institute and approximately fifty regular students enrolled. The following year enrollment increased another twenty-five. These special May Institutes, as they were called, continued each year until the year-round institute opened formally in 1889. However, other special events were occurring that soon would change the Bible work in Chicago into a larger, more permanent organization.

THE CHICAGO EVANGELIZATION SOCIETY

Sometime in January 1885, Moody consented to attend a special meeting in Farwell Hall to discuss city evangelization. T. W. Harvey presided, and two papers were read and discussed. Later, Moody addressed the group and laid the problem squarely on the line: if they wished to carry on their plans to start the Chicago training school, the first step must be to raise the money to finance the work.

Even though Moody showed great enthusiasm for the Chicago work, he wondered whether Chicago was really ready for such a school. The need was there—of this he was convinced. But were the people of Chicago ready to support such an endeavor? Before he left he confided to Miss Dryer that perhaps it should be started in New York.

Whatever Moody's feelings at this time, one thing was clear—he was not interested in starting the school without the full support and interest of the people in Chicago. According to Blanchard, Moody was candid in letting the people know that he himself would not spend time in Chicago raising money. His broader work was very demanding, and he felt it was up to someone else to raise the funds.[10]

Before departing, Moody left his characteristic challenge with Miss Dryer. "Keep it before them," he said, "that I won't come until they raise that $250,000." Evidently Miss Dryer did this. Moody's doubts about starting the school were soon dispelled as the needed money started to come in. Mrs. Nettie F. McCormick and her son, Cyrus H. McCormick, pledged a total of $50,000. John V. Farwell promised $100,000 in stock, and the long hoped for and prayed for training school was turning into a reality.

A year later Moody, again in Chicago, spoke at Farwell Hall on the subject of

9. Frances C. Blanchard, *Life of Charles Albert Blanchard,* pp. 85-86.
10. Unpublished manuscript of Charles A. Blanchard (February 1916), p. 12.

city evangelism. The next day, on January 23, 1886, a Chicago newspaper recounted Moody's address:

> I tell you what I want, and what I have on my heart. I would like to see $250,000 raised at once; $250,000 for Chicago is not anything. Some will be startled, but see how the money is pouring in upon you. See how the real estate has gone up, and how wealth is accumulating, and how you are gaining in population, and a quarter of a million is not much. Take $50,000 and put up a building that will house seventy-five or one hundred people, where they can eat or sleep. Take the $200,000 and invest it at 5 percent, and that gives you $10,000 a year just to run this work. Then take men that have the gifts and train them for this work of reaching the people.
>
> But you will say: "where are you going to find them?" I will tell you. God never had a work but what he had men to do it. I believe we have got to have gap-men—men to stand between the laity and the ministers; men who are trained to do city mission work. Every city mission in this country and Europe has been almost a failure. It is a fact. I have looked into it. I have been in all the great cities of Great Britain, and I have investigated this matter, and there is not a city mission started in these countries that is not almost a failure, because the men are not trained. If a man fails at anything else, put him in city mission work. We need the men that have the most character to go into the shops and meet these hardhearted infidels and skeptics. They have got to know the people and what we want is men who know that, and go right into the shop and talk to men.
>
> Never mind the Greek and Hebrew, give them plain English and good Scripture. It is the sword of the Lord that cuts deep. If you have men trained for that kind of work, there is no trouble about reaching the men who do not go into the churches.
>
> My idea is to have the people study mornings and have some ministers of different denominations give them a good Bible lecture and visit every family in their district and every night preach the simple Gospel.
>
> I do not want you to misunderstand me, but the ministers are educated away from these classes of people. Not that it is too much education, but it is their training that has been away from them. For instance a boy grows up to school. He is kept at school until he is ready to go to college, and then to college, and from college to the theological seminary, and the result is he comes out of a theological seminary knowing nothing about human nature, doesn't know how to rub up to these men and adapt himself to them, and then gets up a sermon on metaphysical subjects miles above these people. We don't get down to them at all; they move in another world. What we want is men trained for this class of people.[11]

In this address Moody's change of emphasis as compared with his conversation with Miss Dryer thirteen years earlier is striking. In 1873 he had been interested in establishing a school for training women workers. He feared that to train men would create problems and misunderstanding with seminary leaders. Now, in this

---

11. *Record of Christian Work,* V (February 1886), 5-6. See also *Chicago Tribune* (23 January 1886), p. 3; and *Chicago Inter-Ocean* (23 January 1886), p. 7.

Farwell Hall address, no mention is made of women. Time and again he refers to training men. Evidently Moody had developed a conviction that there was an urgent need to prepare a certain type of Christian worker who was not currently being trained. He called these workers "gap-men," so designated since they would be able to "stand between" the regular clergy and the lower classes in society.

On February 5, 1887, one year after the Farwell Hall meeting, Moody met with a group in his room at the Grand Pacific Hotel in Chicago. A constitution was presented and adopted.[12] A committee was appointed to secure a charter, which bears the date of February 12, 1887. This was the official beginning of the Chicago Evangelization Society. The original trustees, most of whom had been closely associated with the Bible Work, were Nathaniel S. Bouton, John V. Farwell, T. W. Harvey, Elbridge S. Keith, Cyrus H. McCormick, Jr., and Robert S. Scott. D. L. Moody served as president of the society.

INTERNAL PROBLEMS

Numerous problems developed in the life of the newly organized society, typical growing pains that often characterize a pioneer movement. Since there was no work of this nature anywhere that could serve as a pattern, Moody and his associates had to "feel their way" one step at a time.

Some inner tensions developed in those early years particularly between Moody and Miss Dryer. Those tensions eventually led her to resign from the work.

It is almost impossible to unravel the many factors that created these difficulties. Furthermore, as correspondence among various persons involved reveals, the problems became more complex when Moody and Miss Dryer could not understand the causes themselves. One thing does seen to be evident—the problems existed, not due to one cause, but several. A lack of communication probably was at the heart of the matter resulting in unusual misunderstanding.

Blanchard states:

> Mr. Moody was an inspirer, not an organizer of work. He was so great a man that he could not debate with fellow workers. He directed them, and persons who did not care to do what he wanted them to were not associated for any length of time with him or his work. This is not a criticism, it is a statement of fact, the truth of which all who knew Mr. Moody personally will recognize.[13]

The tension between Emma Dryer and D. L. Moody may have been caused by keen differences in their personalities and backgrounds. Miss Dryer was highly educated, an organizer, and meticulous regarding details. Moody was her opposite. When they eventually started working closely together within this infant organization, Miss Dryer became critical not only of Moody, but of other members of the board.

12. See Appendix A for a copy of the original constitution of the Chicago Evangelization Society (original in the Moodyana files).
13. Blanchard, unpublished manuscript, p. 4.

Sixteen full years of waiting to start the school and Miss Dryer's persistent health problems probably made misunderstandings between Miss Dryer and Moody unavoidable. The problems became even more pronounced by Moody's long absences in evangelistic work during the early days of the society.

In spite of these difficulties, the work continued. It was almost dissolved in July, 1887, when Moody, in a moment of haste, resigned. Having received a letter from Mrs. McCormick in which she expressed some discontent regarding the constitution of the Chicago Evangelization Society along with some suggestions for improvement, he immediately offered his resignation. Mrs. McCormick was aghast at his actions and immediately wrote and offered her own resignation in place of his. Moody immediately reconsidered.[14] He had misunderstood her intentions, and his quick decision probably reflects the tension that existed as a result of the general misunderstanding among the leaders of the evangelization society.

Moody's wife played an important part in convincing him he should change his mind regarding the resignation. On July 26 she wrote a lengthy note to Mrs. McCormick and explained that her husband had made his decision to resign because he believed it would be to the best interest of the group. James Findlay, in an article treating the origin of Moody Bible Institute, seems to capture Mrs. Moody's spirit during this time:

> Most illuminating was the role Moody's wife played in the crisis. Emma Moody was shy and retiring in the extreme, and few people knew the influence she exerted on her husband. Little record is left of the esteem Moody held for his wife's opinions and the deep affection that existed between them. In her own special way Emma Moody acted constantly as a counterbalance to her ebullient spouse. No better illustration is available to demonstrate how quietly yet effectively she aided her husband.[15]

During this trying period Miss Dryer decided to disassociate herself from the work. However, she never lost interest in the ministry of Moody Bible Institute. Shortly before she died in April, 1925, she still spoke of the "large and better work" that grew out of the Chicago Evangelization Society.[16] She continued to be a great admirer of D. L. Moody and often spoke of his many virtues and of her pleasant, rewarding association with him through the years. In her later writings Miss Dryer referred little to the problems that led to her withdrawal from the work of the Chicago Evangelization Society. It seems she gained a great amount of self-insight as well as understanding of the problem that caused her so much personal confusion and difficulty during the last decade of the nineteenth century.

To Miss Dryer goes much credit for the founding of Moody Bible Institute. For

---

14. Unpublished letter from N. F. McCormick to D. L. Moody (15 July 1887); unpublished letter from D. L. Moody to N. F. McCormick (18 July 1887); telegram from D. L. Moody to N. F. McCormick (27 July 1887).
15. Findlay, "D. L. Moody," p. 331.
16. Unpublished letter from Miss Dryer to Mrs. Waite (18 July 1924).

sixteen years she encouraged D. L. Moody to start a training school and supported that vision with her faithful leadership of the Chicago Bible Work. Through this effort she helped to lay the foundation on which the Chicago Evangelization Society and, later, the Moody Bible Institute was built. During those early years, Moody provided the encouragement and motivation, but Miss Dryer and her staff did the work. The original idea of the work was his, and his keen interest in the work and full support as he talked about it to others contributed much to its basic success. However, without Miss Dryer's educational know-how, organizational ability, and unfledging dedication to the work, it probably could not have survived.

Then, too, when Moody became overburdened with the demands on his time elsewhere and faced the great challenges for evangelistic work at every turn, it was Emma Dryer who helped to keep Chicago before him. She never let him forget the need for a school and his original hopes, aspirations, and plans. In her many visits with him at his Northfield home, as well as when he passed through Chicago, the possibility of a Chicago training school always seemed to be foremost in their conversation.

One of the most significant contributions Miss Dryer made to the founding of a permanent training school was the inauguration of the May Institute. Though conducted for a short period of time each year from 1883-1889, they comprised the first efforts to give concentrated and consecutive instruction. The year-round formal training program that was eventually initiated grew out of the last May Institute held in 1889.

FORMAL BIBLE INSTITUTE

During 1887 and 1888, the Chicago Evangelization Society emphasized evangelistic meetings in churches, missions, and tents. However, beginning in January, 1888, the society also held a three-month term for women, called the Bible Work Institute. The design of the institute was "to give thorough instruction in the Word of God, and a practical training in the various forms of Christian work."

Finally, beginning in April, 1889, the largest and most elaborate May Institute was held in the Chicago Avenue Church. The interest was so high, this "May" Institute began one month early and continued for sixty days. From San Francisco, Moody wrote leaders of the society to "push" the planned institute "for all it is worth." The planned institute was "pushed" as Moody had directed. One of the news releases printed in various newspapers read:

INAUGURATION OF THE TRAINING
OF THE
CHICAGO EVANGELIZATION SOCIETY

On the fourth day of April, 1889, I will begin holding in Chicago a Convention of Christian workers, similar to those held in the summers at Northfield.

These meetings will continue from 30 to 60 days, and instruction will be given by well-known leaders of Christian thought and action. As this is the beginning of a movement which it is hoped will culminate in a permanent school, to fit men and women for work among the neglected masses of Chicago and other cities, the instruction will from the first, take a practical turn. The mornings will be devoted to study of, and lectures upon the Bible and its application to the wants of this age; and to these meetings the public will be invited.

The afternoons and evenings will be given to "Applied Christianity," and no pains will be spared to bring the workers face to face with the masses who have renounced or are ignorant of the gospel.

The only expenses which those who attend will be called upon to meet, will be those of board and lodgings.

All Ministers, S. S. Workers, city Missionaries, Students and others who are engaged in Christian work or are preparing for it, and are interested in this Conference are invited. . . .

D. L. MOODY,
In behalf of Board of Managers[17]

While Moody was still in San Francisco, he was interviewed by the press shortly before he left for Chicago. This interview, quoted at length, contains many significant statements by Moody himself, especially about the proposed permanent training school:

Question: What do you aim to accomplish through a Bible Institute?

Answer: To raise up a class of men and women who will help pastors in their work: who will visit from house to house and reach the non-church goers. In other words, we must have a class of men and women between the laity and ministry to do the work that must be done.

Question: Will not such an organization antagonize theological seminaries?

Answer: I think it will help the seminaries. Many who go into the work will see the need of more training and study, and after a year or two will go into some theological seminary and take the regular course.

Question: What do you intend to teach at Chicago?

Answer: The great fundamental doctrines of the Bible, such as repentance, regeneration of the Holy Spirit, atonement, conversion, justification, redemption, faith and assurance, law and grace, sanctification and consecration, resurrection. Of course a great deal of the instruction will be in methods of practical work, as "How to interest non-church goers," etc. Such matters will be discussed at many of the sessions.

Question: Do you intend to work independent of the churches?

Answer: No sir; but in full sympathy with all evangelical churches.

Question: What class of men and women do you want?

Answer: I want consecrated men and women from all classes, graduates of ladies' seminaries, and it would be a good thing for theological students to take a year or two in this way before becoming pastors of churches.

Question: How will you select from those who apply?

17. *Pen and Scissors* (2 March 1889).

Answer: I expect to open a training class in Chicago during April and May. The sessions will be open to all, and I expect that trial in the work will develop those who are fitted for it. I don't know any better way to find out who have gifts.

Question: Will your society be undenominational?

Answer: Yes; all my work has been and will be undenominational. . . .

Question: What will be the length of the course?

Answer: The first course will be for two months.

Question: What will be the cost?

Answer: Instruction will be free; the workers will board and lodge themselves.

Question: Do you know any scheme like this in the country?

Answer: I do not, nor in any other country, but I think it is the crying need of our churches today. Three-fourths of the workingmen in all our large cities are entirely neglected, and we must train men and women to reach them.

Question: What will you say to those who appear on trial, who have no gifts for the work?

Answer: Advise them to take some other calling. Sixty days' experience will test their fitness.

Question: Do you intend to fit workers for the foreign field?

Answer: Any field on earth that God calls to. I think the training will be good for foreign work. Persons who cannot lead souls to Christ in America, can't do it in Africa or China.

Question: Why not start such an enterprise right here in San Francisco?

Answer: I think Chicago is more central and less expensive to reach. San Francisco is too far to one side.

Question: Will you take persons of any nationality?

Answer: Yes; any one who can understand the English language.

Question: Can you find work for laborers thus fitted?

Answer: Yes; I could put a thousand in the field today. There are hundreds of Christians out of employment today who could do grand service. Many can't take a full student's course in college and seminary, to whom this will be a short cut to the fields of usefulness. I want to raise up workers to help the pulpit. Many ministers have too much to do. They can't visit the non-church goers. Our churches want such assistance. I want to get hold of a large number of consecrated men and women who are willing to give all to God. There are many persons of wealth in this country, as in Great Britain, who could and would give their time and money to such work if they once had the joy of winning souls to Christ.

Question: What will be the order of exercise in this preparation of workers?

Answer: The mornings will be for drill in the Bible, where I find my system of doctrine, also for reports of the previous day's work. The afternoons will be spent in visits from house to house. In the evenings meetings will be held in cottages, halls and churches—small meetings in order to get nearer the people than in large mass meetings. Such work as is done in the McAll Mission in Paris will thus be carried on.

Question: Who will assist you in training these workers?

Answer: I shall take charge of the work during April myself, and shall have a few teachers from abroad, besides the Chicago ministers.

When Moody arrived in Chicago, he discovered many more people in attendance than he had anticipated. When the sessions were finally ended on May 10, 1889, there was a great interest on the part of almost everyone. A. W. Williams described the scene:

> All hindrances seemed to vanish before the rising tide of Christian enthusiasm and a large property contiguous to the church, lying diagonally back of it, fronting on what is now Institute place, was bought and a fine building, costing $50,000, was at once begun. It was a three-story building, one hundred by one hundred and seventy-five feet in dimensions, in the form of a hollow square, thus affording abundance of light and air in the heart of a closely built-up section. Three dwellings just north of the church and adjoining, on LaSalle Avenue, were bought as the home of the Women's Department. Having spent $20,000 in completely furnishing these various buildings, the "Chicago Bible Institute" was formally opened with a week's conference, beginning September 26, 1889.[18]

In view of the manner in which many schools trace their history, at least five dates might serve as a point of origin for Moody Bible Institute (see figure 1, p. 204). For example, 1873 could be cited. This was the year D. L. Moody first encouraged Miss Dryer to start training classes. Another possible date could be ten years later, in 1883, when the first May Institute was held. Third, as currently done, 1886 could serve as a date of origin when D. L. Moody delivered his famous Farwell Hall address, although it should be noted that he also spoke in Farwell Hall in 1885. Fourth, 1887 might be more accurate since the Chicago Evangelization Society was not officially organized until February of that year. If a formal constitution were the criterion for determining a founding date of a school, this would be the date of origin.

Finally, 1889 could serve as a founding date, particularly if a year-round curriculum were the criterion for date of establishment. However, as previously mentioned, Dr. Gray stated in the year 1929, "I would not wish to reopen the old controversy as to the date of the founding of the Institute. We have always held it to be 1886." In view of the complexity of the problem, perhaps that is the date that should remain.

18. A. W. Williams, *Life and Work of Dwight L. Moody*, p. 282.

2

Why MBI Became So Influential

Most religious schools in America have come into being as a result of a period of planning and development, but few carried out the process for nearly two decades. When Moody Bible Institute finally opened for business on a full-time basis, it did so as a result of nearly twenty years of planning. It is no doubt true that this prolonged period, though disappointing to many people, became a decided asset when the school was eventually established. The school soon developed into a strong and penetrating force within evangelicalism. Several factors in those early days seem to stand out as reasons Moody Bible Institute became so influential.

STRATEGIC LOCATION

Perhaps a basic factor in explaining the unusual success and influence of Moody's school, particularly in its early days, was its location. By 1886, Chicago was rapidly becoming one of the most important cities in the world. According to B. L. Pierce, in her monumental *History of Chicago,* "the years 1871 to 1893 were the most crowded and dynamic the city had known." In spite of the great fire that destroyed large sections of the city, "untouched was her strategic location with reference to lake, river and canal, thus assuring the city a continuing leadership in the waterborne commerce of the middle west."

By October, 1872, only a year after the fire, and a year before D. L. Moody and Miss Dryer first conversed about a Chicago training school, a new city had risen. Within ten years, the population rose to 503,000 and by 1890 it had passed the million mark to make Chicago the second largest city of this continent. This growth of nearly 268 percent in twenty years, even in an era characterized by urban expansion, was phenomenal.

During this period, Chicago was also rapidly becoming a great industrial center. By 1890 she became the second manufacturing point of the country, and had already become known the world around for her business transactions in grain, lumber, meat-packing, merchandising, banking, investments, and finances.

It was in this great city that Moody Bible Institute had its birth, and there is no doubt about the school's nationwide influence, particularly in causing other, similar schools to come into being.

Contributing to the Institute's rising influence was the World's Fair, held in Chicago in 1893, just four years after the permanent school was opened. Moody conducted one of his most successful evangelistic campaigns at the fair and thus communicated with thousands of people from all over the world. The Bible Institute became his base of operation. This great international event became a potent means for publicizing the unique ministry of Moody's new school.

URGENT AND PRACTICAL OBJECTIVE

The first Bible school in America, The Missionary Training College founded by A. B. Simpson, focused on the needs of the foreign mission field, although Simpson did not exclude from his thinking the importance of meeting needs in the homeland. Though Simpson, like Moody, was thinking of "gap-men," he was thinking of preparing individuals who would not need a full theological and technical course in order to be effective foreign missionaries.

Moody, on the other hand, was very much concerned about urban Americans and the need for evangelism in the large and growing cities. He envisioned a school that would prepare a variety of Christian workers who could perform all types of Christian services not then being carried out by the regularly ordained clergy.

To many Christian people in urban America, Moody was setting forth an urgent and practical objective—one based on a need of which they were very much aware and about which they were deeply concerned. James Findlay, in reconstructing the social and economic conditions that existed in growing Chicago, in the late nineteenth century, gives the following significant information:

> For a long time tension had been developing between working class groups and the native American managerial segments of the city's population. The general hard times of the late seventies had caused intense distress and strikes among the laboring classes of the city, as it had through the nation. Chicago's large immigrant population also included a nucleus of men nurtured on anarchism and Marxian dialectics then spreading over Europe. They provided the seed bed for the growth of a strong radical movement among Chicago's lower classes in the eighties.
>
> After a brief economic upturn between 1881 and 1884 Chicago followed the rest of the country into a new tailspin. As wages fell and unemployment rose, strikes again became common in 1884 and 1885, centering at the Pullman Palace Car Company and at Cyrus McCormick's harvester works. A renewed interest in the eight-hour day, first advocated vigorously in the 1860's, also stirred labor circles in the city. In early 1886 tension again developed between management and the workers at the McCormick plant. The conflict there smoldered until early May when discontent eventually culminated in open violence and the horror of the Haymarket riot.[1]

1. James Findlay, "D. L. Moody" (unpublished Doctoral dissertation), pp. 257-58.

In view of these conditions in Chicago as well as other large cities, it is obvious that urban evangelization would take on added significance to Moody. "Either these people are to be evangelized," said Moody in March, 1886, "or the leaven of communism and infidelity will assume such enormous proportions that it will break out in a reign of terror such as this country has never known."[2]

Evangelical leaders seemingly sat up and took notice when Moody spoke in these terms, and the new Bible Institute in Chicago soon became what many Christian leaders felt was needed in other large cities in America.

WELL-KNOWN FOUNDER

D. L. Moody was no stranger to the people of Chicago when he launched his campaign for city evangelization in 1885-1886. But Moody was not only well known in Chicago—he had become a popular figure throughout America, as well as in Great Britain. His numerous and successful evangelistic campaigns, which were conducted for nearly two decades prior to the founding of the Chicago school, made him a well-known personality. In addition, his Northfield Conferences, which began in 1880, as well as his two Northfield schools, which were founded even earlier, had contributed to his popularity.

It must be remembered too that Moody's ideas and ventures, though new and revolutionary, did not have a history of failure. He was known as a man who was both innovative and successful in implementing his ideas. Consequently, when he proposed his school, there was no lack of interest in this endeavor. "If D. L. Moody proposed it, and is pushing it, it must be worthwhile or at least worth watching." This no doubt represented the feeling of most of those who knew his work.

It should also be noted that Moody lived more than a decade after the Institute began. During that period, he traveled widely in evangelistic work. Wherever he went he promoted his school, as evidenced by the degree of financial support he was able to obtain. He alone carried the main burden for all of the institutions that he founded.

A CIRCLE OF IMPORTANT FRIENDS

Perhaps as important as Moody himself in helping to establish the reputation of the Chicago school were his many friends, not only in Chicago but throughout the nation and on both sides of the Atlantic. Significantly, several of Chicago's most outstanding businessmen became associated with the Chicago Bible Work. As early as 1873, N. S. Bouton, who became superintendent of public works in 1857, served as the first treasurer and auditor. By 1877, T. W. Harvey, one of the greatest retail lumber dealers in the world, was serving as president of the board.[3] Working with him were Mrs. Cyrus H. McCormick, wife of C. H. McCormick,

---

2. Ibid., p. 258.
3. Bernard R. DeRemer, *Moody Bible Institute: A Pictorial History*, p. 18.

the famous inventor of the reaper; E. S. Keith, one of the organizers and president of the Metropolitan National Bank; and other well-known individuals.

When Moody organized the Chicago Evangelization Society in 1886-1887, the six members of the board were well known both in Chicago and overseas for their great business enterprises and financial wisdom. This was particularly true of Farwell, Harvey, McCormick, and Scott.

The keen interest shown by these men in Moody's new idea for reaching the lower classes of the city with the gospel is not surprising. Many poor laborers, often dissatisfied and frustrated with their jobs, created labor unrest for these industrial leaders trying to oversee their plants, factories, and other business enterprises. These Chicago leaders, all thoroughly evangelical in their religious convictions, believed that the Christian message would be able to change and transform lives. They no doubt hoped that this new venture would not only serve as a vital spiritual investment, but that it would also solve some of the social problems that were so prevalent in the tense and mushrooming city.

But it was not only the corps of Christian businessmen that helped make Moody's school a success. From its inception, he brought some of the most eminent evangelical Bible expositors and Christian leaders from all over the world to teach in his new school. In addition to his regular staff, which included such well-known persons as R. A. Torrey and D. B. Towner, the following evangelicals had by 1900 already served as guest lecturers at the Institute: A. J. Gordon of Boston, W. G. Moorehead of Xenia, F. B. Meyer of London, John Smith of Edinburgh, R. W. Mowell of London, C. I. Scofield of Dallas, James M. Gray of Boston, Andrew Murray of South Africa, and G. Campbell Morgan of London.

These men became outstanding "publicity agents" as they left the premises of the Institute and traveled back to their native states and countries. A number of testimonies are on record by these visiting lecturers. F. B. Meyer, after a series of lectures, wrote:

> I cannot conclude my lectures at the Institute without expressing my profound thankfulness at all that I have seen. My knowledge of the work goes back almost to its inception, and it is delightful to find the same spirit, devotion and admirable training as of old. Mr. Moody still seems to be the inspiring and leading force of the whole institution; and, after a considerable experience, I do not hesitate to say that there is nothing better than the training of the human material which pours into your lecture-rooms, for the great work of evangelization and Christian service.[4]

INTERDENOMINATIONAL VENTURE

A very important factor in helping to explain the rapid growth and influence of the Institute in its early days was the increased denominational cooperation that was becoming more apparent toward the end of the nineteenth century. Interdeno-

---

4. *The Moody Bible Institute of Chicago Bulletin* (January 1915), p. 9.

minational activity related to the Moody school in at least three areas: Sunday school work, missionary endeavor, and the churches themselves.

The Sunday school convention era was at a peak period of activity in 1886. The Institute maintained good relationships with those responsible for these conventions, led by Moody himself, who was actively engaged in convention work. Furthermore, the International Sunday School Lesson soon became a regular part of the Institute's curriculum.

The second major area of denominational cooperation benefiting the school was missionary activity. Cairns points out the "cooperation among missionaries in foreign lands preceded the rise of the ecumenical movement at home and stimulated the expansion of that movement in the homeland." In fact, Moody's Mount Hermon Conference in 1886, where a hundred college young people decided to go to the mission field, led to the formation of the Student Volunteer Movement, "which became a great recruiting agency for missions" and contributed to interdenominational and nondenominational activity.[5]

Cooperative effort on the mission field provided a wide open door for students from the school to enter this type of service. Since the Institute was interdenominational, it attracted students from all denominations and, in turn, supplied workers to serve with many different evangelical groups.

A third important area in which interdenominational activity contributed to the success of Moody Bible Institute was church cooperation at large. Prior to 1865, the Protestant churches of the United States "seemed to be bent more on schism and disintegration than on cooperation and reunion or integration." However, after the trials and tensions created by the Civil War subsided, "a trend toward interdenominational cooperation and later organic reunion and confederation became evident about 1880."[6] The later development of liberalism contributed to this movement, as well as the impetus and previous cooperation already created by other interdenominational and nondenominational organizations that were already in existence, such as the American Bible Society, the American Tract Society, the American Sunday School Union, the Sunday school convention movement, the YMCA, Christian Endeavor and the Student Volunteer Movement.

Moody students found many opportunities of service within all of these organizations and movements. But in addition, the Institute was soon pressured by leaders of various denominations to inaugurate a pastoral training program to meet needs the theological seminaries were not meeting. This was probably one of the surest signs of the increasing acceptance of the Institute's program and students by the churches at large.

All of these factors blend together to show that the Institute, as an interdenominational venture, was very much in tune with trends on the larger scene in America. This alignment no doubt contributed to the immediate growth and influence of Moody Bible Institute in becoming a leader in the evangelical world.

5. Earle E. Cairns, *Christianity in the United States*, p. 168.
6. Ibid.

IMMEDIATE GROWTH AND OUTREACH

The old cliché "Nothing succeeds like success" probably points to another important factor. As is shown in the following chapters, success was immediate in terms of fulfilling Moody's objectives.

A key factor in attaining these objectives was what is considered basic to success in every school—good student interest. As early as 1883, when the first May Institute was held, student interest was high, as indicated by an enrollment of fifty students the first year and seventy-five the second. When the permanent school was opened in 1889, again there was no dearth of students. Within three years the school added two more stories to the three-floor building, providing dormitory facilities for nearly two hundred men.

By the end of 1900, a total of 3,413 students had already attended the school, and many had become active in all types of Christian work and were literally serving all over the world. No one thing promotes a school like an enthusiastic former student. A recent alumni survey indicates most who have studied at MBI are enthusiastic about their training; most students, 93.5 percent, would recommend an MBI education to a person who wanted to prepare for a Christian ministry.[7]

IMPETUS FROM THE THEOLOGICAL CLIMATE

The American theological war, known as the fundamental-liberal controversy, had not yet become an open issue when Moody first proposed his training school. Although a number of ministers scattered throughout the land were introducing modern thinking to their congregations, not many professors were openly teaching liberal theology in the seminary classrooms.[8]

But that was soon to change, and by the turn of the century Moody Bible Institute had already become widely known as a school that dared to teach the Bible as the authoritative Word of God.

Moody did not live to observe the budding theological debate. In his later years he had become increasingly aware of conflicting viewpoints among religious leaders, but he seemingly never fully realized the significance of those trends and how they were to affect his institutions.

Some who have lightly studied the life and ministry of Moody have concluded that he himself had liberal leanings in his later years, and have interpreted the liberal spirit that now exists at Northfield as the true spirit of the founder. There is no historical evidence to confirm that conclusion. All of Moody's sermons in print, as well as the literature written about his life and work by those who knew him, confirm the fact that he was thoroughly orthodox to his dying day. He never changed his thinking to accommodate theological liberalism.[9]

---

7. Kenneth Bosma, *Moody Bible Institute Alumni Survey 1984*, p. 4.
8. Henry Kalloch Rowe, *The History of Religion in the United States*, p. 191.
9. For an extensive defense of D. L. Moody's conservative position, see a letter to the editor, written by R. A. Torrey in *Moody Monthly* (October 1923), pp. 51-52.

It does seem to be true, however, that Moody did not seriously face the problem. He was not a scholar and never claimed to be. He was an evangelist, and his busy schedule in preaching the gospel and promoting his institutions seemingly did not allow time for a realistic appraisal of the new thinking that was becoming so prevalent just as he passed from the scene in 1899.

Shortly after the founder's death, the Institute became a focal point in this religious debate. R. A. Torrey, superintendent of the Institute since 1889, had been educated at Yale and Leipzig in historical criticism of the Bible and ordained a Congregational minister. Though his faith was greatly challenged, he eventually became convinced that theological conservatism was the correct approach to biblical interpretation and Christianity. After Moody's death, he became a strong spokesman for Moody Bible Institute and evangelical conservatives in defending the absolute authority of the Bible and other evangelical doctrines.

James M. Gray, who came to the Institute on a permanent basis after Moody died, soon became the dean and later the president. For the next thirty years he guided MBI through the fundamental-liberal storm and brought her through with what appeared to be a stronger evangelical position than she held when the threatening winds began to blow some thirty-five years earlier. Gray never hesitated to speak out in defense of the Institute's fundamental position in biblical things. The Institute's publications during this period of leadership are replete with his writings, which invariably reflect his concern for maintaining a historic theological position.

There is no question that MBI contributed greatly to evangelicalism during these strategic years. Writing in 1923, Hart said, "In my judgment, the constituency that has gone out from the Moody Bible Institute during the last ten years has saved the evangelical churches of the country."[10]

INNOVATION

As shown in following chapters, Moody Bible Institute early became known for its pioneering spirit in inaugurating the new and different. Innovations in curriculum, programs, and methods, not only in the religious world but also in the educational world generally, all served to make the Institute known throughout the world.

Furthermore, Institute leaders did not hesitate to adopt the new and different from the secular world in order to fulfill its purposes. For example, though the Institute was not the first religious organization to use radio, only several years after radio appeared, MBI was already broadcasting over its own station.

The film medium also became a dynamic tool at Moody in direct correlation with the rapid development and use of the educational film in the secular field. In more recent years particularly, the films produced at Moody Institute of Science have made Moody Bible Institute known on all levels—in government circles, in the military, in colleges and schools, and within business organizations.

10. Rollin Lynde Hart, "The War in the Churches," *The World Book* (September 1923), p. 472.

DIVINE GUIDANCE AND INTERVENTION

Historical research has shown that many human factors contributed to MBI's growth into a large and dynamic organization whose influence reaches around the world. But behind, within, and throughout this unusual story has been a force and influence unknown perhaps to the secular onlooker, but very much sensed and felt by Institute leaders. The human factors themselves point to specific guidance and intervention by the sovereign and divine hand of God.

To the evangelical Christian this is not strange language. Admittedly, it incorporates a dimension not recognized by researchers whose presuppositions preclude supernatural intervention in the course of history. But to biblical theists who ''seek to find the glory of God in the historic process,''[11] the origin, development, and outreach of an institution such as Moody Bible Institute cannot be divorced from the concept set forth so forcibly by Augustine. In his historic masterpiece *The City of God*, Augustine declared that man is helpless apart from the grace of God. That helping grace surely has contributed to the success of Moody Bible Institute.

---

11. Earle E. Cairns, *Christianity Through the Centuries*, p. xvi.

3

Before MBI

The modern, soaring skyline that surrounds Moody Bible Institute today may deceive campus visitors. The world's tallest building, the Sears Tower, stares down from the Chicago Loop one mile south. Several blocks east, the John Hancock rises skyward. Next to those great structures, the smaller brick complex called Moody Bible Institute can appear less significant. Five major buildings, the tallest standing nineteen stories, cluster around a central plaza, seeming to form a citadel on this city block.

The impression of a citadel is not out of place when one considers the heritage of the school. Holding firmly to a conservative Protestant theology, Moody Bible Institute has become well-known as a training institution for the preparation of evangelical ministers, missionaries, church musicians, and Christian educational leaders. It has made extraordinary contributions to evangelical education, set the pattern for many other schools that prepare Christian leaders, and developed a worldwide educational outreach by means of literature, traveling Bible teachers, radio, and films. Through the years, the school has repelled attacks by modernist theologians and withstood attempts to move it from the city to the suburbs.

But this formidable institution did not arise in lonely isolation. MBI began because of a need that D. L. Moody and his friends were determined to meet. And before MBI was founded, that need was great.

Initially, schools of higher education in America had been founded to train men for the ministry, and the first schools were evangelical in nature.[1] Two main trends, however, changed this academic situation drastically. First, as public education became prominent, people began to express general dissatisfaction with church-oriented higher education, and secularization grew.[2] Second, as religious liberalism began to penetrate theological thinking near the close of the nineteenth century, many schools that had maintained evangelical purposes in spite of in-

---

1. At the close of the colonial period nine colleges existed, all with strong denominational ties: Harvard, William and Mary, Yale, Princeton, Academy and College, King's College, Brown, Rutgers, and Dartmouth (Ellwood P. Cubberley, *The History of Education*, pp. 702-3).
2. Newton Edwards and Herman G. Richey, *The School in the American Social Order*, pp. 250-51.

creasing secularization shifted from evangelicalism to liberalism.[3] Consequently, conservative Protestants soon discovered that few thoroughly evangelical schools of higher learning still existed to train pastors and other types of Christian workers.

Although the fundamental-liberal controversy had not yet become an open issue when D. L. Moody founded his school, this religious development was destined to have a profound effect on the place Moody Bible Institute was to occupy during and following this theological storm. As many schools of higher education became liberal, the Institute's evangelical influence became more prominent.

Perhaps only a dozen evangelical liberal arts colleges existed when Moody Bible Institute was founded. Although approximately sixty to seventy Protestant seminaries were in operation, these schools were preparing young men primarily for pastoral work. Many needs for other types of full-time Christian vocations were becoming apparent, and even the supply of seminary graduates was falling far short of the number of men needed to fill pulpits throughout the land.

Even as secularism in higher education increased during the nineteenth century, a counterforce began to emerge in America, particularly beginning with the last quarter of the century. Great religious revivals created a new motivation among evangelicals. As the number of individual Christians increased, so did new churches. Soon doors began to open for Christian service in pastorates, in Sunday school work, in evangelistic endeavor, and on home and foreign mission fields. It became clear that colleges and seminaries could not fill these vocational positions with trained leadership. The number of such schools was limited, and their objectives and curricula were not comprehensive enough to meet the variety of needs that had appeared on the religious scene. Bible institutes became the solution.

THE FIRST BIBLE SCHOOLS

Although the Bible institute-college movement is distinctly American in origin and development, several schools in Europe seem to have been forerunners of the movement. The pietistic influences during the nineteenth century caused several European groups to organize missions to carry the gospel to foreign lands. Consequently, these missions organized training schools, similar to Bible institutes, to prepare workers for this foreign service.[4] A well-known school was the Gossmer Mission founded by Johannes Gossmer in 1842.

Another important European school that antedated the American movement was the East London Institute for Home and Foreign Missions. Founded in 1872 by H. Grattan Guinness, this school along with several others would "inspire Dr. A. B. Simpson to urge the establishment of similar schools in America."[5] Schools of this nature, however, did not grow and expand in Europe and "today there are few Bible schools of any size in England or on the continent."[6]

3. James DeForest Murch, *Cooperation Without Compromise*, p. 13.
4. Charles B. Eavey, *History of Christian Education* pp. 337-38.
5. S. A. Witmer, *The Bible College Story: Education with Dimension*, p. 33.
6. Eavey, p. 338.

The first two Bible schools in America, still in existence, were Nyack College, located in Nyack, New York, and the Moody Bible Institute. Nyack College, first known as the Missionary Training College and later the Nyack Missionary College, was founded by Albert B. Simpson in 1882. Moody Bible Institute as a full-fledged school was founded several years later, although its roots can be traced as far back as 1873.

Even though Nyack College was the first significant Bible institute founded in America, D. L. Moody's Chicago school "was destined to become the largest" and "the most renowned."[7] McBirnie calls the Institute "The mother of most Bible institutes."[8] The editors of one religious periodical have switched the metaphor calling MBI the "Father of the Bible Institute movement in America."[9]

Whichever metaphor is used, the Institute soon became a model for similar schools. Shortly after Moody's death, other cities had sent representatives to Chicago to study the curriculum and operation of the Institute, and "institutions on precisely similar lines sprung up in various parts of the land."[10]

LOCAL CHURCH EDUCATION

Before Moody Bible Institute began, evangelical education within the local church was limited primarily to Sunday schools and youth meetings. No vacation Bible schools, clubs, Christian day schools, or camps existed.

D. L. Moody was particularly interested in the Illinois conventions of the American Sunday School Union. On the eve of its fifth annual convention, he remarked: "This thing so far has been a dead failure; we must do something to give it power." He and about a dozen others began at prayer meeting. Brown remarked, "Within a day or two the whole city was moved. When the delegates went back to their homes they carried a spirit of the meeting over all the state."[11]

Moody's new training school was to contribute significantly to Sunday school work, not only in terms of personnel but in curriculum materials and leadership training. All of these developments as well as numerous other influences were no doubt far beyond D. L. Moody's original aspirations.

YOUNG MEN'S CHRISTIAN ASSOCIATION

The Young Men's Christian Association had its beginning on June 6, 1884, when a group of twelve young men met together in London, England, for Christian fellowship. Other young men's groups that had already been started in various parts of the world eventually merged with this group and formed the national

7. Witmer, p. 35. "The lay college" of T. DeWitt Talmage may have been the first U.S. Bible institute in 1872. But it was discontinued a few years later when Talmage closed his Presbyterian Tabernacle in Brooklyn, New York.
8. William S. McBirnie, Jr., "A Study of the Bible Institute Movement" (unpublished doctoral dissertation), p. 19.
9. Editorial, *Our Hope* (March 1953), p. 520.
10. William R. Moody, *The Life of Dwight L. Moody*, p. 345.
11. Arlo A. Brown, *A History of Religious Education in Recent Times*, pp. 58-59.

Young Men's Christian Assocation. The association had its beginning in America in 1851 in Montreal and Boston.

The Chicago association was formed in 1858, two years after Moody came to Chicago. The original institution demanded the "evangelical test" for all voting members. Thus "any male member of good standing in any evangelical church, which holds the doctrine of justification by faith in Christ alone"[12] could join.

Moody became very active in the Chicago association and, in 1865, was elected president, a position he held for four years. "In 1879, at the International convention held in Baltimore, Mr. Moody was enthusiastically elected president of this larger body."[13] However, he declined this office because he felt he could not give himself both to evangelistic work and the national leadership of the YMCA.

Toward the end of the nineteenth century, the YMCA, though evangelical in its early days, was beginning to feel the impact of liberal theology. Though originally engaged in evangelical education, the Young Men's Christian Association was beginning to move away from this theological position by the time Moody Bible Institute was founded. The YMCA began to emphasize a social gospel and stressed social services and recreational facilities for the community. Moody eventually disassociated himself from the work.

MASS EVANGELISTIC EFFORTS

Mass evangelism also influenced evangelical education prior to the founding of Moody Bible Institute. During her first three hundred years, America has been aroused by four distinct "awakenings." McLoughlin says of these four periods: "Each of them has been national in scope and each of them has lasted about a generation. Roughly speaking the first of these extended from 1725 to 1750; the second from 1795 to 1835; the third from 1875 to 1915, and the fourth from 1945 to, perhaps, 1970."[14]

During the first period, George Whitefield was the primary figure as he preached an "evangelical Calvinism." The outstanding person in the second interval was Charles G. Finney, who advanced the "pietistic ideals of evangelical Protestantism." The third period involved two men—D. L. Moody and Billy Sunday. Concerning Moody's influence, McLoughlin states that his "revivals in the 1870s were the opening and half-unconscious battle of the modernist-fundamentalist schism. Theistic evolution, progressive orthodoxy, the 'new theology,' and the higher criticism were significant elements in the same reorientation." [15]

The fourth period, of course, is now underway, led by outstanding evangelists like Billy Graham.

Moody Bible Institute had its origin during the third period (1875-1915). D. L. Moody, active in this period of American revivalism until his death in 1899, took

12. James Findlay, "D. L. Moody" (unpublished doctoral dissertation), p. 36.
13. Moody, p. 127.
14. William Gerald McLoughlin, *Modern Revivalism*, p. 8.
15. Ibid., p. 10.

sufficient time to become active in educational endeavors, but with the primary purpose of multiplying his own efforts through training others to carry on the work of evangelism.

FOREIGN MISSIONS

Moody Bible Institute was organized during the period classified as "modern missions," which began with the work of William Carey in India. When the Institute was founded, evangelical missionaries had already entered nearly a hundred countries of the world, and a short time later the world Protestant missionary staff totaled approximately nine thousand.[16] However, Moody's new school was destined to make a profound impact upon foreign missions (see chapter 11).

EVANGELICAL LITERATURE

Several agencies were actively printing and distributing literature when Moody Bible Institute came into being. The American Sunday School Union had published and circulated volumes of literature, particularly for children. The Religious Tract Society, founded in London in 1799, and the American Tract Society, organized in 1825, were distributing in increasing numbers evangelical books, tracts, and periodicals in numerous languages and dialects. The various Bible societies that have specialized in printing and distributing copies of the Scriptures since the early 1800s also participated in this unique educational outreach.

Thus Moody Bible Institute was founded at a time when general Protestant activity was evangelical in nature. However, this new school was organized on the eve of what was to become a period of severe theological conflict and crisis — a time when numerous educational agencies were to be profoundly influenced by religious liberalism. Yet the school leaders remained convinced of the truth of evangelical doctrine and set out to influence the Protestant world.

16. James S. Dennis, *Foreign Missions After a Century*, p. 35.

4

The General Objective of MBI

Just as the founding of MBI encompassed almost two decades (1870-1889), similarly the establishing of objectives for this new training school required time. Like most educational institutions, MBI began with the original idea of its founder but continued to refine its objectives after its formal opening.

A direct statement of a general objective was not published in the official literature of Moody Bible Institute until 1911. However, certain specific objectives were listed prior to that time and are included here.

Originally Moody wanted to establish a home in Chicago to train women workers. He drew inspiration for this idea from the deaconess home in England, which was part of the Mildmay Institutions and which had as its basic objective the preparation of women for home and foreign missionary work.

However, the Chicago Bible Work began in spring 1873 as a general missionary ministry among the needy people of Chicago. The program emphasized immediate service and outreach, rather than training, although the latter was not excluded. The first annual report on March 1, 1874, indicated that Emma Dryer had conducted a daily morning school for children who could not attend the public school, and a sewing school on Saturday. The Bible was taught in both. In addition, she maintained a daily Bible reading ministry from house to house, particularly in visiting the sick, and she also conducted special mothers' meetings and cottage prayer meetings.

The first published statement of the objective of the Bible work appeared in the 1875 annual report:

> The ultimate object of this Bible Work is to make known salvation through Christ by reading the Bible to individuals in their homes and in small meetings collected for the study of the Scriptures. That this may be done, those engaged in the work meet regularly to study the Word, with reference to the best way of presenting it, and to pray for those persons in whose salvation and Christian growth they have become interested.[1]

1. Annual report of the Chicago Bible Work (1875).

When Miss Dryer inaugurated the May Institutes in 1883 as a part of the Chicago Bible Work, she planned for these to be "trial sessions," with the definite objective of training people to serve as evangelists, pastoral helpers, missionaries, and other types of religious workers. It was her hope that these sessions would be successful, thus encouraging Moody to enlarge the work as originally planned.[2]

According to annual reports of the Bible Work, the May Institute each year was "a training class in systematic Bible study for Christian workers—for both young men and women."[3] Late in November, 1885, a special brochure was published by the Bible Work and included the following aim: "to reach the poor and neglected of this city, and to train Missionaries for Home and Foreign Fields." Thus to the original objective of service and outreach the May Institute added an emphasis on equipping workers through a program of special training, at least on a periodic basis.

D. L. MOODY'S OBJECTIVE IN 1884

When Moody spoke at Farwell Hall in 1886 proposing a permanent training school, he clearly articulated his objective. He wished to establish an institute that would train what he termed "gap-men"—men who could "stand between the laity and the ministers." He was particularly burdened for people in Chicago and other cities who were in the lower strata of society. He wished to see men trained to reach these people with Christian teaching. He was not interested in teaching them Greek and Hebrew in order to prepare scholars; rather, he wanted men trained in the English Bible so they could in turn communicate the Scriptures to people who never came to a church—people who, if they did attend a church, were not being reached because ministers were not able to "get down to them at all."

Moody's Farwell Hall address brought about the Chicago Evangelization Society. The society's original constitution, adopted on February 5, 1887, stated: "The object of the 'Chicago Evangelization Society' shall be to educate, direct, and maintain Christian workers as Bible readers, teachers and evangelists; who shall teach the Gospel in Chicago and its suburbs, especially in neglected fields."[4]

This objective involved more than training and educating workers. This new society was first "to educate," but second "to direct and maintain Christian workers." Moody and his coworkers were interested not only in a training institution, but also in a home mission organization to serve as a sponsoring agency for the workers who would be trained in the Bible Work Institute sponsored by the society.

The first Bible Work Institute was planned and conducted for women by Miss Dryer the first three months of 1888. According to one brochure, the aim of this institute was "to give thorough instruction in the Word of God, and a practical training in various forms of Christian work."

2. Frances C. Blanchard, *Life of Charles Albert Blanchard*, pp. 85-86.
3. Annual report of the Chicago Bible Work (1885-1886).
4. See Appendix A for copy of Constitution.

From 1887-1888 the Chicago Evangelization Society concentrated on missionary activity through tent campaigns and other evangelistic meetings. Unforeseen problems prevented a regular training program from operating at full capacity. It was not until 1889 that training became a regular and permanent part of the program, and "home missionary work" was incorporated as a part of the curriculum through a student practical Christian work program.

MOODY'S OBJECTIVE IN 1889

The program Moody had asked for in the Farwell Hall meeting was finally ready to be launched with a two-month test institute in 1889. The evangelist spelled out the school's goals starting before the institute opened. The school was designed to "raise up a class of men and women who will help pastors in their work; who will visit from house to house and reach the non-church goers. In other words, we must have a class of men and women between the laity and the ministry to do the work that must be done."

Since his earliest conversation (1873) with Miss Dryer about a training school, Moody had been crystallizing his objectives. Instead of a school just for women, he was thinking of a coeducational institution: rather than a school to train home and foreign missionaries, he was thinking primarily of preparing a special type of home missionary who would serve in the large cities reaching the working classes. Though preparation for foreign missionary work was not ruled out of his objective in 1889, Moody's primary concern was America and its urban needs.

MEN'S DEPARTMENT

One of the earliest published brochures describing the course of study in the new Bible Institute appeared in 1889. The following objective appeared:

> There is a great and increasing demand for men skilled in the knowledge and use of the Word of God, and familiar with the aggressive methods of work, to act as pastors' assistants, city missionaries, general missionaries, Sunday school missionaries, evangelists, and in various other fields of Christian labor, at home and abroad. All over the land are men who could, with a little directed study, become most efficient workers in these fields. There are also many men called of God into Christian work at too late a period of life to take a regular college and seminary course, but who would, with such an opportunity of study as our Institute affords, be qualified for great usefulness. There is a third class: men who do not intend to devote their entire time to Gospel work, but who desire a larger acquaintance with the Bible and methods of Christian effort, that while pursuing their secular callings they may also work, intelligently and successfully, in winning men to Christ. The object of our Institute is to meet the needs of these several classes.

A later brochure contained the same information listed under "object" in the 1889 brochure, but also included an additional class of men who were being trained at the Institute: "Many ministers and theological students, who have enjoyed the advantages of the regular training, have spent their vacations with us, getting a better knowledge of the English Bible and how to use it in personal work, and a larger experience in aggressive methods of Christian work.''

By 1892-1893, the ''classes'' of men being trained at the Bible Institute had increased from four to six. In addition to those already mentioned, the following classes were added:

> Graduates of colleges or theological seminaries who wish to supplement the valuable education received at these schools by a thorough study of the English Bible and methods of aggressive Christian work.
>
> Men who wish to fit themselves to meet rapidly increasing demands for teachers of the English Bible in colleges, schools, conventions, Young People's Societies of Christian Endeavor, etc.

By 1893-1894, still another class of men was added under the section entitled ''object'' to bring the total to seven: ''men who expect to enter the pastorate in fields where a knowledge of the Word of God and a knowledge of men is regarded as more important than a thorough scholastic training.''

WOMEN'S DEPARTMENT

A separate four-page brochure also appeared in 1889 to describe the Women's Department, including its objective:

> The object of the Ladies' Department of the Bible Institute is preeminently Bible Study. Its aim is to give Christian women of devoted piety such thorough and ready knowledge of the Word of God as shall render them skillful and effective laborers for Christ in home and foreign fields as missionaries, or in the more quiet circles of home and church life to which in the providence of God, they may be called.

MUSIC DEPARTMENT

Shortly after the formal opening of the school, the term Musical Department was used in the official literature of the school. This is easily understood in view of Moody's statement to the press shortly after the dedication of the men's building in 1890, which, in a sense, outlined his philosophy of education. ''What studies will students pursue in the new school?'' a reporter asked. Moody replied,

> Mainly three. First I shall aim to have given a sufficient knowledge of the English Bible; so far as may be, a practical mastery of it. Second, I would have workers trained in everything that will give them access practically to the souls of the people, especially the neglected classes. Third, I would give a great prominence to the study of music, both vocal and instrumental. I believe that music is one of the most powerful agents for good or for evil.[5]

5. Bernard R. DeRemer, *Moody Bible Institute: A Pictorial History*, p. 30.

A promotional piece printed by early 1891 suggests the role Moody envisioned for music in evangelism. This release indicated that the aim of the Musical Department was "to train pupils who have musical ability to become singers, leaders or organists who can assist Evangelists and Pastors, and do work on the mission fields, both at home and abroad."

Objectives from 1895-1911

In 1895 the first formal catalog appeared. By then the program of the Institute was built around three courses: the Biblical Course, the Musical Course, and the Practical Work Course. Specific objectives for each of these courses are treated in later chapters. Under the section in the 1895 catalog termed "object," the first statement appeared regarding the *general* purpose of the school:

> The object of the school, stated in general terms, is to train men and women in the knowledge and practical use of the English Bible.
>
> The study of music is made a prominent feature, so that men and women may be prepared to lead choirs and teach music. Every encouragement is given to develop talent along this line.
>
> It is not the aim of the Institute to do the work of theological seminaries or conservatories of music, but rather to aid and supplement these.
>
> Great emphasis is laid upon a development and deepening of the spiritual life of the student. If any student should go forth from the school without a more intimate acquaintance with Jesus Christ, and more of the power of the Holy Spirit in his life and work, the Institute would have failed in his case at the most important point.

The same seven "classes" of men mentioned previously in the smaller brochures were also included in the first catalog. In addition, however, a section was given to describe the Women's Department.

> There is an increasing number of earnest Christian women who desire to become successful workers for their Lord and Master. They desire to know how to win souls for His glory, and how to be used by the Holy Spirit. They are conscious of a need of larger knowledge of the Word which shall secure their own growth in divine life! They are also in earnest to know how to use the Word so as to be a blessing to others.
>
> The Bible Institute affords the opportunity for such study of the Bible as shall meet these needs, and also for entering into all forms of practical work.
>
> The aggressive methods of work now taken up by many churches are creating a demand for skillful and effective workers, and for much of this service woman is naturally well fitted. This department of the Bible Institute will be especially helpful to all who may enter such fields of usefulness. House visitation, cottage meetings, children's meetings, women's meetings, and industrial schools, are carried on in variety, according to the tact and skill of workers and leaders. Also, opportunities are afforded of service in tent meetings, inquiry meetings and mission meetings.

Those looking forward to foreign and home missionary work may here receive much that is valuable by way of test of one's ability and suggestions of methods of work.

Few changes were made in the objectives of the school from 1895-1900. Those made at the turn of the century related primarily to the Women's Department. Women were now coming to the school with a variety of objectives. The Women's Department was especially intended:

1. For those who feel called of God to enter some definite form of Christian work, and who desire not only a thorough knowledge of the Bible, but also training in all forms of missionary effort. Such students after completing the course are enabled to fill the positions of pastor's assistants, home missionaries, Young Women's Christian Association secretaries, city missionary and deaconess work, rescue work, Bible class work, etc.

2. For those who are looking forward to foreign missionary work and who desire thorough equipment in knowledge of the Bible, methods of teaching it and wisdom in leading souls to Christ.

3. For missionaries home on furlough who welcome the opportunity to pursue further Bible study, and to examine methods of work before returning to their fields of labor.

4. For those whose home duties are such that they cannot leave them for any length of time, but who long for better knowledge of the Word of God and how to do personal work in order that they may be more useful in their own home, churches and community.

5. For Christian women of leisure who feel that they have no definite call to Christian work, but who desire further opportunities for systematic and thorough Bible study. There are an increasing number of such residents in the Women's Department.

In 1906 the concept of two separate departments for men and women was abandoned, and the objectives for men and women being trained at the Institute were combined into one section.

THE GENERAL OBJECTIVE SINCE 1911

The wording of the general objective in 1895 remained essentially the same until 1911. In the catalog of that year it was condensed into a single sentence and used until 1916: "The object of the school, stated in general terms, is to train men and women in the knowledge of the English Bible, Gospel Music, personal evangelism and practical methods of Christian work, emphasis being laid upon the developing and deepening of the spiritual life."

Beginning in 1916 the leadership of the Institute began quoting from the articles of incorporation to describe the school's general objective. The objective was "to educate, direct, encourage, maintain, and send forth Christian workers, Bible readers, gospel singers, teachers and evangelists competent to effectually teach and preach the gospel of Jesus Christ."

This objective was a revised statement of the original purpose of the Chicago Evangelization Society. The new statement added the terms "encourage" and "send forth."

This new statement is significant, for it reflects in a formal way what had already taken place at the Institute. From 1886-1889 the primary emphasis of the society was "missionary and evangelistic work" in Chicago with periodic "training institutes" to equip workers. From 1889 to the present the primary emphasis has been the "Bible Institute training program," and the "missionary and evangelistic work" in Chicago has been incorporated as a part of the curriculum to eventually prepare workers for a greater and wider ministry. Chicago has served not only as a mission field, but also as a "field work" program for students in training. The constitutional change in 1900 merely reflected formally what transpired almost immediately in 1889 with the formal opening of the Bible Institute for Home and Foreign Missions of the Chicago Evangelization Society.

The statement from the revised constitution was included in every annual catalog from 1916 until 1946. At that time the general format of the catalog was changed, and along with this innovation came a new and condensed objective: "Neither a college nor a seminary, but a school for intensive Bible study and practical experience in soul winning—that is Moody Bible Institute." Though a more general statement, it still reflected the same emphasis, that of Bible training and practical experience.

This condensed statement was used until 1961, when MBI officials returned to the objective stated in the articles of incorporation. However, this time a revised form was used as found in Article II of the bylaws. The purpose of Moody Bible Institute was stated as "the education and training of Christian workers, teachers, ministers, missionaries, and musicians who may competently and effectually proclaim the gospel of Jesus Christ."[6]

This general objective is a segment of the statement that appeared in the bylaws by the board of trustees in 1939. At this time the radio ministry had again merged with the Moody Bible Institute. The complete objective is as follows:

> The establishment of this corporation is for the purpose of conducting and maintaining a Bible Institute for the education and training of Christian workers, teachers, ministers, missionaries and musicians who may competently and effectually proclaim the Gospel of Jesus Christ: the operation and maintenance, without profit, of a radio broadcasting station to stimulate men and women to Christian service through the preaching and teaching of the Gospel of Jesus Christ as set forth in the Bible by spoken messages, song and instrumental music; and the maintenance of such facilities as may be properly used in the publication, distribution and sale of Christian Evangelical literature, any profit from which shall be used in promoting the general objects of the corporation; to acquire and retain for said purposes, real estate, money and personal property, and to do any and all things necessary or reasonable to carry out said corporate purposes.

6. School Catalog (1961-1962), p. 12.

The first part of this enlarged objective is included in the current catalog. More clearly than any other, this statement sets forth what the Institute had actually been doing almost from the time of its formal opening in 1889. The terms "directing" and "maintaining" were dropped, and appropriately so, since they were carried over from the original objective of the Chicago Evangelization Society, which served as a "home mission board" as well as a "training organization."

EDUCATIONAL OBJECTIVES AND PHILOSOPHY

In 1960, the school began a careful self-study and reexamination program as part of an evaluation by the Accrediting Association of Bible Colleges. The goal of the MBI Self-study Committee "was to set forth the avowed objectives of the Institute and to make an honest appraisal of these objectives in the light of all available factual data."

The subsequent 121-page report led to a statement of objectives in 1962. A three-fold objective resulted:

> The purpose of Moody Bible Institute is (1) to develop in students those qualities of mind and character which make for effective Christian living and service; (2) to prepare students to enter Christian service at home or abroad, primarily in church vocations, and also as Christian witnesses in other occupations; (3) to offer professional training on an undergraduate level to enable the student to make a contribution in one or more of the following areas: Bible teaching, work, pastoral ministry, evangelism, Christian education, or sacred music.

Since 1974, MBI has stipulated a series of ten intellectual objectives in its annual catalog. These educational goals include:

1. General knowledge of the theological teaching of the Bible with awareness of the history of doctrines and problems which have arisen.
2. Knowledge of and skill in the use of the tools of exegesis and application of the Bible.
3. Knowledge of the nature, mission, and ministry of the church, including its history and organization, and standards governing its unity and purity.
4. Awareness of God's calling and of one's natural and supernaturally-bestowed abilities.
5. Understanding God's plan and method of world evangelization and the Christian's place in this.

In addition, the school embraces a specific educational philosophy based on "the conviction that the Bible in its original manuscripts is the verbally inspired, inerrant, and authoritative Word of God."

The Bible, therefore, is the central integrating factor of the total curriculum. All truth ultimately is related to and unified by the revealed Word.

THE OBJECTIVE: PAST AND PRESENT

Having traced the development of the general objective, we conclude that Moody's idea in 1886 to prepare leaders who could "stand between the laity and the ministers" as a special type of urban home missionary soon expanded to include other types of Christian workers. The very first official publications of the school had already spelled out in more detail what type of workers these "gap-men" were to be: pastors' assistants, city missionaries, general missionaries, Sunday school missionaries, evangelists, singers, song leaders, organists, and Young Men's Christian Association secretaries.

Workers were being prepared to carry on tasks that were much broader in scope than Moody had probably envisioned. In addition, ministers and missionaries came to the Institute for refresher courses, and graduates of seminaries and colleges came to receive more Bible training before engaging in their chosen vocations. This Moody had anticipated, as indicated in his San Francisco interview, but perhaps not in so great a measure.

This does not mean that Moody's Farwell Hall objective was not being carried out; however, that objective was being enlarged. A. W. Williams describes the work of former students:

> Nearly two hundred are now engaged in city rescue and home mission work. Many are engaged in gospel work as evangelists or singers. Two hundred more have gone on with their studies and now are either pastors or pastor's assistants; 117 have gone out as foreign missionaries to Japan and China, India and Africa, and the islands of the sea; while others are to be found engaged in every kind of Christian work along educational and philanthropic or distinctively religious lines.[7]

The original objective of the school was primarily to prepare leaders who would give their full time to religious work. In all that planning from 1873 on, Moody and Emma Dryer were thinking of this type of training school. When Moody made his ideas known in 1886 and began to "push" to start the work on a permanent basis, he definitely focused on preparing full-time Christian workers. "I could put a thousand in the field today," he said in his San Francisco interview. "There are hundreds of Christians out of employment today who could do grand service."

On the other hand, Moody did not plan to limit his school to this type of student. When asked if persons coming to the school would "have to bind themselves to continue in special Christian work," he answered: "Christian wives and mothers and fathers are just as important as any other workers." This concept was carried out in practice. The very first official publication of 1889 indicated the school's intent in training men who desired to have a greater acquaintance with the Bible and methods of Christian work, "that while pursuing their secular callings" they could "also work intelligently and successfully in winning men to Christ."

7. A. W. Williams, *Life and Work of Dwight L. Moody,* p. 298-99.

Today Moody Bible Institute still trains people, both for full-time Christian service and also for volunteer work as lay men and women. As in early days, the Day School still prepares the majority of students for full-time religious ministries but does not exclude the other category of students. On the other hand, the adult education programs of both the Evening and Correspondence Schools are geared primarily to persons who are interested in volunteer Christian service. It should be noted, however, that both these schools also attract some who are preparing for full-time Christian service or who are already in the ministry but want refresher courses.

5

The Leadership and Organization of MBI

The present structure of Moody Bible Institute results from a process that began in the 1880s. It's six main leaders, D. L. Moody, R. A. Torrey, James M. Gray, Will H. Houghton, William Culbertson, and George Sweeting, have all made distinct contributions to this development.

The organizational structure has never been static. As the work expanded, it was revised; as new areas were added, they were integrated into the whole. By 1946 MBI had grown to the point that additions and integration were not as easily accomplished as before. It was time for a complete reevaluation and reorganization.

The Institute was not slow in purchasing property to keep up with its expanding work. By the time James M. Gray took over the leadership of the Institute in 1904, the plant consisted of about eight buildings. When Will Houghton became president in 1934, the number of buildings had expanded to nearly forty. Today, however, a number of these smaller buildings have been demolished, and in their place stand major structures.

Financially, too, the Institute has grown. Beginning with the $250,000 requested by D. L. Moody from Chicago leaders, it has grown into a multimillion-dollar operation. As a nonprofit corporation, all funds are used to fulfill its purposes to train young people for Christian service and to communicate the Christian gospel and its moral and ethical principles by means of radio, literature, films, and traveling Bible teachers.

The Chicago Bible Work, the forerunner of what is now Moody Bible Institute, had no formal organizational pattern when it was founded in 1873. D. L. Moody inaugurated the work, and it was implemented and carried on by Emma Dryer. N. S. Bouton, who was superintendent of public works in Chicago, served as the first treasurer and auditor.

By 1877 the work had become more organized. According to a special report that appeared that year, the Chicago Bible Work was governed by an official board of trustees. T. W. Harvey was president; Miss Emma Dryer, superintendent; Mrs. Cyrus H. McCormick and Mrs. D. L. Moody, vice-president; E. G. Keith, secretary; J. S. Helmer, treasurer; E. S. Albro, auditor.

By 1886, the year in which definite preliminary steps were taken toward the establishment of the Chicago Evangelization Society (CES), the board of trustees of the Chicago Bible Work had increased from seven to eleven. In addition to those mentioned above, with the exception of Helmer, it included D. L. Moody himself, N. S. Bouton, J. V. Farwell, Major D. W. Whittle, and H. J. Wiling. Evidently no constitution or bylaws existed to govern the Chicago Bible Work. Furthermore, CES was not organized formally as a corporation in the State of Illinois, although that would have been a distinct possibility since the Act Concerning Corporation was approved in the State of Illinois and put in force in 1872.

THE CHICAGO EVANGELIZATION SOCIETY (1887)

The Chicago Evangelization Society began February 13, 1887, when the state of Illinois certified the organization.[1] (The CES had adopted its constitution on February 5, 1887.) According to the original constitution[2] this new organization seemingly was planned to function as illustrated in figure 2 (see p. 205). Any person who was "in sympathy with the 'object' of this organization" and who contributed "annually to its support" could "become a member of the Society." The organization was governed by a board of trustees consisting of seven men: Bouton, Farwell, Keith, Moody, Turlington Harvey, Cyrus H. McCormick, and Robert Scott.

In order to administer the affairs of the society more effectively, the board of trustees could appoint a general manager to serve as a promotional and fund-raising person. In addition they could create a "Board of Managers" consisting of nine persons, who in turn would be entrusted with the actual work of the society.

This second board could also appoint special committees to carry out various phases of the work, as well as appoint a faculty to "plan and supervise the daily work, direct the studies, recitations and united meetings of the workers, and their general duties in the society and in their respective fields."[3] The special school for training these workers was to be called "the Bible-Work Institute."

The Chicago Bible Work was to be made an organic part of the new society at once, but due to disagreements about the constitution and the actual function of the work, this was not accomplished until March 12, 1888, when the trustees approved a revised constitution.

But problems still were not solved internally, and shortly after the Bible Work became a part of the CES, it again separated, and eventually was dissolved. Nevertheless, the work went forward, with primary emphasis on evangelistic ministry although several Bible work institutes were also conducted.

THE BIBLE INSTITUTE FOR HOME AND FOREIGN MISSIONS (1889)

The Bible Institute for Home and Foreign Missions of the Chicago Evangeliza-

---

1. Certificate of Incorporation (see Appendix A).
2. Original Constitution of the Chicago Evangelization Society (see Appendix A).
3. Original Constitution, Article III, entitled "Trustees and Managers." The term "faculty" here is used in the sense of an administrative group, not as a teaching staff.

tion Society, founded September 26, 1889, shifted the primary emphasis from field work to training. Figure 3 (see p. 205) visualizes the organizational and administrative function of the full-time institute.[4] The same board of trustees was responsible for the school, and Moody, who had been president of the society, now became the first president of the new school.

R. A. Torrey, who had received his B.A. from Yale College and his B.D. from the Yale Seminary, served as the fist superintendent of the Institute. Earlier, while still a young student at Yale, Torrey had been influenced by Moody's life and ministry. Now, as a well-educated man, he came to give direction to the new school that Moody had founded.[5]

Torrey began his work on September 26, 1889, the day the Institute formally opened. Since Moody was often away in evangelistic work, the new superintendent was given the responsibility for developing the original curriculum and the program for practical Christian work. He was also charged with the supervision of the Men's Department, and served as the school's permanent Bible teacher, although many guest lecturers taught at the Institute in those early days.

Sarah B. Capron, a former missionary, became superintendent of women in the new school and Gertrude Hulburt was appointed principal of the Women's Department. H. H. McGranahan directed the first Department of Music, and George Sanborn served as the first business manager in promoting the activities of the school.

The work of the school had expanded considerably by 1895, particularly in curriculum development. In essence the administrative system remained the same. The "course" plan was introduced, so that students could specialize in a particular area of of interest. In December, 1893, D. B. Towner became superintendent of the Musical Course, replacing McGranahan. R. A. Torrey became director of the Biblical Course, while continuing as general superintendent. W. W. White served as the associate director of the Biblical Course. Torrey continued supervising the practical work program, now called the practical Work Course. A. F. Gaylord became the business manager (see figure 4, p. 206).

AFTER MOODY'S DEATH

D. L. Moody died on December 22, 1899. Three months later the board of trustees voted to change the name of the school to The Moody Bible Institute of Chicago. During their eventful meeting, the trustees also voted to enlarge the general objective of the school.

The newly-named Institute faced two major problems following Moody's death. Without its founder and major promoter, the school was missing a definite leader. Second, the school did not have a great number of friends to support MBI financially and regularly.

---

4. The organizational charts in figures 2 through 4 have been constructed from information contained in annual catalogs as well as from constitutions and bylaws. They were carefully evaluated in a group meeting of H. E. Stockburger, Robert L. Constable, and Rollin Sherwood in the summer of 1965. The 1985 organizational chart was prepared by Fred Rudy, vice-president.
5. DeRemer, p. 16.

One of the men who "stood in the gap" was A. P. Fitt, Moody's son-in-law, to whom the founder had committed Moody Bible Institute. Fitt, who had served on the board in 1894-1895, agreed to return as trustee after Moody's death and to serve as full-time secretary. Although he did some teaching, he spent most of his time caring for executive and administrative details.

Fitt served well as a connecting link between the Institute and the Northfield Schools, and as a liaison between the new school and D. L. Moody's interests and friends all over the world. He served the Institute in this position until he resigned in 1908 to go into business.[6]

The most influential individual in helping the infant organization to become a strong and thriving institution was Henry Parsons Crowell. Elected to the board of trustees on April 24, 1901, Crowell became president of the board on April 24, 1904, and continued in this position for over forty years.

In the business world, Crowell directed three large enterprises: the Quaker Oats Company, the Perfection Stove Company, and the Wyoming Hereford Ranch. In the religious world, he is credited by his biographer as being the "guiding light" for the Moody Bible Institute. At his funeral, Will Houghton, then president of the Institute, substantiated this statement when he said, "Without wishing to take anything from the records of past Institute leaders, in all honesty the admission must be made that this man has been more responsible than any other for the success of the Moody Bible Institute from early times to this hour."[7]

In those difficult days at the turn of the century, Crowell was responsible for three significant steps that helped the Institute to move out of its crisis. The first was Crowell's influence on James M. Gray. He encouraged Gray to become dean of the Institute.

Gray, who had served as rector of the First Reformed Episcopal Church in Boston, as well as lecturer in English Bible at the Reformed Episcopal Theological Seminary in Philadelphia, was not primarily interested in administrative work. A tentative plan to have three deans direct the program of the growing Institute had been abandoned, and Gray felt he could not handle the top position alone. But because of the constant encouragement from Crowell, he accepted the position of dean of the Institute in 1904 and became a strong and successful leader for the next thirty years.[8] Although Moody's enthusiasm and R. A. Torrey's administrative and teaching abilities set the Moody Bible Institute in motion, James M. Gray probably did more than any other man to guide MBI through its most crucial years.

Enlisting Gray as dean, then, was the first significant thing that Crowell did for MBI. Without Gray's leadership, the Institute could have moved in one of two directions—either toward fanaticism with an emphasis on "healing" and "emotional demonstrations" or toward theological liberalism, as happened in the Northfield schools.

Second, Crowell established an "executive committee" to handle the affairs of

6. William M. Runyan, *Dr. Gray at Moody Bible Institute*, p. 136.

7. Richard Ellsworth Day, *Breakfast Table Autocrat*, p. 306.

8. Day, *Breakfast Table Autocrat*, p. 167.

the Institute between regular meetings of the board of trustees. This arrangement has proved to be both functional and successful. Originally the committee was composed of three members of the board who met each week at the Institute to consider matters brought before it by the executive secretary and to establish policies for that official to carry out.

Third, Crowell provided strong financial leadership while MBI developed a corps of reliable friends. Though he contributed great sums of money to the work (he supplied at least half of the money to build Crowell Hall, the eleven-story administrative building), he never allowed the Institute to become dependent upon him. The personal honesty and Christian ethics of H. P. Crowell are still reflected in the financial operations of Moody Bible Institute.

Today the school is financially dependent upon the thousands of donors who contribute regularly to the work. This is, to a great extent, the result of the wise and business-like guidance given to the Institute by Crowell himself.

Organization Expansion

By 1907 the organizational structure of Moody Bible Institute had changed significantly. In October 1905, the board of trustees had voted to extend the management of the Institute to a board of fifteen trustees from the existing seven. The executive committee functioned to handle business matters and decisions between regular board meetings. A. P. Fitt continued to serve as executive secretary, A. F. Gaylor as business manager, and James M. Gray as dean. In addition, the two separate departments for men and women were discontinued.

MBI had added a Correspondence Department in 1901 and an Evening Department in 1903. The extension work of the Institute, begun in 1897, officially became a department in 1906. In 1907 A. F. Gaylord, the business manager, was responsible for both the correspondence and extension ministries. The number of instructors in Bible and music totaled twelve at that time.

By 1917 the business staff had become a single group of departments under the direction of Gaylord, while the Education Department was considered a separate area of work and the heart of MBI's ministry.

In 1925, James Gray became president of Moody Bible Institute. Up to that time, this term was reserved for the president of the board of trustees, and the term "dean" was used for the top administrative position. Hereafter, this position was to be known as "president." and the "dean" was to be "dean of the education department," including both the day and evening schools.

Several new courses had been inaugurated in the educational area by this time, including the Swedish-English Course (1916), the Pastors Course (1922), and the Jewish Missions Course (1923). The former Sunday School Course had been expanded and was called the Christian Education Course. By 1928 the teaching staff, both full and part-time, totaled forty-nine.

COMPLETE REORGANIZATION (1946)

The most sweeping organizational changes took place in 1946. With the rapid development and expansion came a need for rethinking the total structure of the Institute's program. For example, the business manager, who had served as a liaison between the functional departments and the top administrative position and the board of trustees, eventually bore too much supervisory responsibility and power for effective administrative action. By 1944, the business manager supervised nine large areas.

The Institute had grown into a large and complex educational organization involving numerous departments in addition to its direct classroom ministry. The board of trustees, after consulting with top administrators, implemented the new organizational structure in 1946. This was toward the end of the presidency of Will H. Houghton. Houghton, a former pastor in Atlanta and New York City, had become president on November 1, 1934.

Many significant advances occurred under Houghton, fueling the drive to reorganize the corporate structure. Under the new structure, MBI adopted a branch system. Those heading each branch were designated vice-presidents. Within their respective areas of operation, these men had great creative liberty and responsibility. They reported to an executive vice-president. H. Coleman Crowell became the first executive vice-president in 1945. It was the responsibility of this person, "in the absence of the president of the Institute, or his inability to act," to "perform all duties which would be performed by the president . . . were he present or able to act."[9]

President Houghton, however, was not able to administer this new, more efficient plan; after several years of lingering illness, he died in office on June 14, 1947. Five days later, William Culbertson became acting president. On February 4, 1948, the trustees elected Culbertson to the presidency, where he would serve for twenty-three years.

President Culbertson had been dean of education at MBI since 1942, after having served as rector of three churches. At the age of thirty-one, he had been elected bishop of the New York and Philadelphia synod of the Reformed Episcopal Church and had also been a member of the board of trustees at the Reformed Episcopal Seminary.

Under the new plan, President Culbertson was "subject to the control of the Board of Trustees," but had "the general charge and supervision of the affairs of the corporation."[10]

On August 1, 1971, Culbertson passed the leadership mantle to Dr. George Sweeting, an evangelist and then pastor of nearby Moody Memorial Church. Culbertson was appointed the school's first chancellor,[11] serving only three months before death brought him to his Lord. Culbertson had personally approached Sweet-

9. Bylaws, Article V, Section 6.
10. Bylaws, Article V, Section 5.
11. Flood and Jenkins, *Teaching the Word*, p. 91.

ing about the presidency while Sweeting was on the board of trustees.[12] An author, artist, evangelist, pastor, and gifted speaker, Sweeting showed definite administrative skills as well. At this writing, Dr. Sweeting begins his fifteenth year as president of Moody Bible Institute.

THE CURRENT STRUCTURE

The current organizational chart (see figure 5, pp. 208-209) still reflects the fundamental structure of the 1946 revision. The branch plan remains the organizational approach. Six major branches head the operation of the Institute: administrative services, development, education, investment and legal counsel, publishing, and treasury. The vice-presidents of these divisions report to the executive vice-president. In 1985 a change in the bylaws designated the president as the chief executive of the Institute and the executive vice-president as the chief operating officer.

Growth at MBI has also resulted in the creation of divisions within the branches, each headed by a manager. In 1971, the Institute established the position of vice-president and legal counsel to handle its legal affairs. As Executive Vice-President Donald E. Hescott explains,

> With all the legal matters and documents, the Institute had to use outside counsel. Dr. Culbertson had recommended that we have on staff a counsel and with the growth under Dr. Sweeting, he felt we needed this [expertise] on the cabinet level. Marvin E. Beckman had headed the legal affairs of the Institute since 1966 and was named general counsel in 1970.

Beckman, the first and only general counsel, is a former attorney and judge in Washington state, and is admitted to practice before the Supreme Court. With this strong legal background, he has been instrumental in negotiations to buy land for expansion, in growth of the radio broadcasting and evening school programs, as well as in representing MBI in legal matters involving bequests.

An executive committee still handles school affairs during intervals between official meetings of the board of trustees. Three to seven members comprise the committee, each serving a one-year term; the committee may exercise all powers of the board of trustees in their absence, "subject to revision and alteration by the Board." Occasionally ad-hoc committees are appointed, such as the centennial committee and the former presidential search committee.

Approximately seven hundred full-time and six hundred part-time employees keep this large operation functioning smoothly and moving in the direction of its avowed objectives.

FINANCES

The earliest financial support for the Chicago Bible Work came from interested friends. The main contributors were T. W. Harvey, E. G. Keith, J. S. Helmer, N.

12. Ibid.

S. Bouton, and J. V. Farwell. Mrs. Cyrus McCormick and her husband also took keen interest in the work and devoted large sums of money. This same group of individuals donated most of the $250,000 that Moody requested in 1885 to launch the new training school.

While D. L. Moody was alive he continued to be the main lifeline in obtaining financial support. Wherever he went he promoted his new school, and many people responded to his requests. When he died, however, the Institute found itself in a precarious financial position. Though many people had supported the work, the Institute was left without a strong fund-raiser and without a corps of "regular" supporters.

Henry Parsons Crowell bridged the gap, both financially and administratively. Though he was financially able to support the work of this infant organization, he began immediately to guide the school in developing a corps of regular friends— people who would support the Institute as faithful donors year after year. Although Crowell personally donated large sums while the Institute was in the process of building a solid financial base, he was careful not to make the Institute dependent upon himself. His financial philosophy for Moody Bible Institute was that it must be financially dependent upon each succeeding generation. Through the years this has proved to be a prudent philosophy.

From its inception, the board of trustees has served as a policy-making group in financial matters. These men, all staunchly conservative in their theology, have also adopted a conservative approach in handling the funds of the Institute. Holding to a high view of biblical authority and Christian ethics, they have attempted to maintain the same ideal in finances.

As prudent money managers, the trustees will not allow the Institute to go into debt. Consequently, they never give a green light to construct a new building, to purchase property, or to expand the facilities in any way unless the funds are "in hand" or "in immediate sight." By the same token, they seldom approve borrowing money to keep the present program moving. Rather, when financial stress is creating problems, they call for a reduced operating budget.

Closely aligned with these conservative financial principles are several ethical principles. The Institute accounts very carefully for designated funds. Specified monies from donors are never used for other purposes without the consent of the donor. If for some reason the donation cannot be used in the way it has been requested by the donor, it is returned.

The trustees are also watchful of financial reserves. A committee composed of members of the board of trustees gives guidance in investments, and reserves are evaluated annually for annuities. Ernst & Whinney have served as an auditing firm for Moody Bible Institute since 1910. Through their auditing process, the accounting firm has helped the Institute to maintain strong accounting controls.

Moody Bible Institute has never charged tuition of its Day School students. Students pay only for room, board, miscellaneous fees, and a nominal student benefit fee. The academic training received is free, provided by interested donors.

Though the Institute has several revenue-generating ministries, the funds received do not provide the bulk of resources for the operations. Primary resources consist of donations, bequests, and the surplus from annuities. Direct mail and personal contact provide most contributions. Regular reports of the Institute's work are sent to interested friends. Solicitation is often indirect. Needs are presented, but with discretion and good taste.

Approximately fifteen full-time stewardship representatives call on donors and prospects in almost every state. All of these men are employed on a straight salary basis with no commission. According to an Institute directive, their work is first, a spiritual ministry to individuals, and second, a fund-raising ministry.

Part 2

THE HISTORY AND IMPACT OF THE SCHOOLS

6

The Day School Curriculum

During its first one hundred years of training Christian workers, MBI has expanded and reshaped its Day School curriculum, always keeping in mind the needs of the religious community it serves. Programs have been added; others have been dropped when they no longer served a purpose. For instance, during the past two decades MBI began offering an undergraduate baccalaureate and a one-year Advanced Studies Program in Bible and theology for graduates of secular colleges and universities.

As indicated previously, the Bible has remained a foundational text, yet there is balance in course offerings to prepare students for ministry in a complex world. The MBI philosophy of education is to strike a balance in subject matter and application.

While Bible and doctrine courses are the core of every major, general education subjects also are necessary to prepare a student to relate to the needs of contemporary man and to be effective in his ministry of the Word of God. All subjects are integrated into the biblical world view.[1]

First Formal Curriculum

After the opening of the year-round Bible Institute in September 1889, the first formal curriculum appeared and was described as follows:

> The English Bible is the principal textbook. The study of the Bible is divided into five departments:
>
> I. Introductory. The Inspiration of the Bible. The Structure of the Bible. Methods of Bible Study.
>
> II. Study of Bible Doctrine. God, Attributes, Trinity, etc. Divinity of Christ, Person and Work of the Holy Spirit. The Fall, Sin, Redemption, Persons of the Redeemer, Offices of the Redeemer, Justification, Adoption, Regeneration, Sanctification, Repentance, Faith, Good works, etc.

1. School Catalog, 1985-1986, p. 9.

III. Study of the Bible—in sections and in books. The first year study, under this head, includes, The study of Luke and John, The Acts of the Apostles, The Epistle to the Romans, Colossians and some other Pauline Epistles. All of the general Epistles and Revelation. The Books of Genesis and Leviticus, studies in the historical books, Psalms and Prophets.

IV. The Analysis by the students of texts and passages of Scripture, together with exercises in the construction and delivery of Bible Readings, addresses, etc.

V. The Study of the Bible in its application to various classes of men, the special object of this study being to give the students facility in using their Bibles in the Inquiry room, home workshops, etc.

In addition to the study of the Bible, the study of music is made a special feature of the Institute.

Methods of city, home and foreign mission work are studied under those who have had successful experience in these efforts.

The method of study is in part through lectures, with frequent examinations, and in part by assigning topics or books to be studied by the student, the results to be examined and criticized by the instructor.

Study and work go hand in hand. A portion of several days each week is devoted to actual work in homes, cottages, meetings, missions, and inquiry meetings, the object being to teach students not only the theory of work, but also the work itself.[2]

Classes were open to all men and women who wished "to acquire proficiency in Christian work." The school was "open during the entire year" and students could "enter at any time." All students followed the identical course of study.

The same basic curriculum with a few refinements was offered from 1889 until 1895, when the school introduced the "three course plan." Students now could choose from the Biblical Course, the Musical Course, or the Practical Christian Work Course.

If a student wished to be awarded a diploma (the term "graduation" was not used at this time), he had to "spend two years at the Institute" and had to complete satisfactorily the Biblical or Musical Course. The schedule of three academic terms allowed no planned vacation periods, though students could arrange for periods of absence on an individual basis. All students were required to attend two Bible lectures each day, except those in the Musical Course, who were required to attend one Bible lecture.

The Biblical Course, so named in 1895, maintained the subjects it had been offering since 1889. R. A. Torrey, director of the course, taught a sequence of Bible studies that covered a two-year period as did W. W. White, the associate director, thus enabling students to have some choice as to teacher and subjects.

Torrey's basic outline was as follows:

I. Biblical Introduction
II. Exegetical Study in Sections and Books

2. Men's Department of the Bible Institute for Home and Foreign Missions of the Chicago Evangelization Society, p. 2.

   III. Biblical Doctrine
   IV. Study of the Bible with an Immediate Reference to its Practical Use
   V. Study of the Best Methods of Construction and Delivery of Bible Readings, Gospel Talks, Sermons, etc.
   VI. Study of Methods of Work[3]

The Musical Course, under the direction of D. B. Towner, included notation, sight reading, harmony, solo and part singing, vocal training, conducting, normal training for teachers, and composition. The basic purpose of this course was "to equip men and women with a practical musical education," to serve as "pastor's assistants, evangelistic singers, choir leaders, organists and teachers."

From the time of the first curriculum, students were required to complete practical service in various types of Christian Work. However, in 1895, a special Practical Work Course was introduced with the more formal objective "to test students as well as train them." This program was designed to help students discover their various gifts by actual experience. They engaged in church work (preaching, singing, visiting, and so on), evangelistic work, city and rescue mission work, open-air preaching, house-to-house visitation, hospital visitation, jail services, and literature distribution.

The Missionary Course became part of the curriculum in 1900. For one hour each week students learned about home and foreign missions. The Biblical, Musical, and Practical Work courses remained essentially the same, except that new subjects were added and the staff of teachers was increased, particularly for the Biblical Course. Two years of study and satisfactory completion of either the Biblical or Musical Course were still required in order to obtain a diploma.

BIBLE STUDENTS, MUSIC STUDENTS

Beginning in 1906, the term "course" was reserved for a full program of study covering a two-year cycle. As a result, the Missionary Course became Missionary Study, and the Practical Work Course became Practical Work. The Biblical Course and the Musical Course remained essentially the same but were called simply the Bible Course and the Music Course.

Students soon were classified as Bible students, Bible-music students, or music students. The minimum period for study and recitation was twenty-seven hours per week. Those preparing primarily for Bible work were advised to take the full Bible Course. Those interested in a combination of Bible and music were advised to take eighteen hours each week in the Bible Course and a maximum of nine hours in the Music Course. Students interested in preparing for a ministry in music enrolled in the Music Course and were required to take eighteen hours each week in the Music Course and a maximum of nine hours in the Bible Course.

Beginning in 1906, students who satisfactorily completed a term of work were awarded a certificate. When a student eventually earned six certificates, represent-

---

3. Annual Catalog (1895), pp. 16-18. This is basically the same outline that Torrey used in 1889.

ing two years of work, he received a diploma. Final approval of each term's work depended primarily on satisfactory grades earned in final examinations.

In 1907, the terms "graduates" or "graduation" were used for the first time. Previously, those who completed the two-year program were spoken of as "those awarded diplomas."

COURSE EXPANSION

Course expansion began in 1911 and continued for several decades. During this time, in addition to having "regulars" or "special" partial program students, MBI permitted interested alumni to return for additional studies. These students were known as "postgraduates."

ENGLISH COURSE

An English Course appeared in 1913 with Hanna May Thomas as the instructor. This was not a full-fledged program, but several subjects areas were instituted to meet student needs. Classes emphasized grammar, rhetoric, and composition, as well as conversational speech for foreign-speaking students.

The following year, proficiency in rhetoric and composition became a requirement for graduation. During those formative years of the MBI curriculum, school officials were concerned with training students who could communicate competently in both speaking and writing.

D. L. Moody was not a master of the English language. His messages were replete with grammatical errors, and his letters frequently contained misspelled words. However, he recognized the need for a good education. In the initial program he was not concerned primarily with a study of the English language; he wanted people trained in the English Bible. Moody had a distinct type of Christian worker in mind who would not necessarily be ministering to the upper classes in society. However, those who came to the Institute, even in the early years of the school, became involved in all types of Christian service ministering to all types of people. Therefore competency in English became a necessary requirement for effective Christian service.

SUNDAY SCHOOL COURSE

Various subjects that were directly related to Sunday school work had been offered at the Institute since 1900. In 1914 a specific Sunday School Course began following the counsel and help of the International Sunday School Association. The purpose of this course was to equip young men and women "to make Sunday school work their life calling." Students who wished to enroll in this program did so at the beginning of their fourth term of study. Graduates of the course received both the diploma of the Institute and a teacher training diploma from the Illinois State Sunday School Association.

By 1915 five full programs of study were offered: the Bible Course, the Bible-

Music Course, the Music Course, the Sunday School Course, and the Missionary Course. Diplomas could be earned in any one of these five areas.

SWEDISH-ENGLISH COURSE

In 1916, MBI added a sixth full course of study, the Swedish-English Course. Designed to train Swedish young men for Christian work, it included the regular subjects offered at the Institute, plus special courses in English, Swedish language and literature, New Testament Greek, homiletics (in the Swedish language), and history. By 1918 this program became more formalized with a working arrangement between MBI and the Swedish Evangelical Free Church of the United States of America; in effect MBI served as the training school for the denomination's young men who wished to prepare for the ministry or for missionary work.

This program continued until 1928 when it became part of a separate school in Chicago. Eventually Trinity College emerged, as the Evangelical Free Church of America began a four-year liberal arts program. Both the college and the seminary, called the Trinity Evangelical Divinity School, now are located in Deerfield, north of Chicago. However, MBI still offered a limited Swedish-English Course until 1934.

PASTORS COURSE

After receiving encouragement from outside groups, and careful deliberation, MBI instituted a new program in 1922 called the Pastors Course, "to provide adequate pastoral training for the benefit of certain qualified students" who wished to enter the Christian ministry. Initially this course represented an additional year of specialized studies for graduates of the regular Bible, Bible-Music or Missionary courses. In addition, qualified students who had taken comparable training elsewhere also could enroll for these specialized subjects. Later, a full program was offered especially for those interested in the pastoral ministry.

JEWISH MISSIONS COURSE

The Jewish Missions Course was added in 1923. The first of its kind, it covered a period of three years and was designed to prepare Christian workers to minister among Jewish people. Specialized subjects were offered such as Hebrew, Rabbinics, Jewish history, Messianic prophecy, Yiddish, and Jewish feasts and customs. With the exception of a change in the length of the course and a few other minor alterations, the course remained essentially the same until the major curriculum revision in 1966.

The third major curriculum reorganization occurred in 1925 when certain courses were combined and some new programs were added. The Missionary, Pastors, Jewish Missions, and Swedish-English courses remained essentially the same. However, the Bible, Bible-Music, and Music courses merged into one program, called the General Course. Now students interested in Bible and/or music enrolled in the General Course and chose a major in either Bible or music or in both Bible and music. In 1929 a separate Music Course reappeared for students desiring specialized training in piano, organ, or voice. Two specialty courses began in the 1920s. In 1924, MBI opened its Religious Education Course to train directors of Christian education. This course replaced the Sunday School Course. In 1927 MBI inaugurated the Missionary Medical Service Course to provide medical workers in areas where qualified medical assistance was not available. The program was not planned to lead to a medical degree or to provide credits recognized by medical schools, but rather to give practical knowledge in the areas of anatomy, physiology, hygiene, sanitation, various diseases, minor surgery, and obstetrics. In 1929 it combined with the regular Missionary Course and both required eight terms for graduation.

As a result of additions and consolidations, seven courses existed by 1929: The General Course, the Pastors Course, the Missionary Course, the Christian Education Course, the Jewish Missions Course, the Swedish-English Course, and the Music Course. The next year MBI began its Christian Education-Music Course, which continues today as the C.E.-music major. The course helped to prepare students to serve in a dual position as directors of Christian education and music. The program was three years in length and consisted of "all of the subjects of the Christian Education Course and the most essential studies of the Music Course."

With the addition of the Christian Education-Music Course in 1930 and the elimination of the Swedish-English Course in 1934, the Day School curriculum remained unchanged until 1949-1950, when the Missionary Technical Course appeared. The first of its kind, this program prepared specialists for mission-field operations in aeronautics, radio communications, and photography. Since its beginning, this course has undergone many changes that reflect changing educational and missionary needs. Today the Missionary Technology-Aviation Department trains pilots and ground personnel for missionary service (see chapter 11).

Curriculum Revision of 1951

MBI adopted a semester academic plan in 1951, resulting in major curriculum changes. Instead of following a year-round "term plan," students now could attend two semesters per year and an optional summer school program. All eight courses were revised, and with the exception of the Missionary Technical Course, each consisted of six semesters of work that required three years to complete. Some new studies were added, but many of the one-hour subjects offered under the term plan were reorganized and formed into two- and three-hour subjects.

The basic objectives of all eight courses remained essentially the same with the exception of the General Course. Rather than providing a choice in one of four areas of specialization (Bible, music, home missions, and Christian education), the General Course was renamed the General Bible Course and was arranged so that students could elect subjects in any one or all of these four areas.

The objective of the General Bible Course was the same as before: to give students a knowledge of the Bible and skills to be effective Christian workers. In other words, this course was non-specialized while the other courses were designed to train people for specific church vocations—pastors, missionaries, church musicians, directors of Christian education, directors of youth, children's workers, and specialized home and foreign missionaries.

NEW UNDERGRADUATE PROGRAMS

Beginning in the fall of 1966, MBI introduced a new degree program. A self-study report by the educational branch (1961) had examined the academic programs, while an alumni survey by Getz (1964) had evaluated the educational experiences of graduates. Both reports revealed that students needed an undergraduate degree for many types of ministry. The new B.A. option allowed students to earn a Bachelor's degree by completing sixty semester hours of course work in the liberal arts at an accredited college or university in addition to the course requirements of Moody Bible Institute. This credit from another school may be earned before coming to Moody Bible Institute or after the three-year diploma program has been completed.

With the new program, MBI replaced the historic "course" plan with a system of majors offered by academic departments. The new plan allowed students greater flexibility in their choice of subjects. A diploma or a Bachelor of Arts degree could now be earned in eight majors, including Bible-theology, Christian education, pastoral training, church music, foreign missions, and communications.

Since the Baccalaureate Program has been in operation, other majors have been added, including evangelism. As MBI begins its one hundredth year of service, diplomas or degrees are available in the following majors: Bible-theology, Christian education, Christian education-music, communications, evangelism, international ministries, American intercultural ministries, Jewish and modern Israel studies, pastoral training, missionary technology-aviation, and sacred music.

Beginning in August 1986, entering students will be able to complete requirements for an B.A. degree in four years through a new baccalaureate curriculum (see chapter 21).

First-year students enroll in an identical core curriculum. This foundational year program features introductory subjects necessary for subsequent course work. In addition, the foundation year courses provide freshmen with essential Bible knowledge and spiritual guidance at an early point in their undergraduate education. The foundation curriculum includes: elements of Bible study; Christian life and ethics; church at work in the world, a study of the church fulfilling its missionary function in the world, and the issues of a biblical, educational ministry; concepts in physical education; English composition; Bible survey; personal evangelism; and speech communication.

During the early 1970s MBI officials became aware of a special type of student who already had a college degree but needed training in the Bible. Mission agencies recommended a one-year Bible program for their college-trained missionary applicants who lacked formal Bible and theological education. In addition, other college graduates who wanted better training for lay work and graduates who had become Christians while in college looked to a short but comprehensive biblical education.

MBI became one of the earliest schools to offer a one-year certificate of academic studies, when in 1972 it began the Advanced Studies Program. Students having bachelor's degrees from acceptable colleges and universities can complete thirty-two semester hours of courses from the Day School curriculum, including such specialized courses as spiritual life and ministry, survey of theology, and principles of Bible study.

Day School enrollment reached 1,330 students in 1985, reflecting the significant increases of the past twenty-five years (see figure 6, p. 206). Today's student studies in one of the larger theological libraries in the Midwest, containing more than 107,000 volumes and more than 1,000 current periodicals.

MBI also operates a Christian school for children in St. Petersburg, Florida. More than seven hundred students attend grades kindergarten through twelve at Keswick Christian School. Bible is considered the most important subject, as at the Institute, and the school has a strong academic tradition. For example, high school seniors score consistently above the national average on the Scholastic Aptitude Test (SAT), and the school has produced three National Merit Scholars.

7

The Evening School Curriculum

When D. L. Moody first challenged Emma Dryer to start a training school in 1873, he was eager that she start teaching at once, even before he left for England. Accordingly, Miss Dryer "appointed evening meetings for the young people" and "they began to study the Bible in Genesis." These sessions were first held in Moody's Northside Tabernacle. Thus, the first classes ever conducted in relationship to the origin of Moody Bible Institute were evening classes.

As the Bible Work expanded, much of the training during those early years occurred in the evening. One brochure describing the Bible Work in 1884 referred specifically to the night schools that were held. One school met in the Chicago Avenue Church, a second in the West Side Tabernacle located at the corner of Morgan and Indiana streets. The basic purpose of those schools was to teach foreigners "to read the English Bible, and to use a Sunday School Quarterly."

The type of courses and students changed greatly during the one hundred years that followed. As of the fall semester of 1985, twenty-two campuses located in seven states provide both adult-level and college-level courses. Students can earn an Adult Bible Studies Certificate with thirty semester hours of credit or an Associate of Arts degree by completing sixty semester hours of college-level study.

The increasing emphasis on continuing education and aggressive expansion of extension campuses resulted in steady growth during the 1970s and a record enrollment during 1985, when over 2,500 students attended fall semester classes (see figure 7, p. 207).

EVENING DEPARTMENT ORGANIZED

The first reference to evening classes in the official literature of the school appeared in 1889, during the Institute's formal opening. "Special Evening classes" for those whose business engagements prevented attendance regularly in day classes would be offered. These night classes were continued for three or four years. Finally in October 1903, a special Evening Department began offering classes four nights a week; attendance during the first term averaged 125 each evening.

Beginning in 1904 three nights were set aside, with Tuesday and Thursday evenings being given over to Bible study and Wednesday evenings to the study of music. The three-evenings-per-week program was continued until 1952 when the evenings were reduced to Tuesday and Friday. This general plan continued until the fall of 1967, when Evening School was again held on three nights—Monday, Tuesday, and Thursday, the present schedule.

From the beginning of the regular evening program, students enrolling at night could choose either the Bible Course or the Music Course. Although the subjects offered were limited in number, Moody Bible Institute was attempting to offer "a similar course of training in evening classes" as those offered in the Day School. In 1906 it was stated "that the evening program was practically the same as that covered in the Bible and Music Course of the regular department" and that it was "carried on by the same teachers."

The curriculum in Evening School was arranged so that four terms per year were offered: fall, winter, spring, and summer. The summer term, though, had to be completed by correspondence study since no evening classes met during the summer months. The total program could be completed in three years, and students who successfully completed this program were awarded an MBI diploma.

When the Evening Department was established, its general objective was similar to that of the Day School. The main purpose was "to furnish a practical course of training in Bible study and approved methods of aggressive Christian work for men and women employed during the day." Even though this general objective was the same in both schools, the Day School was geared to preparing students for full-time church vocations. The Evening School, on the other hand, trained lay workers who would, though active in secular work, become more effective workers in their churches and in other types of Christian service.

Although Evening School initially had emphasized the training of lay workers, students with plans for full-time Christian ministry were also enrolling; therefore beginning with the fall term of 1918 the Evening School program was revised to parallel the Day School curriculum.

The new curriculum required four years of thirty-seven weeks, covering three terms per year. The summer term and correspondence study were eliminated, and all instruction was confined to the classroom as in the day classes.

The six courses available in Day School could now be completed in Evening School: the Bible Course, the Bible-Music Course, the Music Course, the Missionary Course, the Sunday School Course, and the Practical Work Course.

REVISING THE PROGRAM

From 1918 to 1924, Moody Bible Institute, with few exceptions, continued to offer the same program in the Evening School as in the Day School. However, as the Day School curriculum expanded its offerings, it became impracticable to duplicate the complete day program in Evening School. After the general curriculum reorganization in 1925, only four full programs offered in the Day School were offered in Evening School: the General Course, the Missionary Course, the Religious Education Course, and the Swedish-English Course.

Soon it was impossible to offer even these four courses. By 1930 the only complete course of study available in the Evening School that matched the Day School was the General Course. Foundational subjects from all of the other Day School courses were included in the Evening School curriculum, but to complete any other program than the General Course, a student would eventually need to enroll in the Day School.

With the narrowing of curriculum offerings in the Evening School came a narrowing of the Evening School objective. In 1930 the school again began to promote the "layman" objective, as indicated by a statement in the Moody Bible Institute Bulletin:

> The Evening School of Moody Bible Institute is intended primarily to instruct laymen—both men and women, who by virtue of their training may become elements of strength and usefulness in the home church; whose intelligence shall become a source of inspiration to discerning pastors; who may, on occasion, be ready to teach a Bible class, give a prayer meeting exposition, or even fill the pulpit.

Though a renewed emphasis was placed on attracting laymen, the objective of preparing or helping to prepare full-time Christian workers was never excluded. The Evening School continued to attract men and women of this nature and still does today.

Helping the Church Worker

When the Day School curriculum converted from the term to the semester plan in 1951, the Evening School curriculum was also revised. Previously, students had pursued the General Course and received the same diploma as Day School students. In the new curriculum the course of study was reduced to thirty-six semester hours, with graduates earning a Certificate of Graduation.

By carrying six subjects per week, a student could complete the program in three years; many students chose to complete their studies over a longer period of time. Students who did not wish to take the full complement of subjects could enroll as "specials" and take fewer subjects per week. Those taking a full course of study could enroll in one of four branches: the Bible branch, the Christian education branch, the music branch, or the evangelism branch.

In 1959 a new Basic Bible Course allowed students with academic deficiencies to receive instruction in the Bible. While the General Evening Course still required a high school diploma, students without a diploma could now enroll in the Basic Bible Course. The new course could be completed in two years and a certificate of recognition was awarded upon completion of the program. The General Evening Course still required at least three years to earn a certificate of graduation.

The reduction in class hours and the creation of a curriculum that was independent from the Day School represented an important shift in the purpose and philosophy of the Evening School. Changes in the philosophy of local church ministry mandated the new approach. The church worker was becoming a vital part in church ministry, and the Evening School adjusted to meet that need, said Jay Fernlund, former Evening School director and dean of continuing education. Fernlund, now director of the Correspondence School, explained the shift in an article to alumni:

> There's been a real shift in emphasis on how churches perform their ministry. When Dwight L. Moody began our school, the concept was very strong that you had a professional staff who did the church work. The pastor, the music director and his assistants performed the work of the ministry. But Moody felt that the scriptural way is for the whole church, the laypeople, to be involved. The pastor and his staff become trainers or facilitators.[1]

THE PRESENT PROGRAM

Two major changes have resulted in an Evening School curriculum that more closely follows adult education principles. In 1966 a new plan granted students more flexibility in their studies toward graduation. Rather than enrolling in one of the four branches, students could graduate from the program by completing six series of six credits each. In 1982, graduation requirements were reduced to five series. Students now can select these five series from many areas, including Bible, theology, Bible background subjects, Christian education, Christian communications, Christian psychology, missions, evangelism, and sacred music. Upon completion of a single series of six credits, a special certificate of recognition is awarded, and when the student receives five of these certificates (thirty semester hours), he earns the Adult Bible Studies Certificate.

Beginning in 1984, students in the college-credit courses could earn an Associate of Arts degree by completing sixty semester hours of course work. The sixty academic hours include studies in Bible, theology, ministry, and general arts, including English composition, speech, and music. Most of the courses are eligible for transfer credit to a four-year Bible College, and thirty of the semesters hours duplicate the first-year program of the Day School.

EXTENSION CAMPUSES

The specter of Vietnam and civil unrest rolled into Middle America in the late 1960s, and metropolitan Chicago immediately felt its presence. In the hot summer of 1968, leaders of anti-Vietnam rallies protesting U.S. policy focused on Chicago, site of the Democratic National Convention.

Demonstrators gathered in nearby Lincoln Park and police watched warily. The inevitable clashes—sometimes violent, always controversial—raged for several nights, resulting in tensions and numerous arrests. Chicago suffered civil unrest

---

1. "Education After Hours," *Moody Alumni*, Summer 1980.

for several years as militant opponents to American policy sought to change that policy.

In the midst of such unrest, Chicago suburbanites hesitated to travel to the big city at night. Many of the students attending evening school had been from surrounding suburbs as well as the Chicago neighborhoods; now some declined to continue or begin studies. As a result enrollments declined in the late 1960s and then leveled off.

The temporary fears soon abated, and attendance began a slow growth, but Evening School officials recognized a need to provide adult education outside Chicago. In the early sixties, an extension campus in Moline had been considered, but the plan was dropped. Now the zeal to expand returned. Instead of suburb-dwellers going to the campus, the campus would go to the suburbs.

The first extension campus opened in September 1972 in Joliet, a distant southwest suburb, but its beginnings were a bit shaky. PCM officials, the school registrar, and enrollment clerks accompanied Dr. Fernlund, then director of the Evening School, to the Joliet YMCA one September evening for the 5:00 P.M. registration. But by 5:10 only one woman had shown up. The officials stared across the empty room. Forty-five minutes later Fernlund turned to the registrar and invited him to dinner. The others stayed at their stations. Fernlund recalls the scene: *"That's the end*, I thought. *There is to be no Evening School outside Chicago.* We walked to a hamburger stand and had a hamburger and malt. . . .We had been gone almost twenty minutes and walked back. The room was full of people! We could not believe our eyes."[2]

They blinked again and noticed the line was forty-people deep. They ran to their positions, slightly embarrassed, and began to write. "The people kept pouring in all evening. We didn't leave until 9:00 P.M." At nine o'clock Fernlund walked downstairs to a pay phone and dialed the dean of education back in Chicago. A tired but jubilant Fernlund announced, "Well, your extension program is off and running."

More than 140 students enrolled that first semester, assuring the continuation of satellite campuses for the Evening School. During the next five years four more schools began, and MBI began expanding outside Illinois. The year following the Joliet opening, the program expanded into Ohio. A group from the Center for Christian Studies asked MBI leaders to start a school in Akron following the closing of the Akron Bible Institute. The group provided initial funding and MBI agreed. The active search by the CCS and Akron's immediate success confirmed the wisdom of expanding the Evening Schools. "The success in Joliet showed that going into a suburban location was a viable approach. In Ohio we were going four hundred miles away from the central campus and the historic strength of Moody Bible Institute," Fernlund noted. The success there assured officials that the school could succeed at remote locations.

Enrollment figures soared in the 1970s. From 678 students in 1970, more than

2. Jay Fernlund, interview, 5 September 1985.

1,800 had enrolled by 1977 (see figure 7, p. 207). Throughout the 1970s the expansion of extension campuses continued, aided by an unusual ruling of the Federal Communications Commission. The FCC ruled that educational FM radio stations must have an educational branch of their organization in the area to be eligible for a station license. Evening School officials started schools in the Iowa-Illinois Quad Cities area in 1977, which allowed licensing of WDLM-FM. In 1980, an extension campus opened in Boynton Beach, Florida, in connection with the Moody FM outlet, WMBW.

Recent additions to the extension system include schools in Peoria, Illinois; Sarasota, Florida; and Dayton and Warren, Ohio.

8

Impact on a City

Tens of thousands of men and women have walked through the archway of Moody Bible Institute during the past one hundred years to receive training in the Day and Evening schools. These students have come from all over the United States and from many foreign countries, representing numerous denominations. While engaged in their studies, either as full-time day students or part-time evening students, they have not only been preparing to serve in positions of Christian responsibility, but they have immediately participated in various types of practical service throughout Chicago.

After graduation, these men and women have entered church vocations that have taken them to all parts of the world to serve as missionaries, pastors, musicians, youth leaders, children's workers, and Christian educators. Ranging from college presidents to Christian workers serving in isolated and almost unknown sections of the South American jungles, graduates of Moody Bible Institute circle the globe.

ENROLLMENT STATISTICS

Since the opening of the formal school in 1889, through spring semester 1985, a total of 57,800 students have enrolled in the Moody Day School. Since the opening of the Evening Department in 1903, through spring semester 1985, 65,000 students have attended the twenty-two Evening Schools around the country, for a total of 122,800 in both schools. In both schools there is a fairly equal division between men and women.

Enrollments in both the Day and Evening schools have been relatively constant since 1920, with certain notable exceptions. By 1911 the Day School enrollment for the year had climbed to 614 (annualized) and the Evening School to 353. By 1920 the annual Day School enrollment had more than doubled the 1920 figure and the Evening School had tripled. Day School attendance climbed steadily following World War II, and semester enrollment reached 1,000 in 1970. During the five years ending 1985, an average of 1,350 students attended each fall semester.

Attendance in the Evening School topped 890 students (fall semester) by 1965, before dropping below 700 in 1970 during the height of civil unrest in Chicago (see chapter 7). But enrollment tripled during the next seven years, and by fall semester 1985, Evening School enrollment reached 2,500, an all-time record. Four new extension campuses, preregistration, and elimination of enrollment fees—students now pay only course fees—were major factors in the record enrollment.

Students have been attracted from a variety of geographical areas and a number of denominational groups. Only six years after the opening of the formal school, 196 women students and 350 men students had traveled from thirty-two states and thirteen countries to attend Moody. Together they represented more than thirty denominations.[1] Today students come from almost every state in the union. In 1984 students from twenty-six countries studied at MBI. Through the years, the number of denominations represented has increased, reaching seventy-nine in 1984. The endorsement of so many denominations seems to reflect a trust in the consistent, fundamental doctrinal position of the school.

Students in Evening School represent a variety of backgrounds. One year after the Evening Department organized, forty of the students held secular employment, three were pastors, twelve were Sunday school superintendents, and 167 were Sunday school teachers. There were 152 churches represented from twelve denominations.

This type of student has continued to attend Evening School over the years. In 1956 a special questionnaire returned by 75 percent of the evening students indicated most of these adults were active in the local church. Of the total group, 41 percent were Sunday school teachers, 22.7 percent were choir members, 14.5 percent were boys' or girls' group leaders, and 13.8 percent were young people's leaders. In addition, 10.2 percent were members of church boards, and 5.8 percent were either pastors or assistant pastors.

Students enroll in Evening School courses for several reasons, but the primary reasons to attend are increased Bible knowledge, 93 percent of respondents, and "being a better witness for Christ," 83 percent, according to a 1983 study of students enrolled at extensions in Illinois and Ohio, as well as the main campus.[2] The number of lay workers in churches and Sunday schools appears to remain high, as 63 percent of respondents indicated they enroll "to become a better teacher or preacher," and 56 percent indicated a primary reason they attend Evening School is to become more effective church leaders.

CHRISTIAN SERVICE IN CHICAGO

The first brochure published by the Bible Institute in 1889, stated "study and work go hand in hand." Rather than spending all their time in the classroom, students were to give "a portion of several days each week . . . to actual work in

1. *The Annual Catalog for Home and Foreign Missions of the Chicago Evangelization Society* (1895), pp. 22-24. It should be noted that not all of these students were in residence at one time. At the close of the year 1894, 75 women and 140 men were pursuing studies.
2. Richard VanDyke, "A Study to Evaluate the Current Evening School Program: Societal Factors," unpublished paper, February 1983.

homes, cottage meetings, missions and inquiry meetings.'' The purpose of this emphasis "was to teach students not only the theory of the work, but also the work itself.''

Later, when the first catalog appeared in 1895, a regular Practical Work Course had been organized. Since that time students have been able to discover and develop their particular gifts, talents, and abilities by actual participation in Christian work. They have preached, sung, visited, canvassed, and taught Bible classes. In addition, students have participated in evangelistic meetings, mission work, children's work (choirs, Brigade and Awana groups, and released-time classes), open-air work, hospital visitation, jail work, and literature distribution. The term "course" was soon dropped, and practical Christian work became an integral part of all other courses. But the purpose and program of practical Christian work (PCW) has remained largely unchanged since 1889.

In recent years, PCW directors have emphasized quality and supervision rather than mere quantity. Increasingly students have engaged in PCW activities that correlate with their field of study. But practical Christian ministry at Moody Bible Institute has always been more than a field work program—it has served to give students many practical experiences, even in areas in which they may never work and minister in their vocational calling.

In 1982 the PCW Department became the Practical Christian Ministries Department (PCM). Most Bible institutes and colleges had begun designating required service as "Christian service," and that spurred the name change. There also was concern that the term "work" was misleading.

" 'Ministry' better reflects what we are all about," noted PCM Director Leonard Rascher. "The experience is not just part of student training but actual ministry. Students don't have to wait until they have a diploma to start ministering. And the ministry *is* practical."

Through its PCM program, the school has contributed directly to evangelical education in the Chicago area. The impact of students on the spiritual needs of Chicago cannot be directly known, but statistics kept by the Practical Christian Work Department suggest a positive effect on evangelical training in Chicago. Consider these four areas:

1. *Bible classes.* These classes have included Sunday school classes (the most popular type), mission classes, weekday church school classes, child evangelism classes, and released-time classes in public school. In addition to these classes in which the Bible has been taught directly, there also have been personal evangelism and teacher training classes, which have been designed to teach others how to carry out certain types of Christian work.

Statistics on the number of "classes taught" are available for only forty-three of the ninety-five years since 1889. Conservative projections reveal that Moody students have taught, since 1889, approximately 17 million individual class sessions. This equals the efforts of one thousand Sunday school teachers presenting classes every Sunday morning for thirty-three years.

2. *Visitation and personal counsel.* Through the years personal calls have been made by teams of students going from house to house in order to converse with people regarding spiritual concerns. In addition, teams of students have regularly visited hospitals to talk with patients and offer spiritual and emotional comfort and help.

Statistics regarding individual visits are available for forty different years. Projecting from these figures, students at the Institute have made an estimated 2.2 million calls and visits in homes and hospitals since the turn of the century.

While teaching, attending various meetings, and doing visitation, students have also counseled with individuals personally regarding spiritual matters. Statistics are available for forty-nine years of such activity since 1900. Conservative estimates indicate that over 4.7 million people have been counseled since the opening of the formal school, or about 1.3 times the number of people currently living in Chicago.

3. *Literature distributed.* Distribution of literature—including Bibles, New Testaments, Bible portions, and gospel leaflets—is usually handled person-to-person and often requires conversation. Bibles and portions of the Scriptures are usually given out to people who indicate a strong interest in learning about Christianity. More than 32 million pieces of literature have been distributed since the turn of the century.

4. *Personal responses.* As noted earlier, the spiritual impact of the PCM outreach cannot be fully measured. However, objective data supplied by students is revealing. During twenty years, 1965-1984, students reported that 62,000 people whom they had counseled professed belief in Jesus Christ as personal Savior, and almost 10,000 determined to live a more dedicated Christian life. Since the turn of the century, more than half a million people have made one of these two responses.

Many of these decisions have come from individuals who are non-churchgoers or those previously uninterested in Christianity. Since much of the work has been carried on in rescue missions on skid row, in prisons, in mission Sunday schools, and the homes of non-churchgoers, many of the individuals responding did so as a result of an initial contact with students from Moody Bible Institute.

New ministries have arisen in the 1980s to meet the needs of the city. Chicago is a world-class metropolis drawing immigrants from around the globe. PCM assignments include ethnic ministries to Chinese, Japanese, Korean, Mexican, native Indian, and Vietnamese residents of the city. In Operation Good Samaritan, students visit city facilities for the elderly. Here students wash windows, scrub floors, even take individuals shopping. Typically students work as teams, one student performing a task while the other provides companionship. Often there is a chance to present the gospel as friendships develop.

The nature of the PCM activity is as varied as the student body. When a student raised in Hong Kong and a frequent visitor to China wanted to tell American church members about conditions in China, he was offered a special PCM project. Each Sunday he visited a different church, giving Americans an inside view of worship and persecution in the Christian church in China. Students have used their talents to present the gospel message through song, drama, pantomime, and magic.

Perhaps the most unusual gospel witness involved aiding stranded motorists. When two Moody students driving home to a Chicago suburb spotted and helped a stranded motorist get moving again on a busy highway, he offered to pay. They refused, and the surprised motorist asked why. The two students explained the love of Christ had prompted their actions, and they began to share the gospel. The man did not accept Christ as his Savior, but the two men students recognized a unique ministry opportunity.

With PCM approval, they developed a new ministry. Using a citizen's band radio, they cruised area expressways once a week, looking for disabled vehicles. They aided dozens of motorists one semester. When cars had mechanical problems too severe to solve immediately, the duo notified local service stations for emergency help. During most of their stops, the two students were able to present the gospel. In this fashion the PCM Department seeks to give students *practical* assignments using their spiritual gifts and natural abilities.

CHURCH VOCATIONS

From earliest days, students, upon graduation or after additional training in other schools, have entered a variety of church vocations. For example, those who left the school during the year 1894 served as foreign missionaries, home missionaries, matrons in charitable institutions, ministers' wives, YMCA secretaries, evangelists, evangelistic singers, pastors, colporteurs, Sunday school workers, Salvation Army workers, and school teachers. Wilbur Chapman reported that of the nearly 3,000 who studied at the Institute during its first ten years, at least one-third were already "engaged in active Christian work throughout the country."

The latest, most thorough investigation of vocations chosen by Moody graduates is the 1984 alumni survey. The report surveyed 1,250 graduates and 400 non-graduates since 1900, with more than 72 percent of the respondents graduating or attending after 1970. Almost two-thirds of all Moody alumni, 61.1 percent, have participated in full-time religious vocations. One-third of those in full-time Christian service work for a church; more than one-fourth are in foreign missions.[3]

Though the terminology used to describe various types of Christian work has changed over the years, MBI alumni lead and assist at a variety of Christian agencies. Table 1 indicates the extent of alumni involvement during the past twenty years. (Data also are included from the 1974 alumni survey by Glenn Arnold and the 1964 alumni survey by Gene Getz.) The many types of work represented may

---

3. Kenneth Bosma, "Moody Bible Institute Alumni Survey 1984," 19 November 1984, pp. 9, 46. The researcher reports a sampling error of only 2.5 percent for the entire MBI alumni population.

be listed under the following broad categories: pastoral ministry and church education, and Christian media (broadcast and print).

Table 1
Percentage of Moody alumni serving at various Christian agencies

	1984	1974	1964
Churches	32.1	40.3	43.6
Home missions	9.8	9.0	9.2
Foreign missions	27.3	33.3	34.3
Schools, K-12	6.2	3.1	2.6
Higher education	10.5	9.6	---
Evangelism	5.7	---	---
Other (primarily publishing and broadcasting)	8.4	4.7	10.3

Source: Kenneth Bosma, "Moody Bible Institute Alumni Survey 1984," p. 54.

9

Impact on a Nation: Correspondence School

The typical student is between twenty-five and forty-years-old, a blue-collar worker, and has already completed some college courses. If enrolled in the college-level program, the student probably is male; if in the adult-level program, most likely female.[1] Whatever the program, these students all have one thing in common: During their evenings and free time they are part of the Moody Correspondence School.

They are studying at home toward a Certificate of Graduation in Continuing Education or an Associate of Arts degree. They may be studying college credit courses that can earn transfer credit in the MBI resident school or other Bible schools offering similar courses. Correspondence School students are part of a tradition reaching back to the turn of the century. A correspondence program at Moody Bible Institute was considered as early as 1895, but it actually began in January 1901, with the following objective: "The Correspondence Department has been organized for the benefit of those of both sexes who cannot, for financial or other reasons, attend the Institute personally. The purpose is to give them, as far as possible, all the advantages of the systematic methods of study here pursued."

The new department paralleled the development of the correspondence movement in general education. Chautauqua, originally founded to train Sunday school teachers, but which later became a secular school, "was the first American institution to establish correspondence courses on a regular basis."[2] The first course was offered in 1879 by William Rainey Harper, then a professor of Hebrew at Yale.

Harper's exposure to this program at Chautauqua inspired him to create a correspondence school at the University of Chicago, where he became president in 1892. It was Harper's work in Chicago that helped establish correspondence study "as a part of the educational scene" in America.[3]

---

1. Richard Patterson, "Continuing Education," *1984 Annual Report of the Vice-President and Dean of Education*, p. 28.
2. Malcolm S. Knowles, *The Adult Education Program in the United States*, p. 38.
3. Clinton Hartley Grattian (ed.), *American Ideas About Adult Education*, 1710-1951, p. 75.

First of Its Kind

As the "mother" of the Bible institute-college movement, Moody Bible Institute launched her Correspondence School at the same time that the secular world inaugurated its own, making the MBI school-by-mail the "oldest of its kind in the Bible institute movement."[4] It should be noted, however, that C. I. Scofield prepared a "Comprehensive Bible Correspondence Course" and began distributing it as early as 1896. Scofield's course, covering the whole Bible, seems to have been the first evangelical correspondence Bible study program ever circulated. Interestingly, Scofield handled this course privately for a number of years, selling it in 1915 to the Institute. The Scofield Course then became a part of the Moody Correspondence School curriculum and has remained so ever since.

In the beginning, Moody Correspondence School offered two courses. *Bible Doctrine* and *Practical Christian Work* were both written by R. A. Torrey and divided into sections for easier study. The sections averaged forty-six pages each and were printed in a separate pamphlet. Students often carried these pamphlets for study on the train or streetcar or would read them during their lunch hour.

When a student satisfactorily completed a course of study with a passing percentage, he received a certificate of progress, which was accepted for credit in the regular Bible Course of the Institute. A pupil studying two or three hours per week could complete the Practical Work Course in a year. Students devoting three hours per week to the Bible Doctrine Course finished that program in two years.

Curriculum Growth and Expansion

The correspondence program increased its offerings steadily from 1901 to 1945. The largest addition came in 1915 when the number of courses doubled from four to eight. One of these, Introductory Bible Course, was designed for those who did not have time for lengthy or deep study. Another, Christian Evidence, presented basic arguments to support the truth of Christianity. A course in evangelism also appeared. The fourth addition was the three-volume Scofield Bible Course covering the entire Bible, which has been the largest single addition to the Correspondence School curriculum.

Two more courses were added in 1924, Fundamentals of Christian Faith and World Wide Missions. During the next sixteen years the Correspondence School introduced seven more subjects, including such courses as Panorama of the Ages and Scriptural Truth.

With seventeen courses in place by 1945, revision now accompanied expansion. Some courses were dropped; new courses were added; older courses were revised and some given new and more popular titles.

By 1955, Moody Correspondence School offered approximately twenty courses. By 1965, more than forty were available.

In 1957 the Correspondence School classified all courses into three divisions:

4. S. A. Witmer, *The Bible College Story: Education with Dimension*, p. 129.

Basic Bible Courses, Adult Bible Courses, and Advanced Bible Courses. Eventually the term "series" was used to describe these groups of courses, and by 1960 there were five different series. At present the five series are: Christian Life, New Testament Studies, Old Testament Studies, Personal Evangelism, and Prophecy.

The Adult Study Program began in 1960 leading to a certificate upon completion of twenty credit units. Today students can earn a certificate of graduation by completing thirty semester hours.

COLLEGE CREDIT

The Correspondence School first offered college credit courses in the 1960s. These courses are identical to those offered in Moody Bible Institute's Day School; they usually will transfer as credits to other Bible institutes or Bible colleges that offer equivalent courses, and are readily accepted by the MBI Day School.

A student receives a certificate in biblical studies upon completion of thirty semester college hours. The certificate meets the requirements of many mission agencies for one year of study in Bible and theology for their missionary candidates. Or the student can chose to earn an Associate of Arts degree in biblical studies by finishing sixty semester hours, normally a two-year program. The Associate of Arts degree is identical to that offered on Evening School campuses and requires the student to participate in a PCM program throughout his time as a student.

The American Association of Bible Colleges and MBI have both approved the college program for college credit. At present, twenty courses are offered by mail for college credit, ranging from Old Testament Survey to New Testament Greek.

INCREASING ENROLLMENTS

The Moody Correspondence School has grown consistently during its eighty-five years. From 1900 to 1953, new enrollments increased steadily from 160 in 1900 to 7,832 in 1953. Enrollment declines year-to-year occurred in only fifteen of these yearly periods. "Enrollments" or "enrollees" designate the number of courses in which individuals are enrolled, and may not represent the total number of people involved, since a person may have enrolled for more than one course.

As could be expected, three of the yearly declines occurred during depression years, 1930, 1931, and 1932. Amazingly, while the National Home Study Council reported that enrollments in other correspondence schools (religious and secular) dropped between 50 percent and 79 percent, at MBI the declines were far less: 3.5 percent in 1930, 7 percent in 1931, and 9.5 percent in 1932. But in 1933, enrollments again increased 8.7 percent. Therefore, while the depression years were severely affecting correspondence study in general, the impact upon MBI study-by-mail was relatively mild.

The ever-expanding productivity following World War II contributed to substantial growth and a baby boom. During this period, correspondence study also shot upward. The number of enrollees in the MBI home study program exploded from 7,800 in 1953 to more than 40,000 twelve years later. During this period an average of 4,600 new enrollees began correspondence courses each year. From 1955 to 1965, the Correspondence School had more than quadrupled its number of new enrollees.

The pace of growth has been less dramatic during the past twenty years, but cumulative enrollments still have risen steadily, reaching 92,600 in 1984. Actual physical enrollments were 48,000 in 1984; 51,000 in 1985.

LARGEST SCHOOL OF ITS KIND

A 1960 survey of Bible correspondence courses offered by Bible institutes and colleges revealed a total of 2,509,000 enrollees. Except for two Canadian schools with 102 students, these services are carried on by Bible institutes in the United States.

However, only ten of the thirty-two schools had more than one hundred enrollees, and only four—Moody Bible Institute, Emmaus Bible School, Lutheran Bible Institute (Minneapolis), and the Bible Institute of Los Angeles—conducted sizeable schools with registrations running into thousands. In fact these four schools accounted for 98 percent of the reported home study education.[5]

Emmaus Bible College (formerly Emmaus Bible School), located in Dubuque, Iowa, specializes in an overseas ministry, working with missionaries, and mission agencies. Their courses have been translated into more than 80 languages and have been distributed in 125 countries.

The Lutheran Bible Institute enrolled 16,732 correspondence students in 1960. The Bible Institute of Los Angeles, now called Biola University, inaugurated a correspondence school in 1914. Its course offerings are similar to those of the Moody Correspondence School.

In 1960 the thirty-two existing schools reported a combined figure of 259,000 enrollees. Since Moody Bible Institute had 39,836 enrollees that year, 15.3 percent of all enrollments were at Moody Bible Institute.

Since the report, MBI and Emmaus Bible College have had proportional increases in enrollment, and other schools have become co-leaders in the movement. Columbia Bible College (South Carolina) and Ft. Wayne Bible College (Indiana) both enroll thousands in their college-credit courses each year. Several mission boards also have become leaders in offering correspondence courses in Bible books. However, the Association of Christian Continuing Education Schools and Seminaries (ACCESS) reports that MBI remains a leader in offering courses for college credit through home study.[6]

CLASSES IN HOMES AND PRISONS

Without need for chalkboard or teacher, Correspondence School students can

5. Ibid., pp. 125-30.
6. Interview with James Wegner, vice-president of ACCESS, 17 September 1985.

meet almost anywhere. Two of the more unusual programs are the Home Bible Classes and Prison Ministry.

The "group study" plan dates to 1915, when Sunday school classes, young people's societies, and Bible study groups could study home courses together. The teacher or leader of the group enrolled the students and supervised the class study. The Correspondence School received student exams for grading, just as if each person were enrolled and studying privately. Now in addition to individual study, each person had the benefits of group discussion and encouragement.

Home Bible classes remain a popular form of learning thanks to a setting that encourages fellowship and discussion and a pace suitable for the group members. The leader receives a teacher's supplement that includes outlines and additional notes, but leaves the grading to Correspondence School officials.

The class study plan represented a first in correspondence school education. Moody Bible Institute led the entire study-by-mail industry by pioneering the home class plan in 1915. Secular universities adopted the plan in the mid-twenties.[7]

Students even study God's truths by mail in prisons and jails. Throughout the country, prisoners study privately and in groups led by chaplains. As early as 1926, prisons had received Correspondence School courses, but that year one inmate wrote *Moody Monthly* magazine (then called *MBI Monthly*) telling how the correspondence courses had changed attitudes. In response, MBI created a special "gift fund" to place Bible courses in the hands of those behind prison doors.

By 1928 eighty-four prisoners were enrolled. By 1965, 5,000 individuals in 170 penal institutions were studying Moody correspondence courses.

Privately or as members of small groups led by chaplains, thousands of prisoners today are enrolled in Moody Correspondence courses.

The Correspondence School has allowed MBI to establish ties with prisoners, both unbelievers and those who became Christians while in jail. Many inmates discover that while prison walls hold their bodies, correspondence courses can free their spirits.

"If it weren't for those courses I doubt very much if I would have gotten through prison as easily as I did," notes Jimmie Johnson, a former prisoner at Sing Sing Penitentiary in New York. Months before his conviction for armed robbery, Johnson requested a Bible from a prison chaplain. He recognized his need for forgiveness of sins and accepted Christ as his Savior. His desire for alcohol, the force behind most of his crimes, immediately left him.

His good behavior at Sing Sing earned him parole after five years. During those five years, Johnson completed twenty-two courses.[8] Since his release Johnson has presented his testimony many times and visited prisons, recommending the Correspondence School. Recently Jimmie and his wife became missionaries to Chad. He considers the Bible and the Correspondence courses to be the lifeline that preserved him during his prison years.

7. Witmer, p. 130.
8. Rosemary Rausch, "Confined to Study Scripture," *Moody Monthly,* November 1983, p. 36.

CORRESPONDENCE BY RADIO

The Correspondence School offers classes by radio as well as by mail. When radio station WMBI began broadcasting in 1926, one of its first programs was Radio School of the Bible. Two class sessions aired each week, and the Correspondence School selected teachers, mailed materials, and scored exams for all listeners.

Radio School of the Bible evidently is the first correspondence study program ever offered by radio in America. The program has grown quickly in listeners and enrolled students. One hundred sixty students enrolled in seven courses the first year; six years later 1,900 registered.

Today MBI faculty teach the courses, which air nationally on the Moody Broadcasting Network in more than 250 cities. In addition, recordings of broadcasts air in five countries overseas. Students receive a textbook and notes upon enrollment, and complete periodic exams during the academic quarter. They earn Correspondence School credits for successful completion of the course.

Many listeners do not enroll formally, but listen regularly to receive the sound teaching. In 1985, for example, listeners could hear lessons on Survey of the Old Testament I, Survey of the New Testament, Teaching with Results, and Making a Christian Leader.

Part 3

THE VOCATIONAL PROGRAMS AT
MOODY BIBLE INSTITUTE

10

Christian Education

Though seminaries introduced the earliest programs in Christian education, Moody Bible Institute inaugurated the most far-reaching emphasis in Christian education within the evangelical world. Since its program began in 1914, MBI has been training students to become skilled Sunday school teachers, superintendents, and Christian education directors. The program today continues to train church educational workers through two majors in the Department of Christian Education.

Christian education operates on two levels: "Professional" church education offered by Bible institutes and seminaries, and local church education offered by the Sunday school and other church-sponsored educational programs. These programs train students from ages five to eighty-five in the truths of the Christian life as revealed in Scripture. Evangelical churches hope such training will confront the non-Christian student with the need and plan of spiritual salvation and challenge the Christian to a godly life of serving and honoring Jesus Christ.

Within schools of higher education, departments of Christian education typically offer professional church education. The primary goal of such church education is to prepare students for church-related educational ministries, such as administering Christian education programs, serving as missionaries and other vocational church workers, or simply becoming volunteer Sunday school teachers in the local church.

The second level of church education operates within the local church itself. The primary educational agency is the Sunday school, but in many churches other educational programs supplement the Sunday school, including vacation Bible school, youth clubs and groups, children's churches, and the summer camp program.

For many years the Sunday school was the primary educational agency within the church. In 1882 the Young People's Society for Christian Endeavor gave impetus to church youth programs that would accompany the Sunday schools. However, the educational ministry of the church expanded most noticeably in the early decades of the twentieth century. Soon Sunday schools and youth groups linked with vacation Bible school, club programs, children's church, and camping to educate children, teens, and adults.

As the educational ministries of the church expanded, evangelical leaders needed some type of professional educational program to prepare workers to administer
adequately the various educational agencies in the church. Sunday school teachers, superintendents, and youth leaders needed to be trained, and in the early part
of the twentieth century it became clear that the church also needed professional
directors and leaders of church education.

DEPARTMENTS OF CHRISTIAN EDUCATION

When D. L. Moody founded his Bible institute, no departments of Christian
education existed. John H. Vincent, who was active in Sunday school work in
1861, "expected the Christian colleges at once to establish chairs for the training
of teachers of religion, but the chairs were not established to any great extent for
many years."[1]

During the first two decades of the new century, seminaries introduced a few
programs with the major purpose of preparing directors of Christian education.
However, Moody Bible Institute was destined to develop the most far-reaching
emphasis in church education within the evangelical world. Most of the seminaries
with these pioneer programs were theologically liberal; interestingly, natural economic conditions prevented the religious education objectives of these seminaries
from being "successfully realized" at that time.[2] A few theologically conservative
seminaries began professional programs of church education during this period.
These programs flourished; some continue today, including those at Southern Baptist Theological Seminary and Southwestern Baptist Theological Seminary.

As early as 1914 MBI organized a Sunday School Course. By 1922 MBI had introduced a special religious education curriculum with the distinct purpose of preparing men and women for a broad educational ministry in the church. The development of this program and its extensive outreach is related closely to the
influence of the Sunday school movement at large, with its new emphasis on curriculum development and teacher training.

SUNDAY SCHOOL MOVEMENT

During the first half of the nineteenth century, the American Sunday School
Union had functioned as the main professional organization in promoting teacher
training and adequate curriculum within the nation's Sunday schools.

However, by the time Moody Bible Institute began, the American Sunday
School Union had narrowed its objective to missionary endeavor—the founding of
new Sunday schools in unchurched areas. In its place, the local and national interdenominational Sunday school conventions have become the primary agencies in
teacher training and curriculum development. Sunday school workers would gather together from various parts of the country, not only for inspirational purposes,

1. Marianna Brown, *Sunday School Movements in America*, p. 143.
2. K. B. Cully, *The Search for a Christian Education Since 1940*, p. 13.

but to be instructed in how to be more effective teachers and superintendents.

At the fifth national convention in Indianapolis in 1872 "among the themes foremost in interest and importance for its consideration was that of a system of uniform Bible lessons."[3] The International Uniform Lesson system, which grew out of this proposal, was beginning its third cycle of seven years when MBI began. This basic plan would continue for years to come, although it would be subjected to numerous criticisms and revisions.

An organized plan for regular teacher training developed in 1908 when the convention became a permanent organization known as the International Sunday School Association. Delegates at the twelfth international convention held in Louisville, Kentucky, created the first standard course and advanced standard course in teacher training. Eventually these courses would have a significant impact on the MBI curriculum.

The suggested courses were established by 1910, consisting of fifty hours of study of the Bible, the pupil, the teacher, and the school. The advanced course required a hundred hours in the same subjects.

DEVELOPMENT OF THE MOODY CURRICULUM

The beginning of professional church education at Moody Bible Institute owes much to the influence of the International Sunday School Convention and later, the International Sunday School Association. Beginning in 1900 the Biblical Course included a subject entitled "international Sunday school lesson," which was "studied weekly." This, of course, was the Sunday school curriculum of the International Sunday School Convention adopted in 1872.

The 1900-1901 catalog described this subject: "Instruction is given by precept and example in the method of teaching, so that this [course] may be considered a Sunday School Teacher's Institute." The course was not only a study of lesson content, but also of methods of presentation—an approach advocated by the Sunday school convention. In 1903 the International Lesson became segmented, with one section for primary teachers, the other for intermediate and senior teachers.

The next major development occurred in 1911. Three years after the 1908 Louisville convention had designated standard and advanced training courses, MBI combined the international Sunday school lesson course into a broader subject called Sunday school methods. The 1911 catalog stated:

> Experts of the International Sunday School Association give weekly instruction in the theory and practice of Sunday school work, including organization, teacher training, visitation, primary, adult, and home departments. The International Sunday School diploma is awarded those passing the required examination in this work.
>
> The International Sunday School lesson is taught weekly by a member of the

---

3. Executive Committee of the International Sunday School Association, *Organized Sunday School Work in America*, p. 5.

Institute faculty, with special reference to the needs of Sunday school teachers.

SUNDAY SCHOOL COURSE

In 1914 the International Sunday School Association made another important contribution to Moody Bible Institute. In addition to the Bible teacher training class and the Sunday school methods class offered within the Bible Course, MBI added a new course called the Sunday School Course, with E. O. Sellers as director. According to the 1914 catalog, "This course is to equip young men and women who desire to make Sunday-school work their life calling. At the beginning of the fourth term, those who desire may enroll in the special Sunday-school course, receiving upon its completion, a special diploma for the work done in that course."

The Sunday School Course at the Institute became the forerunner of what are now called departments of Christian education in evangelical schools of higher education. The subjects included at that time were child study, religious pedagogy, Sunday school organization and management, history of religious education, blackboard drawing, and practical Christian work.

All these changes aided the development of professional church education at MBI. However, the most significant change was yet to come. Until 1922 the Sunday School Course was described as having been "planned at the suggestion and with the advice and assistance of the General Secretary and other representatives of the International Sunday School Association." But in the 1922-1923 catalog the Sunday School Course was dropped from the curriculum. The subjects previously offered in this course were simply listed with the following statement: "These subjects are of special interest to those who desire to take up Sunday-school work as their life calling."

The International Sunday School Association, of course, had ceased operation, having merged with the Sunday School Council of Evangelical Denominations to form the International Council of Religious Education. The strong influence of the International Sunday School Association was over. No other outside organization would affect professional church education at MBI. Instead, the Institute itself became the most influential agency in promoting evangelical professional church education.

RELIGIOUS EDUCATION COURSE

In 1922, the same year when both the significant merger took place in the Sunday school world and the Sunday School Course no longer appeared in the curriculum, Clarence H. Benson joined the MBI faculty. Benson had been a successful pastor as well as a missionary in Japan. Upon coming to the Institute, he was asked to teach the Sunday school subjects that were formerly in the Sunday School Course.

Benson was not content to continue without a definite program of professional church education and, in 1924 he helped to organize a Religious Education

Course. The course operated similar to a department of Christian education. A "growing demand for directors of religious education" spurred development of the course, explained President James Gray, who added,

> The Institute would have preferred not to have assumed such an added responsibility under present circumstances, but it yielded to the same urge that forced it recently to add to its other courses that for the preparation of pastor. The urge is that religious education as a vocation is in danger of being monopolized by the Liberals, who believe neither in a supernatural Bible or a childhood indeed of a new birth. "Christian" Education Course rather than "Religious" Education Course might have been a better title for the new department in the Institute, but it was felt that the latter was a technical designation of value because it was well-known and easily recognized. . . .[4]

Ever since the turn of the century, liberal theology had gradually permeated the Sunday school convention movement. Similarly, liberal leaders also had influenced the formation of the International Sunday School Association. The formation of the Sunday School Council of Evangelical Denominations revealed even deeper inroads of liberalism. By the time of the significant merger in 1922, the International Council of Religious Education was largely influenced and controlled by leaders who were liberal in theological convictions.

OBJECTIVES AND A NAME CHANGE

Under the leadership of Benson, MBI proceeded to develop its own professional program. Institute leaders believed they now had a superior program to that of the International Council, pointing to the new academic requirements necessary for the MBI certificate. Students would study such subjects as Bible storytelling, biblical geography, manual arts, personal evangelism, and blackboard drawing.

The 1926 catalog included a complete statement of objectives for the new Religious Education Course. The course would "train as directors of Christian education, men and women of executive ability who do not feel called to the pastorate or the mission field, but who desire to use their talents in the organizing and directing of such education in churches when pastors lack time or training for it." Subjects included history of religious education, correlation of religious education, music in religious education, psychology, child study—adolescent period, and curriculum making.

In 1928 the course name was changed to Christian Education Course due to reaction in the evangelical world against the liberalizing term "religious." Initially MBI leaders had wondered about naming the new course the Religious Education Course. They had decided, however, to use the term "religious" since it was a technical term and better known in relationship to the term "education."

As the Christian education program evolved, changes took place in the basic

4. James M. Gray, "Religious Education Course," *Moody Bible Institute Monthly* (December 1923), p. 163.

curriculum structure. Then in 1931 a new three-year course was added called the Christian Education-Music Course, which was designed to prepare students for the dual position of director of Christian education and director of church music.

MBI began its program of departmental majors in 1966, allowing students to earn a Bachelor of Arts degree within five years. A new department of Christian education replaced the Christian Education and Christian Education-Music Courses. Students now could receive a degree in Christian education by completing the MBI three-year curriculum and sixty hours of liberal arts courses at an accredited college or university.

Beginning in fall semester 1986, students can receive their B.A. degree within four years, through an articulation arrangement with two Chicago-area universities (see chapter 21).

The curriculum for Christian education changed more than any other area in the 1966 revision. This was primarily due to an extensive three-year research study of Christian education conducted by the Accrediting Association of Bible Colleges from 1961-1963. The curriculum outline suggested in the Witmer report became a basic guideline for revising subject offerings in order to bring them into conformity with current needs and standards.[5] Some of the new and revised subjects offered in the new curriculum included educational work of the church, principles and methods of teaching, Christian counseling, camping, supervised leadership training, curriculum and history, and philosophy of Christian education.

The Department of Christian Education has expanded and revised its curriculum during the past twenty years. In 1985 course offerings included family education in the church, Christian education administration, curriculum development, the Christian day school, developmental psychology, and educational psychology.

VOCATIONAL MINISTRIES

Students who have completed Christian education at Moody enter many different kinds of church vocations. In addition to those becoming directors of Christian education, graduates also have entered international and U.S. missions work as well as the pastorate. About 53 percent of graduates of the C.E. department have held at least one position in full-time Christian service, and 28 percent held such positions in 1984, according to 1984 alumni survey.[6]

Young women comprise the largest specific segment of C.E. graduates who have chosen a full-time Christian ministry. Many are wives and coworkers of missionaries and other types of full-time Christian workers. For example, during the period 1954-1962, almost 25 percent of C.E. Course graduates were wives of

5. S. A. Witmer, *Report: Preparing Bible College Students for Ministries in Christian Education*, pp. 95-115.
6. Kenneth Bosma, *1984 Alumni Survey*, pp. 46, 48.

Christian workers.[7] This is not surprising, as women have always been the majority enrolled in the C.E. Course and later the Department of Christian Education. Among graduates of the program women have outnumbered men in all but two years since the program began in 1924.

In the world of evangelical Christian education, MBI has also been directly responsible for two major evangelical training organizations. Through the efforts of Professor Benson, MBI has been influential in the founding of a third. Through these organizations the school has multiplied its own outreach through church education many times.

EVANGELICAL TEACHER TRAINING ASSOCIATION

As first secretary of the International Bible Institute Council of Christian Education, Benson began work on a standard training course that would conserve the high standards of the International Council of Religious Education without the objectionable features of the Standard Leadership Course. The "objectionable features," as later pointed out by Benson, were: (1) limited Bible study, (2) neglect of personal evangelism and mission study, (3) lack of sequence in studies, (4) the inadequate recognition of academic training, and (5) a restricted list of approved textbooks.[8] In 1930 the council formed the Evangelical Teacher Training Association (ETTA) to continue the work. The four purposes stated in the preamble to the Articles of Incorporation have remained unchanged through the years, namely to: (1) foster a closer cooperation among evangelical Christian institutions; (2) certify to the public a deep interest and concern for Christian education; (3) provide and promote a common course in teacher training that will give adequate attention to Bible, personal evangelism, and missions; and (4) recognize and encourage the use of textbooks of approved orthodoxy.[9]

The ETTA offers three certification programs: the Christian education diploma, the standard teacher's diploma, and the teacher's certificate. The fourteen preliminary and advanced certificate courses prepare lay teachers for more effective ministry in the local church, while the diploma courses qualify individuals as ETTA teachers of the certificate courses.

Diploma courses can be taught only by ETTA member schools. Moody Bible Institute is among sixty-five active-member schools that award the C.E. diploma of ETTA. Thus, MBI students in the Department of Christian Education receive two diplomas upon graduation, one from MBI, the other from ETTA. The association also offers training toward the C.E. diploma through an additional 150 associate and affiliate schools.

Students can earn the C.E. diploma by completing thirty-four semester hours of Bible and specified Christian education courses. Graduates may teach all ETTA certificate courses for ETTA credit to local church teachers and leaders. Students

7. Gene A. Getz, *Report of the Presidential Questionnaire*, I, 53.
8. Clarence H. Benson, *The Sunday School in Action*, pp. 127-31.
9. "ETTA — What and Why?" (special form prepared by the Evangelical Teacher Training Association, Wheaton, Ill., n.d.).

can earn the standard diploma by completing twenty-four academic hours in Bible, teacher training, evangelism, human development, church educational program, and a child, youth, or adult education speciality. This diploma qualifies the graduate to teach ETTA leadership courses.

Because of the two-fold emphasis on professional lay training, ETTA has been a major contributor within both higher Christian education and the local church. Palmer states that "the Association legally belongs to the Bible Institutes, but it also belongs to the people in the churches."[10]

ETTA has had a significant impact on the Bible institute-college movement. According to C. B. Eavey in *The History of Christian Education*:

> The Association was first and at the time the only agency affording Bible institutes means for obtaining some kind of uniformity among themselves. Its work and objectives met with the approval of most institutes as well as some colleges and some seminaries. A large proportion of the institutes became members of the Association immediately, and others endeavored to qualify as soon as possible.[11]

Relative to the local church, Frank E. Gaebelein points out in *Christian Education in a Democracy*, "this association has done much for the improvement of teaching in the evangelical Sunday schools of America."[12] Eavey adds that ETTA "has raised the level of teaching wherever its courses have been used."[13]

Thirty evangelical denominations have adopted the ETTA certificate program as their official denominational training program, and churches in another thirty denominations use ETTA material as part of their training program. During the 1980s, certificate courses have been taught in more than eighty countries.[14]

ETTA AND MOODY BIBLE INSTITUTE

The direct contributions of ETTA to evangelical education are the indirect contributions of Moody Bible Institute. Although the idea of an evangelical organization of this type was instilled in Benson's mind by a public school teacher from New York City, it was Benson who developed and initiated the idea. The MBI educator largely developed the curriculum and materials.

MBI's direct contribution to ETTA can be observed in the association's curriculum plan. Benson used as the basis for the ETTA curriculum essentially what he had produced at the Institute prior to 1930. The Institute's Christian education subjects in 1930 had changed little from those included in the Religious Education Course organized by Benson in 1924. When MBI joined the ETTA in 1932, the school's C.E. curriculum was affected only slightly. In fact, the Moody curricu-

10. Joy E. Palmer, "The Contributions of Clarence H. Benson to the Field of Christian Education" (unpublished master's thesis), p. 68.
11. C. B. Eavey, *History of Christian Education*, p. 343.
12. Frank E. Gaebelein, *Christian Education in a Democracy*, p. 226.
13. Eavey, p. 415.
14. "Christian Education Diploma," pamphlet of the Evangelical Teacher Training Association.

lum went on as usual after ETTA was developed while many other schools adopted the ETTA pattern. Put another way, they also adopted the Moody pattern.

Another factor that indicates that similarity of the two curricula is that Benson wrote several textbooks that were used for both programs. Five textbooks written for his MBI courses and published by Moody Press also were used by ETTA: *An Introduction to Child Study, The Sunday School in Action, History of Christian Education, Techniques of a Working Church,* and *The Christian Teacher.*

In addition to these textbooks, Benson prepared a number of manuals for use in the ETTA Certificate Courses on the local church level. Originally these manuals were published by Moody Bible Institute, but are now, through special arrangement, the property of ETTA.

The research commission of the National Sunday School Association in 1959 surveyed sixty-three Bible institutes, colleges, Christian liberal arts colleges and seminaries to learn which books were used most frequently in teaching courses in professional church education. Out of forty different books used in the sixty-three different schools, Benson's *The Sunday School in Action* was used more frequently than any other book. The textbook survey listed three more of his books as third, sixth, and ninth in usage.[15]

Benson served as ETTA president from 1952 until his death in 1954. However, the influence of MBI educators upon ETTA still continued. Professor Harold Garner became vice-president of ETTA in 1955, and beginning in 1958, Garner served fourteen years as vice-president and chairman of the board while teaching at MBI. Garner was a former pastor who strongly endorsed the ETTA program. He taught at MBI twenty-five years and became the first chairman of the Department of Christian Education in 1966.

When Garner retired from MBI in 1972, he continued as ETTA chairman of the board for three more years, helping administer an organization that has been called "the interdenominational leader in the field of local church . . . leadership development in Christian education throughout the 20th century."[16]

Garner served on the ETTA executive board for twenty years. What Benson had helped to start, Garner enthusiastically promoted.

SCRIPTURE PRESS AND MBI

Shortly after Professor Benson arrived at MBI in 1922, he became concerned about teacher training as well as the lack of adequate evangelical curriculum materials. He objected to the uniform lessons in use since 1872 because they were planned to cover "only 35 percent of the Bible." He also objected to the lesson outlines because they "were framed, prepared, and worked out from the adult point of view" and "not adapted to children."[17]

Benson also disagreed with the closely-graded systems, saying they were re-

15. National Sunday School Association, "Textbook Survey Report," pp. 8-9.
16. Kenneth O. Gangel in "ETTA: 50 Years Serving Christ Thru Leadership Training," booklet, p. 4.
17. Benson, *The Sunday School,* pp. 143-49.

stricted in their use because of "numerous small Sunday schools," and the "lack of trained teachers [and] suitable literature."

Meanwhile the International Council of Religious Education was developing new experienced-centered lessons. Benson considered the underlying philosophy of this new educational approach to be out of harmony with the basic presuppositions of evangelical theology. In addition he criticized the council for substituting "methodology at the expense of content." However, Benson still recognized in this new approach several commendable points:

> Its advocates remind us that they are only reviving the interlocutory and catechetical methods of the early church, who said it was the teacher's part to listen and the pupil's part to question. There is no doubt that we have laid too much stress upon instruction. Education has been considered a pouring-in instead of a drawing-out process, and the teacher was supposed to have fulfilled his function when he passed on to his pupils the knowledge he possessed. Modern education has put a new interest and enthusiasm into study by making the child a part of it. It relies on the point of contact for kindling intellectual zeal and upholds the joy and spontaneity of childhood. The will of the pupil and his interest and good feeling at the moment are the teacher's only dependency. Instead of "discipline and repression," modern education sets up the motto of "development and expression."[18]

The strengths and weaknesses in the old as well as the new materials challenged Benson, and "hundreds of requests for orthodox material," spurred him to action.[19] In 1925 the Moody professor began to work with his Christian education students on the development of a new system of lessons. For the task he engaged "a corps of college graduates in his advanced classes, most of whom had had public school teaching experience with different age-groups."[20] They critically examined all existing curricula, trying to construct a new series that would provide comprehensive, "consecutive and complete Bible instruction."[21]

Six principles guided the preparing of materials: (1) The Bible and the Bible alone is the religion of Protestants; (2) all Scripture is profitable for instruction; (3) the lessons should be adapted to the capacity of the pupil; (4) Bible instruction can be made personal and practical; (5) Bible instruction should parallel religious observance; (6) Bible instruction should be adapted to department organizations and public school divisions.[22]

After eight years of investigation, criticism, and experiment, in 1933 Benson and his students offered to the evangelical public a new series of Sunday school lessons that they called the All Bible Graded Series.

Originally, Benson had hoped MBI would publish these materials, but Institute leaders did not feel led to become a publishing firm for Sunday school curricula.

18. Ibid., pp. 144-50.
19. C. V. Egemeier, "Our New Editor-in-Chief," Church School Promoter, III (August 1941), 54.
20. *Story of Scripture Press* (pamphlet), p. 2.
21. Benson, *A Popular History of Christian Education*, p. 229.
22. Benson, *The Sunday School*, pp. 151-54.

However, when Benson's students completed the project in 1933, Victor E. Cory of the Bible Institute Colportage Association became interested in the new materials. Consequently, Benson and Cory teamed up and founded Scripture Press. Cory regarded Benson and the material as innovative.

Benson changed the thinking of evangelicals as to the underlying principles, quite contrary to the trends of the day. There existed the two extremes; the international uniform lessons on one hand; and on the other extreme, the closely-graded lessons inaugurated by the denominations associated with the Old International Council of Religious Education. Dr. Benson was a pioneer in the development of the departmentally-graded lessons, which avoided the disadvantage of either of the two extremes.[23]

Similar to the beginning of ETTA, Scripture Press grew out of the classrooms at Moody Bible Institute and developed into a separate organization. It began with the production of Sunday school and vacation Bible school curricula, but today Scripture Press publishes materials for use in "the total church program." In addition to the materials for use in the Sunday school and vacation Bible school, materials are available for use in Sunday evening youth groups, children's church, and camps.

Scripture Press is not the only nor the largest publisher of evangelical curriculum materials. However, this organization has made a distinct contribution to evangelicalism, because it originated at a time when evangelicals felt a great need for suitable materials. Today most Protestant denominations use the materials and Scripture Press curriculum is printed in ninety-five languages for worldwide distribution. Once again the direct contributions of Scripture Press actually represent the indirect contributions of Moody Bible Institute.

NATIONAL SUNDAY SCHOOL ASSOCIATION

Though more related to Benson personally than to the Moody Bible Institute, it is important to mention the founding of the National Sunday School Association in 1946. Benson also became much involved in the development of lesson outlines that were eventually called the Uniform Bible Lesson Series. He favored these lessons, "not because he was in favor of uniform lessons as such, but because more than one half of the Sunday schools in the country were using uniform lessons. He wanted to contribute the best lessons possible."[24]

The National Sunday School Association (NSSA) actually came into being as a result of concern by The National Association of Evangelicals over the curriculum outlines of the International Council. Benson decried "the modernists who have gained control of the Council . . ." and noted, "the lessons have not been acceptable to the orthodox constituency of the Protestant churches."[25] Benson became very active in this new organization, not only through his interest in the new curri-

23. Palmer, p. 62.
24. Ibid., p. 70.
25. Benson, *The Sunday School,* pp. 155-56.

culum materials but through the national conventions sponsored by NSSA each year. According to Clate A. Risley, executive secretary of NSSA from 1952-1964, "Benson more than any other single person renewed interest in the Sunday school convention movement."[26]

Since the first convention in 1946, an annual three-day convention has been held in major cities throughout the United States and Canada, with registered delegates numbering as many as ten thousand. In addition numerous evangelical state and local associations have been formed as offspring of this parent organization.

26. Palmer, p. 71.

11

Missions

The story of Moody Bible Institute and evangelical missions reaches around the globe into almost every country. Of MBI's many contributions to the evangelical cause, this has been the most far-reaching and influential.

The modern missionary period was already nearly one hundred years old when Moody Bible Institute opened its classrooms. But in its early days, MBI did not have a special curriculum designed for the preparation of foreign missionaries. Though Moody was very interested in foreign missions, he was primarily concerned about preparing "gap-men," lay men and women who could assist pastors and other Christian leaders in reaching the lower classes in urban society. This plan, however, was destined to change. People soon began coming from all over the world to prepare for all types of Christian service, including foreign missions. By 1899, 130 former students were already serving as missionaries in foreign lands. Of those students whose specific vocations were known, this represented 12.5 percent.

Since a number of students were coming specifically to prepare to be foreign missionaries, the objectives and curriculum of the school began to undergo change. By 1895 the stated objectives for both the men's and women's departments included the preparation of foreign missionaries.

The first reference to a missionary course occurred in 1900, an informal program associated with a new student organization called the Missionary Study and Prayer Union. No specific subjects were listed. One hour per week was "regularly set aside for consideration of home and foreign missions," with "general meetings" being held periodically.

By 1904 the term "missionary course" was changed to "missionary study" and became a required subject within the Bible Course. This change indicated an increased emphasis on missions, as all students in the Bible Course were now required to study missions. Previously, missionary study was optional.

A FORMAL MISSIONARY COURSE

The first formal Missionary Course began in 1912 with Edward A. Marshall as director. Students devoted two hours each week to the study of city, home, and foreign missionary work. In addition, students traced the development of the missionary enterprise through the evangelical church.

The Missionary Course added five subjects in 1915, designed particularly for those students who were planning to go to the foreign field: the life of the missionary, comparative religions, the history and science of missions, phonetics and language study, and tropical hygiene.

Thus the first Missionary Course had a dual focus: First-year courses helped all students build an interest in missions, and courses offered during the second year were designed for those who were planning to become foreign missionaries.

Two years later, in 1917, the missionary program established two emphases: home missions and foreign missions. The program in home missions was in essence the regular Bible Course. The foreign missions emphasis concentrated on answering the new demands in missionary training. MBI continued to add subjects to its Missionary Course over the years. Under Director William H. Hockman (1927-1945) the Missionary Course offered increased medical training reflecting the needs and demands on the mission fields during this time. Students could elect either a short or a long course in special missionary preparation. The short course was in essence the program offered previously, while the long course included a number of additional medical subjects, such as anatomy and physiology, diseases of digestive organs, diseases of eye, ear, nose, and throat, minor surgery, obstetrics, and tropical diseases.

This curriculum resulted in a seven-term Missionary Course and a nine-term Missionary Medical Service Course, both offered until 1930. The two programs then merged into one course of eight terms, designated the Missionary Course. When MBI changed from the term plan to the semester plan in 1951, the Missionary Course became a six-semester program. Certain required courses in the previous program became electives in the new curriculum, and students had to complete six weeks of fieldwork in home missions during one summer.

By 1956, the Missionary Course included four majors: Bible, Christian education, biblical languages, and modern languages. In addition, the curriculum was organized so that "graduates of four-year liberal arts colleges or universities could complete the course in two years instead of three."

JEWISH MISSIONS COURSE

The Jewish Missions Course began in 1923 with Solomon Birnbaum, a Hebrew Christian, as director. In the early days, the Hebrew Christian Alliance of America sponsored the program, but later it became a course offered by MBI. The three-year course proposed "to prepare workers to carry the Gospel of Christ to the Jews" at home or abroad.

In addition to the Bible subjects and other subjects already required in the general course, Jewish missions offered the following specialized subjects: Hebrew, Rabbinics (a study of the rabbinical writings), Jewish history, Messianic prophecy, Yiddish, and Jewish feasts and customs.

Four Hebrew Christians have led the Jewish missions program: Solomon Birnbaum, course director from 1923-1940; Max I. Reich, course director from 1940-1946; Nathan J. Stone, course director from 1946-1966; and Louis Goldberg, professor of Jewish studies, who continues to guide the program today as an emphasis within the World Missions Department (see "New Programs, New Names," p.108).

The Jewish Missions Course represented the first complete training program for ministry in Jewish missions. Stone notes, "Though other schools offer a subject or two on Jewish missions, the Institute provides an entire three-year course for those interested in this type of ministry." By 1936 about 50 percent of those in Jewish ministry in the U.S. were former MBI students, Stone has estimated.

Missionary Technical Course

In 1941, Paul Robinson, a pastor and MBI alumnus, began making plans to go to the mission field. Because he believed that an ability to fly would help him as a missionary, he learned to pilot a plane and soloed on December 3, 1941. Four days later, America declared war on Japan, and Robinson was grounded along with other civilian pilots. In order to continue his flying and to get more experience, Robinson joined the Civil Air Patrol and flew under military orders.

When Robinson finally applied for missionary service, the mission board advised him not to go to the field because of his age and family responsibilities. Taking the board's advice, Robinson dedicated his time to teaching flying skills to other, younger would-be missionaries.

In February 1946, Robinson proposed to MBI leaders a plan to train missionaries in aviation. Henry Coleman Crowell, MBI executive vice-president who had been the key man in the development of the radio ministry and the main promoter for Moody Institute of Science, took a vital interest in Robinson's proposal. Three months later the board of trustees approved the plan. One member even offered to buy the first two airplanes.

On May 1, 1946, the flight program lifted off. It would quickly become the premier program in the country for training missionary pilots.

Using a plot of land that MBI had leased at suburban Elmhurst Airport, Robinson intended to teach missionaries to fly. However, it soon became clear that specialists were needed who could serve the general missionaries with transportation and communication to the outside world. Robinson envisioned a "missionary airplane."

Therefore in 1949, a Missionary Technical Course emerged, "to meet the recognized need for missionaries who have technical knowledge as well as Bible Institute training." After spending two years in direct study of the Bible, as well as in missionary subjects, each student was to spend two more years receiving technical training in four areas: radio and communications, photography, aircraft maintenance and repair, and flight and ground work, which would lead to a commercial pilot license.

Since the course's beginning, the technical curriculum has undergone numerous changes in order to provide the most practical program to meet field needs. The current technical program has evolved from refining the curriculum and consulting missionary aviation agencies concerning the changing field needs.

Two distinct majors appeared in the 1954 catalog: aviation flight and mechanics, and radio and communications. Within the aviation flight and mechanics major, a student could concentrate either in aircraft and engine mechanics or in flying during his third year.

Because of an increased interest in the Technical Course, and in order to select the best qualified men, a screening process developed. Aptitude tests and a flight camp narrowed the field of candidates. Based on their aptitude and spiritual qualifications for this type of ministry, a select, qualified group of students entered formal training each year.

To screen students even more carefully, beginning in 1960 all students admitted to the aviation program were required to successfully complete a two-year pre-aviation curriculum in the regular Missionary Course. Students could continue in the regular MBI curriculum if they failed to qualify, and the Institute was assured of higher quality students in the technical major.

The jet age came booming into Chicago in the sixties with the completion of O'Hare International Airport, destined to become the busiest in the world. In 1950, MBI had relocated its flight school to peaceful Wood Dale Airport, less than twenty-five miles from the main campus. However, O'Hare now threatened to crowd the small flight school, limiting air routes and flight times.

MBI trustees wisely approved the purchase of land in Elizabethton, Tennessee, in 1967. The hilly terrain of eastern Tennessee clearly simulated the flight conditions of typical missions work—primitive settings and changing elevations—while providing room for the flight school to expand. Today twenty-one planes and sixteen instructors train future missionary pilots at Elizabethton.

New Programs, New Names

Many changes occurred in the missions program during the 1960s and 1970s, but probably the most significant involved name changes. In 1966 the Missionary Course was renamed the Department of Missions as the school began to offer a B.A. degree in five years. In 1976, the home missions major of the department became the American Intercultural Ministries major, or AIM. The name recognized that rural and urban America had become multicultural, with immigrants and many ethnic groups locating in the cities. AIM provides perceptual and ministry skills by offering students emphases in one of six areas: black American, Asian American, native American, Hispanic, rural American, and urban American ministries.

Leaders in the missions department felt the name change would elevate American missions to the attention of students and supporters as a worthy enterprise. Somehow home missions had become the ugly stepsister of foreign missions, its needs seemingly less important and challenging than missionary service overseas.

Howard Whaley, then chairman of the missions department, explained: "The program at MBI was emphasizing foreign missions, with home missions regarded as preliminary training. But we realized that the field is the world and students are to minister at both Jerusalem and Samaria."[1]

With this new emphasis in place, faculty within the Department of Missions began to reexamine the entire program and concluded the label "foreign missions" major was also misleading. Raymond Tallman, currently chairman of the department, explains, " 'Foreign' had become the term for missionary work that was thought to be cross-cultural. However, with the American Intercultural Ministries we had taken the first step in identifying . . . home missions as cross-cultural."[2]

To recognize the equality between foreign and home missions, in 1981 the foreign missions major became international ministries, while the American intercultural ministries major continued. Both became part of the new Department of World Missions.

The present missions program offers the prospective missionary practical training for the field instead of emphasizing the history and techniques of the missionary enterprise. New courses include missionary relationships, which explore such essential skills as interpersonal relationships, management techniques, and handling stress.

Missions agencies immediately endorsed the new program. Whaley reports, "By 1980 we had people from missions agencies saying to inquirers, 'Go to Moody if you want the best training.' " Enrollment in the department surged 66 percent during the first four years of the new program.

Meanwhile, other missionary programs were also experiencing changes. When the new baccalaureate program began in 1966, the Missionary Technical Course became the Department of Missionary Technical Training. Two separate departments appeared in 1971, Missionary Aviation and Missionary Radio. The Jewish studies major remained part of the Department of Missions but became the Jewish and modern Israel studies major in 1973.

The objective of the Missionary Radio Department was "to prepare missionary technologists in point-to-point communications and missionary radio broadcasting." Initially enrollment was strong, but as student attendance began to decline, officials became aware of a decreasing need. Electronics training had become available at numerous community colleges and technical institutes. Furthermore, students with technical skills now came to MBI for specialized training in Bible and theology as one-year special studies or advanced studies students. Clearly the department no longer needed to train radio technologists, and in 1978 the department disappeared.

Similarly the missionary nursing program ended in 1981 when it was clear that many students were arriving at MBI as nurses already, seeking biblical training prior to missions service. To help these nurses, the Department of World Missions

1. Howard A. Whaley, interview, 10 July 1985.
2. Raymond Tallman, interview, 28 August 1985.

eliminated a nursing major but offered practical supplemental electives on subjects such as nutrition in developing countries and tropical diseases.

Early in the history of the Institute, students organized a missions group called the Bible Institute Foreign Missionary Band. This student group actually functioned as a branch of the national organization known as the Student Volunteer Movement for Foreign Missions.

By 1911 the Student Volunteer Movement for Foreign Missions had bands of students in nearly a thousand institutions of higher learning in North America. Moody Bible Institute was one of these schools, which is not surprising since D. L. Moody was a key figure in helping to found the national movement.

Membership in the band at Moody was limited to those who were definitely planning on becoming foreign missionaries. By 1895 the membership had already reached twenty-five, and ninety of the members were still at the Institute. In 1927 the Student Volunteer Band ceased to function at MBI, probably because of the liberal theological views that had permeated the national Student Volunteer Movement.

The MBI Missionary Union began in 1900 as the Missionary Study and Prayer Union. Originally the MSPU program corresponded closely with the regular curriculum, since the outline for the MSPU meetings formed the basis for the first informal Missionary Course, also introduced in 1900.

By 1913 all students were required to attend the union meetings at 9 A.M. on Wednesdays and received one-half hour credit per term. MSPU became Missionary Union in 1914, with the former MSPU subject requirements shifting to the General Course in Missions.

Until 1921 Missionary Union continued to be both a student organization and a part of the curriculum. At that time the General Course in Missions was rendered Missions and became the introductory subject required of all students. Missionary Union then became a student organization under faculty guidance. Its membership was voluntary, and its constitutional objectives were as follows:

> To stimulate and foster the missionary spirit and purpose in the student body by the holding of stated meetings, voluntarily attended; to promote systematic missionary intercession, and missionary giving through voluntary offerings; to keep in touch with Moody Bible Institute students on the mission fields; to conduct missionary meetings among the churches; and by every possible means to emphasize and forward the supreme Christian task of world evangelization.[3]

STUDENT MISSIONARY FELLOWSHIP

Two significant changes dramatically increased student participation in missions at MBI. Beginning in 1964, all students automatically became members of Missionary Union upon enrollment at MBI, though attendance at meetings and participation remained voluntary. Many students responded to this approach, but a

3. Catalog (1927-1928), pp. 28-29.

second change would have a greater impact: In 1981 Missionary Union became the Student Missionary Fellowship.

The name change eliminated some false impressions. Some students considered Missionary Union a club one had to join first, a "holy club" for the missions elite. "Fellowship" implies that all students can be part of the missionary vision, even those who are not missions majors or planning on a missionary career.[4]

Student participation in the 1980s has been notable. Most contribute to SMU's two missions projects each year. Students contribute between $5,000 and $15,000 to each project. Giving is voluntary, but most respond to the vision. In 1985 they sent hundreds of reference books to Chinese pastors on Mainland China. Working with the African Inland Missions, they have shipped Bibles to Zaire.

In addition, many students attend Prayer Focuses, where they intercede for the lost of different cultures and communities: the Muslims, Latin America, unsaved relatives, and black Americans. SMU leaders help fellow students remain aware of the evangelistic needs of the world through several chapels each semester. Chapels may focus on international students enrolled at Moody, reports on student missions experience, presentations by guest missionaries, or use drama, music, or readings to depict the place of missions in the student's world.

Campus-wide interest in missions can be measured by student response to the annual Missions Conference. More than seventy missionaries and mission agency leaders lead seminars for three days each fall semester. Students can interact, even challenge speakers in these small encounters. In addition they attend plenary sessions to hear a missionary spokesman. Many students respond; in 1983, 52 percent of the students indicated they were seriously considering missions service or sensed God's call to serve Him in missions.

ALUMNI ON THE MISSION FIELD

Three long, brass-trimmed plaques mounted in the entryway of Torrey-Gray Auditorium list the names of students who are active in foreign mission service. The plaques stretch almost forty feet across the foyer wall. As of 1985, 2,500 students are serving on foreign fields. These men and women work under the guidance of hundreds of mission boards and agencies in 108 countries.

Since 1895, 6,100 former students have served on foreign fields. Missionary alumni come from the Bible, Christian Education, Communications, and Pastoral Training Departments as well as the Department of World Missions.

From 1800 to 1954 evangelical missionaries entered approximately 120 countries and territories for the first time. By the time Moody Bible Institute was founded almost one hundred of these areas had already been penetrated.[5] Though MBI did little to contribute to the origin of the modern missionary movement, statistics do show that Moody Bible Institute progressively made a significant contribution

---

4. Tallman, interview.
5. John Caldwell Thiessen, *A Survey of World Missions*. This information was obtained by compiling a table of dates from Thiessen's book showing when each country was entered by evangelical missionaries.

to the development of this movement. In 1893 there were approximately 9,000 Protestant missionaries in the world. By comparison, 85 former students at Moody had already traveled to the foreign field by 1895. This means that six years after the full-time Bible Institute had officially opened, approximately one percent of the total Protestant foreign missionary staff in the world had studied at Moody Bible Institute. In China alone, almost 650 MBI alumni were serving as missionaries by 1900.[6] The number of MBI alumni-missionaries, as a percentage of the total foreign missionary force, continued to climb until 1938 when it had reached over 5 percent. In a matter of a few years MBI had become one of the the most significant evangelical missionary training centers in the world. Today about 3 percent of all foreign missionaries are alumni of Moody Bible Institute.[7]

MBI has had a continuing impact as a training ground in North America. In 1984 about 53,000 Protestant missionaries originated in North America, and one of every twenty had received his or her training at MBI.[8]

IMPACT ON WORLD MISSIONS

MBI has been a major factor in the success of many mission agencies. The Evangelical Alliance Mission increased its missionary force from 228 to 820 under the leadership (1946-1961) of David H. Johnson, an MBI graduate. Johnson's successor as TEAM general director was also a Moody alumnus, Vernon Mortenson. Dr. Mortenson led TEAM for thirteen years, directing the mission as it expanded to include more than one thousand missionaries.[9]

Two MBI alumni, Herbert Griffin and Arthur Glasser, served as North American directors of the China Inland Mission when it was the largest mission of its kind in the world. George Verwer founded Operation Mobilization while still a student at MBI. OM's two ships, the *Logos* and the *Doulos*, dock in ports throughout Europe, and missionary teams distribute literature across the continent. Verwer has directed OM for almost thirty years.

Raymond Davis, general director emeritus of the Sudan Interior Mission, describes the impact of MBI on his organization:

> At the time of our greatest number of missionaries, 1,331 in 1957, about one-third were Moody alumni.
>
> I believe that no other Bible training institution anywhere in the world has made a greater contribution to the training of missionaries who have served in SIM. History now proves that those missionaries in SIM who were pivotal pioneers who God used in the establishing of . . . widespread churches, especially in

---

6. J. Herbert Kane, "The Role of Moody in World Missions," p. 4.
7. Mary Janss-Clary, "Christianity in the World," *World Vision,* January 1981, pp. 3-5; Lawrence E. Keyes, *The Last Ages of Missions*; Interdenominational Foreign Missions Association, Wheaton, Ill.; and Central Records, Moody Bible Institute.
8. Ibid.
9. Flood and Jenkins, *Teaching the Word*, p. 152.

Ethiopia and Nigeria, received their training at Moody Bible Institute.[10]

Other "pivotal pioneers" have left MBI to achieve notable ministries. Walter Post was the first missionary to enter New Guinea. For fifty years Margaret Laird served in the Central African Republic as linguist, nurse, and homesteader. "Almost single-handedly she was instrumental in keeping the government from adopting French, instead of Santo, as the official language,"[11] Kane writes. In 1959 she received the highest honor of the Republic, the "Knight of the Order of Merit," for her work.

MBI also emphasizes the missionary enterprise in America. By 1892 four single women were already working among the North American Indians, according to the *Institute Tie*, predecessor to *Moody Monthly*.

Since that time, MBI graduates have continued to influence missions work in the United States. The 1984 death of Kristin Kent, an AIM major, renewed interest in urban evangelism. Looking forward to evangelizing in the inner city, Kristin died violently a few blocks from campus shortly before her senior year was to begin. A scholarship in her name now assists other MBI students preparing to serve in the U.S. mission field. At her memorial service President Sweeting proclaimed, "From our student body there will be dozens of young men and women who will go not to the jungles of Ecuador but to the jungles of the cities of the United States and the world because of this good testimony."

After graduation, an MBI alumnus usually needs five additional years before entering missions work. Graduates visit mission agencies, receive further training, and obtain financial and prayer support. Despite this delay, about eighty graduates of MBI join the missionary ranks each year.

IMPACT UPON MISSIONARY AVIATION

Moody Bible Institute was the first Christian school to introduce a specialized program with the sole objective of preparing missionary technicians. Ten other schools in America now offer flight training for missions service, but MBI continues to supply about 50 percent of all pilots and technicians at the two major mission aviation agencies, Mission Aviation Fellowship and Jungle Aviation and Radio Service. Furthermore, 80 percent of all Moody Aviation graduates have served or are serving at MAF, JAARS, or one of forty other mission boards using pilots.[12]

During its first forty years, the Department of Missionary Technology—Aviation, known simply as Moody Aviation School, has graduated 504 students. The facilities and need for individualized instruction have always limited enrollment. Founder Robinson once said, "the emphasis has been increasingly on quality, not quantity." In 1985, sixty-five students attended the flight school in Tennessee.

Safety is a major concern, and the Moody aviator will log more than 350 hours

10. Kane, "The Role of Moody in World Missions," pp. 11-12.
11. Ibid., p. 7.
12. Ken Simmelink, interview, 5 September 1985.

before he receives his degree, even though the FAA requires only 200 hours for a commercial license. The grand finale for his training is a taxing cross-county flight into Mexico and California. The cross-country team encounters mechanical, geographical, and weather obstacles en route, and the pilots feel like seasoned veterans upon touchdown back in Elizabethton.

James C. Truxton, a former vice-president of Missionary Aviation Fellowship, believes this intensive training yields the best type of pilot and mechanic for missions work.

> We have by now had abundant opportunity to make a fair evaluation as to the difference in quality and capability for the task between those who come from the mission-geared Moody course, and those who come out of either military or secular avenues of training. There is no question but that the former are far, far ahead, both in their grasp of what is involved; and in their spiritual equipment by which to stick with it through the years.

In 1961, the aviation section of the Moody Technical Department was awarded "examining authority" for private pilots by the Federal Aviation Agency. This appointment placed the Institute among the limited number of aviation schools in the United States that have met training standards sufficiently high to authorize them to issue certain airman certificates without further government (FAA) examination.

Through MBI's unique financial arrangement, many students become pilots and technicians who otherwise could not afford to. Ever since Moody Aviation began in 1946, the Moody Bible Institute has subsidized at least 60 percent of the cost of the operation.[13] As with total educational operation, tuition has been free. The total cost to the Institute to operate its own airport, to pay the salaries of its professional technicians, to purchase and maintain planes, machinery, and radio equipment, represents indirect investments in the total evangelical missionary program.

The student pilots pay only for their own tools, books, and flight fees, about 20 percent of the total costs. They also contribute the final 20 percent through a unique work-study type of program. Students participate in their own commercial charter service, Moody Aviation, and also perform maintenance work at local airports.

The story of MBI missions, told only in summary form here, is a story reaching around the world. The specific contributions of Moody Bible Institute to evangelical missions are abundant. Even the school seems to reproduce itself, as many former students at Moody have started Bible institutes on the mission field patterned after their alma mater. With little exaggeration, leaders at MBI proclaim, "Moody is Missions."

---

13. Annual Report of the Missionary Technical Department (1962).

12

Pastoral Training

Though not a seminary, Moody Bible Institute has a strong impact on the pulpits of America. Even before its Pastors Course began in 1922, MBI saw many of its graduates serving as pastors and pastors' assistants. Today many graduates of the pastoral studies and Bible-theology programs can be found in churches across America. Some are in large, well-known churches, others in obscure small-town locales. All receive the same training at MBI and with fervor proclaim the gospel of salvation through Jesus Christ.

Perhaps MBI's greatest impact has been upon churches in rural America. The need for ministers in villages and small towns originally was a major force behind the Pastors Course, and today many MBI-trained pastors serve in rural communities. In fact, thousands of rural churches have been organized by Moody graduates during the past century—from the north woods of Minnesota to the Arkansas Ozarks, from the mountains of West Virginia to the Pacific Northwest forests.[1]

Neither Dwight L. Moody nor his colleagues originally wanted to develop a pastoral training program at the school. Furthermore, they knew they risked misunderstanding by seminary leaders and church officials if they began training ministers. However, late in the nineteenth century, religious trends and events seemed to merge, making a pastoral program not only acceptable but essential to D. L. Moody and his school. Among the historical factors that caused Moody to rethink his position about pastoral studies at the school were: (1) the multiplication of churches and urban communities and an insufficient number of trained pastors to meet these expanding needs; (2) the rise of interdenominational activity; and (3) the development of the lay movement.

Between 1860 and 1900, the number of churches within major Protestant denominations had more than tripled, reaching 155,000. Thus, during the period that Moody Bible Institute was forming in the minds of its founders, local congregations were multiplying rapidly.

As the number of churches grew, other developments occurred that would signi-

---

1. Flood and Jenkins, *Teaching The Word*, p. 123.

ficantly affect the objectives of Moody's new school. Immigrants began streaming into the United States, resulting in a growing urbanization. W. W. Sweet in his book *The Story of Religion in America* notes, "One of the marvels of the eighties was the astonishing growth of cities. The rapid rise of Chicago, Cleveland, Detroit, Milwaukee and the Twin Cities in the middle west are typical."[2]

Even though churches were expanding more rapidly than the total population during this time, they suffered from several problems. According to Henry K. Rowe in *The History of Religion in the United States* there were three main handicaps to church efficiency. First, there were not enough trained ministers and Sunday school teachers; second, a conservative attitude prevailed regarding new methods; and third, denominationalism held strong sway.[3]

REASONS FOR A PASTORAL PROGRAM

D. L. Moody became aware of some of these problems during his evangelistic travels. There were not enough ministers to reach the growing number of unchurched people, particularly in the large cities. Many of the young people, even though they had been exposed to spiritual guidance in their rural environment, "often neglected their religious life because the city provided them with anonymity." The "immigrant laborers settled in congested areas, and the native groups moved to the suburbs, along with their churches." In addition, "material success [often] created indifference to spiritual life that could only be characterized as secularism."[4]

These conditions also caused Moody to sense the need for what he termed "gapmen." In addition to a trained clergy, he called for men and women who could teach Sunday school, work in missions, and do the type of work that was being neglected by the established churches.

But the ministerial problem was twofold, as observed by Moody. In addition to there being too few ministers to do the job, many of the pastors were unable to reach the lower classes even if they did have the desire and the time. The seminaries, Moody felt, were training these leaders to minister only to the upper classes—the educated and sophisticated strata of society. There was a need to educate people who had a good grasp of the English Bible as well as knowledge of aggressive methods of Christian work who would be able to reach the masses.

The second main problem—a conservative attitude toward new methods—was not unrelated to the first ministerial problem. Moody was aware of the tradition that characterized most ministers as "other worldly." As Rowe comments, "It was difficult, even for Protestant churches in America, to escape from the obsession that the clergy constituted a class apart, with distinct privileges and with functions that could not be performed properly by the laity."[5] One of these functions was preaching.

2. William Warren Sweet, *The Story of Religion in America*, p. 336.
3. Henry Kalloch Rowe, *The History of Religion in the United States*, pp. 190-91.
4. Earl E. Cairns, *Christianity Through the Centuries*, p. 461.
5. Rowe, p. 177.

Moody had first proposed the idea of a Chicago training school to Emma Dryer in 1873, intending to train women missionaries similar to the Mildmay work in England. Asked by Miss Dryer what would be done for the young men who also needed training to do work in the churches, Sunday schools, and missions, Moody replied that they should leave this work to the seminary. Miss Dryer quoted Moody as saying, "We'd find ourselves in hot water quick, if we undertook to educate young men."

Indeed seminary leaders and the clergy were skeptical, thinking Moody would train men in a school that would offer "substandard" preparation. Aware of this attitude, Moody seemed almost fearful of attempting such a plan during the early years. In America, most colleges and universities had been founded originally to train ministers, and this training took place in an aura that was academic and scholarly. The curriculum emphasized philosophy, theology, and the languages, both biblical and classical.

But as the years passed, Moody became even more aware of what Witmer termed "a critical lack of trained personnel." Seminaries continued to come "far short of preparing a sufficient number of men while doing nothing to train women for specialized ministries other than the pastorate."

But the continual exposure to a growing need gradually changed Moody's thinking about having a distinct school to train both men and women. In 1886, when Moody delivered his famous Farwell Hall address that led to the founding of the Chicago Evangelization Society, he had reversed his emphasis from that of fourteen years before. Not once did he refer to "young women" in this address, but always to "young men." He did not intend to exclude women, but the problems of society and the churches had convinced him that "gap-men" could reach individuals among the lower classes, where regular ordained and seminary-trained ministers had been ineffective.

However, Moody's "gap-men" did not include a corps of pastors. His school originally did not train men for the regular ministry. Instead, the Institute prepared men and women to assist the regular clergy in their work. In 1889 a reporter asked Moody if he felt such an organization as the training institute he envisioned would "antagonize theological seminaries." Moody answered, "I think it will help seminarians. Many who go into the work will see the need of more training and take the regular course."

Later in the interview he said: "I want consecrated men and women from all classes, graduates of ladies' seminaries, and it would be a good thing for theological students to take a year or two in this way before becoming pastors of churches."

One month after the Institute opened in September 1889, Moody and his collaborators continued to take precautions to avoid giving the impression that the new training was to compete with seminaries. The next month MBI officials clarified the purpose of the school with an article in the *Record of Christian Work.*

It is not to train preachers that the school is established nor to furnish a short-cut to the ministry. We say, therefore, to young men who intend to be ministers, do not come here to prepare for the ministry. If you are ready for the ministry and want to take a short course of practical training, come to the Institute. If you intend to study for the ministry and desire the practical training before taking your seminary course, then come, but do not come thinking this is a substitute for a theological or a college education.[6]

In those early days, the official school literature never suggested that the Institute existed to train men for the regular ministry. However, beginning in 1892 a gradual transition took place, as the Institute catalog invited "graduates of colleges or theological seminaries" who desired to supplement their education "by a thorough study of the English Bible and methods of aggressive Christian work." The transition from not attempting to train men for the regular ministry to the establishment of a full pastoral training program in 1922, grew out of a need, particularly a need to prepare men as pastors in rural areas and to serve smaller churches among the lower classes — places to which many seminary-trained men hesitated to go.

The changing impact of denominationalism also contributed to the formation of a Pastors Course at Moody. Denominational walls were tall and thick in the nineteenth century, yet congregations were gradually developing a new attitude toward selecting their pastors. Dargan calls this "the voluntary principle in the choice and maintenance of pastors."[7] In many instances individual congregations began to ignore denominational authority and to control their own affairs on a more decentralized basis. This religious trend began to create pressure on MBI leaders to inaugurate a Pastors Course — even against their desire to do so.

Closely related to the establishment of the voluntary principle was the origin of what Henry Rowe calls the "lay movement," which became particularly strong toward the end of the nineteenth century. A keen interest in missions and social service was on the increase. This trend was observable even in the Roman Catholic church. "Laymen took part in evangelism as members of deputations, speakers at shop meetings and helpers and organizers in large evangelistic campaigns."

The voluntary principle and the lay movement both helped to break through denominational walls. These trends also contributed to the success of the Moody school, which from its beginning had as its objective the training of a certain type of layperson.

In addition, cooperation between denominations opened new horizons for evangelical education. Many new interdenominational and nondenominational organizations emerged, and the Sunday school movement gained momentum. Importantly, the fundamental-liberal controversy also helped spur the lay movement.

This theological debate was not yet an open issue when the Institute was founded. But the war soon came with great force, splitting denominations and creating new leadership needs. Moody Bible Institute, already on the scene with its conser-

6. *Record of Christian Work* (November 1889).
7. Edwin Charles Dargan, *A History of Preaching*, I, 563.

vative approach to theology and Christian work, quickly entered the debate. Consequently, MBI found itself in a strategic place of leadership and influence.[8]

DEVELOPMENT OF PASTORAL TRAINING PROGRAM

Six years after the formal school opened in 1889, MBI leaders recognized the need for a "terminal type" of pastoral training at the school. By 1895, 206 former students were already serving as pastors, pastors' assistants, and church visitors. Though a number of these men had previous training before coming to the Institute, or completed additional courses after MBI, many were entering pastoral work with MBI training only and were performing a definite service.

Even though the school was offering a special type of pastoral training, precautions were still taken to not create a public image that MBI was attempting to serve as a seminary. For a number of years statements regarding the relationship of the Institute to the seminaries were included in the annual catalog. G. Campbell Morgan wrote in an early catalog: "The work is not undenominational, but rather it is interdenominational. It is not antagonistic to the work of the church, but its servant. It is not entering into competition with the theological seminaries, but is complementary."[9]

As time passed more men came for training in pastoral work even though there was no program designed especially for this type of education. A special brochure in 1913 included the following statement:

> The standard of scholarship among our men students is advancing, and last year about 29% had a university, college, or theological seminary training. Seventeen came to us from other Bible schools against five the year previously. In the same connection, the number coming to us from the Pastorate for further training and spiritual quickening, is also increasing.[10]

In the same brochure a statement by the secretary of a home mission board of one of the larger denominations was printed as follows: "I do not know how we could get along in our work here were it not for the Moody Bible Institute. We could not man our frontier fields as we do but for the help we secure from you."

In 1915 the school added a course in "pastoral theology" for those who expected "to become pastor's assistants, whether men or women" and for those who were thinking of entering the pastorate without being able to secure seminary training. The next year the school offered a course in New Testament Greek.

PASTORS COURSE ORGANIZED

By 1922 the transition was almost complete when a special Pastors Course was organized. The objective of this course was "to provide adequate pastoral training

---

8. W. E. Garrison, *March of Faith*, p. 273.
9. Catalog (1911-1912), p. 13.
10. *Moving Forward* (pamphlet), p. 3.

for the benefit of certain qualified students'' who desired ''to enter the Christian ministry.''

At first a one-year curriculum was introduced. Transfer students from other schools with comparable prerequisites could also take this special course. The subjects offered included New Testament Greek, Christian theology, history of doctrine, advanced Christian evidences, advanced biblical criticism, Christian philosophy, Bible exposition, practice preaching, and public speaking. In addition students could study church history, biblical psychology, pastoral theology, evangelism, denominational church polity, and music.

The transition was complete by 1925, when a separate three-year Pastors Course became a regular program in the curriculum. MBI leaders gave this statement to explain the rationale behind this program expansion:

> It was not the thought of the founder of the Institute to establish a rival to theological seminaries. . . . But he was obliged to organize his Chicago mission into a church nevertheless, because he was facing a condition and not a theory, and the same may be said of the Institute's training of pastors. In the first decade of its existence, and under Mr. Moody's Presidency, of the thousands of students in attendance, ''368 are pastors, pastor's assistants and a church visitors.'' The proportion of pastors increased with each decade, and finally made it the part of wisdom to put in a pastors course for the better equipment of those whom the churches were calling into that office. Because of the additional expense and for other reasons, this step was taken with reluctance, but when it had been repeatedly urged upon the management by influential church leaders of various denominations, it seemed to be the Divine leading that it should be done.[11]

By 1927 the Pastors Course, in terms of content, was comparable to a seminary curriculum. Subject areas such as practice preaching, comparative religions, historical survey of missions, and inspiration of the Scriptures were added to the course. The program totaled approximately forty-five weeks of study each year, while the average seminary course totaled about thirty-two weeks a year. Thus, the Institute course was equal to four years of study rather than three, as required in many seminaries.

When the general objective of the Institute was revised and enlarged in the Articles of Incorporation in 1939, the preparation of ministers was, for the first time, made a part of this objective. It read in part: ''The establishment of this corporation is for the purpose of conducting and maintaining a Bible Institute for the education and training of Christian workers, teachers, ministers, missionaries, and musicians who may competently and effectively proclaim the gospel of Jesus Christ.''

Since 1927 the basic curriculum in this pastoral program, with minor revisions, has remained essentially the same. The total curriculum revision in 1951 shortened

11. *Moody Bible Institute Bulletin* (June 1925), p. 9.

the course content to accommodate the new six-semesters program down from nine terms.

With the new baccalaureate program in the fall of 1966, students interested in pastoral ministry could earn a Bachelor of Arts degree by taking ninety-three semester hours of professional studies at the Institute and sixty hours in the liberal arts in an approved college or university. The general studies in another school could be earned either before or after coming to Moody Bible Institute.

The program was renamed the Department of Pastoral Studies in 1966. The department continued to offer a diploma for those who completed only the MBI course work, and pastoral students could specialize in either Greek or Christian education. The new program not only allows the pastoral-training student to earn a recognized degree, but also provides studies in the humanities, the social and natural sciences and requires more work in the practical area of Christian education, while permitting students to specialize in an area of personal interest.

Current diploma requirements are ninety-seven semester hours, and B.A. course work requires five years of study. However, beginning in August 1986, a student can earn a B.A. in pastoral studies in four years (see chapter 21).

MBI AND PASTORAL TRAINING

Through its Department of Pastoral Studies, MBI has been filling the pulpits of evangelical American churches for the past 60 years. Almost 5,000 former students, divided evenly between men and women, completed a survey in 1933. Of this group, more than 1,200, nearly 25 percent, classified themselves as pastors. The trend has continued. Among MBI alumni in full-time Christian service who responded to a 1962 survey, 23.5 percent indicated they were serving as pastors. A 1974 survey reaffirmed MBI's role in training pastors; 22 percent of all graduates who were in full-time religious vocations were pastors.[12]

Compared to seminaries, which offer theological degrees, MBI has had a substantial impact in training pastors. We have analyzed seminaries granting bachelors' degrees (mostly Bachelor of Divinity degrees) during three selected years: 1950-1951, 1955-1956, and 1960-1961. Generally these degrees were conferred after the students had completed four or more years of study. Moody's diploma program, of course, represented only a three-year curriculum. However, both degree and diploma recipients (in the theological schools and the MBI program) remain graduates of accredited pastoral-training programs, and the point of comparison is the number of graduates, not length of program.

The seminaries generally are larger and better known, and their average number of degrees conferred are higher than the average for all schools included in govern-

---

12. Glenn F. Arnold, *A Comparative Study of Present Doctrinal Positions and Christian Conduct Codes of Selected MBI Alumni*, p. 86. More than 1,300 alumni completed the survey of graduates of twelve classes between 1945 and 1971.

mental reports. The 1951 government report listed 150 theological schools with an average of twenty-three degrees offered per school.[13] In the same 1950-1951 period, Moody issued forty-four diplomas to Pastors Course graduates.

In the 1955-1956 report, 165 schools were listed with an average of 27 degrees given per school.[14] In contrast, MBI granted 58 diplomas, more than twice the average number for the theological schools for the same period of time. In the 1960-1961 report, 174 schools were listed with an average of 28 degrees conferred per school,[15] while MBI issued 25 diplomas.

These comparative statistics again show that Moody Bible Institute has contributed significantly to evangelical pastoral training. However, in recent years fewer men have left the school to enter pastoral work immediately. Most receive additional training. For example, the 1962 survey revealed that 27.7 percent of those men who are pastors received no training after they left Moody Bible Institute. However, 40.2 percent went on to a Christian liberal arts college, 20.1 percent went to a state or private university, and 30.5 percent obtained seminary training.[16] Though the Institute is still considered a terminal program for some pastors, in the majority of cases, MBI operates as a pre-pastoral program.

THE BIBLE INSTITUTE-COLLEGE MOVEMENT AND PASTORAL TRAINING

The Bible institute-college movement has contributed greatly to evangelical pastoral training. The Accrediting Association of Bible College reported in 1960 that these 250 specialized training schools serve the "smaller and newer evangelical bodies." In addition, several denominations adhere to "the regular college and seminary pattern for ministerial preparation" and have organized Bible institutes "as a type of school that provides the educational services not available in conventional institutions."[17]

As one of the largest of the Bible institutes, MBI already has contributed significantly to pastoral work in evangelical Protestantism. During sixty years (1922-1982), more than 1,850 students were graduated from the Pastors Course and Department of Pastoral Studies, an average of thirty-one each year.

MBI EDUCATORS AND PASTORS

Bible teaching at Moody Bible Institute reaches into many areas of specialization (missions, church education, music, and so on) but has a major impact in pastoral training. Over the years several outstanding Bible teachers have joined the Moody faculty and have contributed greatly to the preparation of men for the ministry. From their pens have come numerous articles and books that have expanded

---

13. Robert C. Story, *Earned Degrees Conferred by Higher Educational Institutions, 1950-1951*, p. 117.
14. Mohel Rice and Hazel Poole, *Earned Degrees Conferred by Higher Educational Institutions, 1955-1956*, p. 146.
15. Wayne Tolliver, *Earned Degrees Conferred*, 1960-1961, p. 206.
16. Gene A. Getz, *Report of the Presidential Questionnaire*, I, 31.
17. S.A. Witmer, *The Bible College Story*, p. 58.

their contribution beyond the classrooms of MBI.

During the early years of Moody Bible Institute the Bible teaching of R. A. Torrey and James M. Gray was certainly noteworthy. Since MBI was relatively small in those days, compared with its present size, both men were actively involved in the classroom, even though they carried top administrative responsibility.

Dr. Torrey served as superintendent of the Institute and also became the first full-time Bible teacher in 1889. He is well remembered by those who sat under his teaching as a man who could make the Bible clear and interesting. He wrote many articles and books, including, *Difficulties in the Bible, What the Bible Teaches, How to Succeed in the Christian Life,* and *Importance and Value of Proper Bible Study.*

James M. Gray's greatest contribution in the classroom was his synthetic approach to Bible study. A master in helping students to see the Bible as a whole, his synthetic method was an innovation in Bible teaching and became a pattern for many evangelical Bible institutes, colleges, and seminaries.

The first graduate of Moody Bible Institute, William Evans, later became a member of the MBI faculty. Greatly influenced by D. L. Moody and R. A. Torrey, Evans served as teacher and director of the Bible Course from 1903-1914. Though well known as a Bible teacher in his day, Evans made a permanent contribution to Bible students and pastors through his writings. He wrote more than forty books on subjects ranging from preparing sermons to memorizing Scripture. His most-read book, *Great Doctrines of the Bible,* is still in print seventy years after publication.

P. B. Fitzwater served at the Institute from 1913-1954. At different times he was director of the Pastors Course, registrar, dean of the Evening School, and dean of education. Most of his time, however, was spent in the classroom teaching English Bible and theology. Former students recall him as a great expositor and organizer of biblical truth. His two lengthy volumes *Christian Theology — a Systematic Presentation* and *Preaching and Teaching the New Testament* have been significantly used by scholar and layman alike.

Wilbur M. Smith was influential in evangelical circles both as a Bible teacher and as a scholar. He served at the Institute as a member of faculty and teacher of English Bible for seven years before resigning in 1947 to accept the position of Professor of English Bible at Fuller Theological Seminary.

Dr. Smith's major works included *The Supernaturalness of Christ, Therefore Stand, This Atomic Age and the Word of God, World Crises and the Prophetic Scriptures, Chats from a Minister's Library,* and *A Treasury of Books for Bible Study. Therefore Stand* became a classic in the field of apologetics and was published while Dr. Smith taught at MBI.

Kenneth W. Wuest, who taught twenty-nine years at MBI before retiring in 1958, was respected by Greek students and scholars alike. Pastoral students enjoyed his practical approach to the Greek New Testament. But perhaps his most significant and lasting contribution was as an author. His books were popular and practical, particularly to the Bible student who had not had the opportunity to study New Testament Greek. Five books offering help in understanding the meaning of the New Testament were: *Nuggets from the Greek New Testament, Bypaths in the Greek New Testament, Treasures from the Greek New Testament, Untranslatable Riches*, and *Studies in Vocabulary.* He also wrote a number of Bible commentaries on New Testament books. His major work was probably *The New Testament: An Expanded Translation.*

Other Bible teachers have helped to make MBI and its pastoral training program what it is today, including William R. Newell, Harold L. Lundquist, Max I. Reich, Robert M. Russell, John Page, and Donald G. Smith.

All these men have been deeply committed to a high view of inspiration and demonstrated a deep respect for the Holy Scriptures. This attitude permeates the total ministry of Moody Bible Institute, but particularly its departments of Bible, theology, and pastoral training.

13

Sacred Music

Some refer to it as "Moody music," but that may be misleading, suggesting emotional melodies or brooding hymns. Actually, the collection of hymns and choruses written and composed by faculty and alumni of the Department of Sacred Music (and its predecessor, the Music Course) span the musical spectrum, from somber hymns to lifting choruses. Such variety in musical styles is guaranteed when a school has been developing church musicians for almost one hundred years.

Moody music certainly is lasting music. "Grace Greater Than Our Sin" and "Only a Sinner," composed by D. B. Towner in the first decade of the twentieth century, remain favorites of the church as the century's final decade approaches. MBI composers and lyricists have penned such stalwart hymns as "Trust and Obey," "Great Is Thy Faithfulness," "Make Me a Blessing," and "To God Be the Glory."

Because the Department of Sacred Music has encouraged both diversity and tradition, modern gospel songs also have been penned by MBI musicians. John Peterson, Dan Wyrtzen, and Larry Mayfield, former students in the sacred music program, are responsible for many Easter and Christmas cantatas currently performed. Their gospel songs and choruses are church favorites, including Peterson's "Heaven Came Down and Glory Filled My Soul," "Surely Goodness and Mercy," and Wyrtzen's "Love Was When" and "Yesterday, Today and Tomorrow."

This great heritage resulted from the disciplined, yet practical training offered in the Music Course and the dedication of one of its earliest directors, D. B. Towner. The composer of more than 2,000 songs, Towner developed the Music Course while serving as a faculty instructor as well.

CREATION OF THE MUSICAL DEPARTMENT

Moody Bible Institute came into existence when the gospel song had just become a popular type of individual, as well as congregational, expression. The Moody-Sankey revivals had popularized this type of music, actually creating the label "gospel song." Here were hymn tunes that were easily sung, readily remembered, and that contained verbal expressions emphasizing a personal conversion experience and relationship to God. Most of these songs had an "evangelistic text," a "tuneful melody," a "catchy rhythm," and "simple harmony."[1] They were closely related in content and musical composition to the emotional and spiritual environment that characterized the "gospel preaching ministry" of the evangelists.

Moody Bible Institute began during the third great awakening in America with D. L. Moody himself being the key evangelist. It follows naturally that his new training school was in a perfect position to train not only evangelists, pastors, and missionaries, but also song leaders, vocalists, instrumentalists, and composers to aid these Christian leaders. For Moody, music was "one of the most powerful agents for good or for evil."

The Musical Department formed shortly after the school opened in 1889. Under the direction of H. H. McGranaham, the department proposed to train students "to become singers, leaders or organists" who could "assist evangelists and pastors, and do a work on the mission fields, both at home and abroad."

TOWNER AND THE MUSICAL COURSE

By 1895 the catalog specifically outlined a program of study called the Musical Course. Subjects included notation, sight reading, harmony, solo and part singing, vocal training, conducting, and composition. The revised objective was "to equip men and women with a practical musical education" in order to serve as "pastor's assistants, evangelistic singers, choir leaders, organists and teachers."

D. B. Towner came to direct the musical program and teach harmony and singing in December 1893. His teaching staff included W. C. Coffin, voice; Kathleen Henry, piano; and Agnes B. Clemens, organ. Students could now develop a variety of musical skills under the supervision of several teachers who were specialists in their fields.

Although McGranahan was the first director of the sacred music program, Towner had the most influence in organizing a music course and in touching the lives of numerous students. He served as director of the Music Course for twenty-five years, until his death in 1919.

Towner's graduates became prominent song leaders and writers, including J. B. Trowbridge, I. E. Reynolds, and George S. Schuler. Towner was able to have such a wide, national influence as he trained evangelical music leaders for several reasons. First, a need existed, for no school was attempting such a program. The revivalistic movement was at its peak at this time, resulting in a demand for song leaders. Second, Towner was at Moody Bible Institute, a school that in all facets of its program was rapidly expanding and reaching out to the evangelical world. The evangelists and pastors alone who were being trained at the Institute helped

---

1. Donald P. Hustad, "Problems in Psychology and Aesthetics in Music," *Bibliotheca Sacra* 117 (July 1960), p. 214.

create numerous job opportunities for music leaders.

Third, it was the school D. L. Moody founded. The very fact that Moody and his song leader, Ira Sankey, were names known throughout the world for their evangelistic activities probably attracted many young people to the Chicago school. Fourth, Towner himself was an unusual musician. He had every potential to develop into a "concert and oratorio singer,"[2] which had been his ambition until he met Moody in an 1885 campaign in Cincinnati.

According to E. O. Sellers, "As a composer, Dr. Towner is credited with over 2,000 published songs. . . . He edited and published many song books, also a line of text books for his class work," and in those days they were widely used.

Beginning in 1906 all students were required to complete one music class, while specializing in one of three programs: Bible, Bible-music, or music. A person interested in a ministry of Bible work and music could take a combination program, while the music program was designed specifically for those interested in a music ministry.

CURRICULUM DEVELOPMENT

In 1925 the three academic programs emerged into the General Course, but music students could still specialize in music or Bible-music. This change was only temporary, for three years later MBI added a new Music Course, enlarged to nine terms or three years of study. The General Course still allowed students to enroll in music classes, but the new course permitted greater specialization. The Music Course included such subjects as advanced theory, counterpoint, history of music, and hymnology, with emphases in piano and organ, and in voice.

This enlarged course provided a terminal program for students who previously had needed "to supplement their Institute training with advanced work in a conservatory or the music department of a university."[3] MBI leaders were concerned about turning out a finished product.

The new course also helped to raise musical standards in the evangelical world. Institute leaders had become concerned about a deterioration in the type of music being used in evangelical circles as well as the way song services and choral groups were being directed. President James M. Gray spoke to this issue pointedly:

> Ira D. Sankey himself never trained or personally led the great choirs which were a feature of the revivals of his day, but there grew up around him and followed him a coterie of singing evangelists, noted also as composers and conductors, who perpetuated the work he so blessedly began, for nearly half a century. We think of Bliss and McGranahan, of Stebbins, Towner, and their contemporaries, men of reverence and dignity in the handling of the baton, whose lives and

---

2. William J. Reynolds, "Twentieth Century Church Music," *Church Music in Dimension*, I (Winter 1964), 1.
3. James M. Gray, "Our New Adventure in Music," *Moody Bible Institute Bulletin* (May 1930), p. 3.

testimony were potent factors in their campaigns.

If there has been a deterioration in the work of some of the successors of these men, the time when the decline began can be pointed out and the reason explained. It was a case of smaller men copying a master and, as is not unusual, making that sometimes ridiculous which he made an art. The Moody Bible Institute, since the days when Dr. D. B. Towner was the director of Music instruction, has set its face against such extravagances, and is not without hope that its advanced Music Course may do much to restore the lost balance to a noble calling without lessening its soul-winning power.

Of course, the personality of a leader is reflected in the character and quality of the songs he sings, and which he asks the congregation to sing, and therefore as he himself becomes better trained in the art of music, his spiritual life will express itself in songs which are more worthy, and hold a larger content of the life-giving Word.[4]

With opportunities for Christian education work increasing in the local church and the need to prepare leaders who could perform in a combination ministry, a three-year Christian Education-Music Course was added in 1930. This course contained all of the subjects in the regular Christian Education Course and the most essential ones in the Music Course. The program particularly helped small churches with limited resources. "There are many churches today in smaller towns and with limited budgets, which desire a director of church music and also a director of religious education, but which cannot afford both" explained President Gray. "Could they obtain the two in one their need would be met, and to meet this need is one of our objectives."

When MBI adopted the semester academic calendar in 1951, the Sacred Music Course expanded to include four programs of study: piano, organ, voice, and composition. In addition, the school organized a separate department of sacred music, which replaced the Sacred Music Course in 1966 when the degree program began.

THE BACCALAUREATE PROGRAM

The Department of Sacred Music in 1966 began to offer its graduates an option to earn either a Bachelor of Arts or a Bachelor of Music in sacred music degree. For the B.A. degree, the student had to complete sixty semester hours of general education in an approved college or university, either before or after completing the regular program at Moody Bible Institute. A student could earn the B.Mus. degree by completing the MBI program and then studying two years (minimum forty-two semester hours) in a conservatory or other collegiate-level school of music.

The Christian education-music major appeared under the new program and allowed the student to earn a Bachelor of Arts degree either before or after coming to the Institute.

Students could earn a B.A. in C.E.-music by taking additional college course work before or after studying at MBI. In both the church music and C.E.-music

4. Ibid., p. 4.

majors, diplomas were awarded to all students completing the MBI curriculum. Course offerings have changed through the years to allow students more flexibility, but the historical curriculum has been largely maintained.

Beginning in August 1986, students can complete work for the B.A. in church music in four years through the new baccalaureate program (see chapter 21). In 1984, the Department of Sacred Music received accreditation by the National Association of Schools of Music. NASM is the professional accrediting agency for schools of music issuing collegiate and post-graduate degrees. The diploma program has been accredited as meeting the standards of NASM, making MBI course credit transferable, and assuring wide recognition of the MBI diploma in sacred music.

PUBLIC MUSICAL PROGRAMS

For more than sixty years, MBI music students have performed for the general public. What began as in-house recitals and choral concerts has spread across America and onto the European continent. Today the well-known choral groups sing throughout the school year, and annual Christmas concerts bring capacity crowds.

Beginning in the 1950s, public performances became a curricular requirement for all students majoring in music. Senior recitals in voice, composition, piano, and other instruments are held each spring semester. In addition, faculty members periodically appear in professional recitals before students and the public.

Besides individual performances, all students are given opportunity to participate in group performances. Choral groups have been a part of the school's musical life almost from its beginning. In 1895, separate men's and ladies' choruses practiced regularly to help all students develop their voices. However, these choruses did not perform regularly.

In 1921 the first performing group appeared, the Auditorium Choir. The Choir sang at church services held in the MBI auditorium. Dr. James Gray presided at the four o'clock weekly meetings, designed as model services for students in the Pastors Course.[5] In fall 1946 the Auditorium Choir became the Moody Chorale, destined to become one of the most well-known choral groups in the religious world. As the first director, James Davies led the Chorale on its first extended concert tour the next year. Donald Hustad succeeded Davies as Chorale director in 1947, and during his fourteen years of conducting, the group developed an international reputation (see next section).

Residents of Chicago are most familiar with the MBI choral groups through two special Christmas programs, Candlelight Carols and a performance of Handel's *Messiah*. Candlelight Carols, originally called Christmas Vespers, began in 1953 with the singing of Christmas carols and a dramatic biblical pageant that retold the Christmas story. The concert has grown during the past thirty years to antiphonal

5. Mary Jean McKinley, "History of Chorale Goes Back to '21," *Moody Student* (21 April 1949), p. 3.

singing, special visual effects, and even congregational singing. Every seat is taken for each of the three performances. "We could fill Torrey-Gray Auditorium three more times, if the choirs could perform [the whole week]," reports a member of the Public Ministries Office, which distributes tickets.

The Messiah features the MBI Oratorio Chorus—two hundred voices of students, including church music and C.E.-music majors and members of the three choral groups. About one of every six MBI students participates in this community presentation. Advanced voice students are featured soloists, and a community orchestra provides full accompaniment.

CHORAL AND INSTUMENTAL GROUPS

The first choral group, the Moody Chorale, began touring almost immediately. In 1953 they replaced the glitter of the Hollywood Bowl with the glory of the resurrection message as the featured choir at the Bowl's Easter sunrise service. The Chorale has toured Europe several times, singing in packed auditoriums and churches. During their 1958 summer tour, for instance, they sang before audiences totaling 65,000. Perhaps the highlight of their ministry abroad was their 1973 tour of Great Britain. They accompanied President George Sweeting on an evangelistic tour that commemorated D. L. Moody's British crusades 100 years earlier. In England, Scotland, and Ireland they sang before filled churches, school assemblies, and civic auditoriums.[6]

Like the other two choral groups, the Moody Chorale regard their concerts as ministries, not mere performances. Evangelism and consecration are among their key goals. According to the Moody Chorale constitution, members sing in order "to bring those [listening] into a relationship with the Lord Jesus Christ by salvation and to bring Christians into a deeper relationship by consecration; and also to aid in the deepening of the spiritual lives of members themselves."

All three groups have such opportunities, and they see results. During one spring tour, the Chorale was returning from a sightseeing side trip to the Grand Canyon and began informal singing as the bus wound its way from the famous site. The bus driver interrupted the singing by taking the microphone and announcing his life was not right with God. "He asked the group to pray with him. Two weeks later the Chorale flew him to Chicago for their annual home concert. The concert crowd was moved by the genuine quality of the bus driver's testimony."[7]

The Women's Glee Club formed as a regular group in 1955. Robert Carbaugh, its first director, served twenty-seven years. In 1958 Carbaugh helped Women's Glee to purchase a set of English handbells. The bells added a unique, sweet sound to the music and were used both for accompaniment and instrumental selections. The Women's Glee was renamed the Women's Glee Club and Handbell Choir. The brilliant sounds of the handbells have been a highlight of concerts ever since.

The Men's Glee Club began in 1956 and has been under the direction of five

6. Flood and Jenkins, *Teaching the World*, p. 92.
7. Ibid., p. 245.

men: Robert Carbaugh, who organized the group; Kerchal Armstrong; John Wilson; Vann Trapp; and Robert Iler, the current director. Later MBI began a concert band featuring woodwinds, brass, and percussion. Their repertoire includes sacred hymns, gospel songs, classical music, and patriotic marches.

STRIVING FOR BALANCE

Since Moody Bible Institute began, its leaders have believed that the content and music of certain gospel songs have a definite place in the music program of the church. However, MBI leaders also have felt that some gospel songs have been written that are not very worthy. They have recognized a degeneration in the type of content and musical expression, as well as in the way these songs have been used by various religious leaders.

In 1929 MBI developed a new music course to help counteract some of the trite and superficial musical activity underway, and, in Dr. Gray's words, "do much to restore the lost balance in gospel music."

MBI has continued to advocate the maintaining of high musical standards. Its conservatory-level curriculum and the quality of its faculty, contribute to these standards, as do the content and artistic value of the music used in recitals and concerts.

But in this upgrading process, the leaders at Moody have not lost sight of the value of the gospel song or hymn. The gospel song may seem overly simple at times, and often subjective, but MBI musicians recognize that this music can be felt and understood by the average person in the pew.

Donald Hustad explains the importance of the gospel hymn this way:

> Gospel hymns are widely used in our constituent evangelical churches. And our interest in and support of them is for spiritual as well as cultural reasons. We believe the gospel hymn is a vital subjective expression of our "know-so, say-so" faith. It is our personal testimony in song, and it is effective partly because it is couched in simple words and music.
>
> However, we are thankful that our churches are also regaining some of their lost heritage of historic hymns of worship and doctrine. I'm thankful for the example set by our church leaders here at MBI; it is not hymns *or* gospel songs, but both. This means spiritual, as well as musical, balance.[8]

MBI leaders and musicians continue to stress balance between an emphasis on "personal experience and emotion," and the "inclusion of theological and Scriptural truth."[9] Hustad adds, "We need songs of testimony, of simple faith, and of invitation; but we also need hymns of worship, of doctrine, and of admonition. We enjoy the fellowship that comes through sharing the gospel solo, but we also need the movement of exaltation in moving worship of God."

In addition to preparing well-trained church musicians, MBI leaders want to

8. Donald Hustad, "Gospel Songs Fading?" *Moody Memo* (May 1961).
9. Hustad, "Problems in Psychology," p. 217.

provide all Christian leaders—pastors, missionaries, and Christian education leaders—with sufficient knowledge of music and its function in the church so that
they will be able to cooperate with the professional church musician.

In certain situations, such as small churches, professional musicians are not
available. Therefore MBI also believes that the pastor can perform his pastoral duties most effectively when he can use music properly. Whether training to be a
pastor, missionary, or teacher, all students must enroll in both introduction to music and introduction to church music. In addition, non-music majors can take music electives, including private lessons. During the ten years 1894 to 1904, probably sixty-five students a year enrolled in private music classes. More recently,
during the thirty years ended 1983, about 250 students received private training
each year in voice, piano, organ, or another musical instrument.

Exposure to the Classics

In the past, a lack of proper exposure to classical music has limited evangelical
education. For a number of years leaders at Moody sensed this need in the lives of
students and have provided greater opportunities for such exposure. As early as
1915, piano and organ students were learning to master the music of Bach, as well
as the masterpieces of other great composers. Those studying instruments continued to be increasingly exposed to this type of music, and gradually, those majoring
in vocal studies were also introduced to the classics.

By the early forties voice students were presenting some of the great masterpieces in student recitals. In the early 1950s students began to present instrumental
and vocal recitals on a larger scale, and well-known concert artists, particularly in
the religious field, presented organ, piano, and vocal recitals at Moody.

This exposure to the classics has benefited non-music majors as well, helping to
provide a cultural background in the arts for all students.

Part 4

LITERATURE MINISTRIES OF MOODY BIBLE INSTITUTE

14

The Bible Institute Colportage Association

D. L. Moody glanced on the shelves of the local bookstore, and his frustration mounted. He had just finished an evangelistic series in Madison, Wisconsin; now he wanted to give the new converts reading materials that would help them mature in their Christian lives.[1] Though the shelves bulged with fiction of all kinds, he could not find a single religious book on Christian growth. Unable to find practical, inexpensive books, he decided to do something about it.[2] He started the Bible Institute Colportage Association (BICA).

The key word in Moody's thinking was *inexpensive*. "Dime novels" about Jesse James and Diamond Dick were popular in those days, but as the *Chicago Daily News* stated, "Inexpensive religious literature was as scarce as mosquitoes in Antarctica."[3] Few people bought evangelical books once they saw the cover price.

"Their price must come down" was Moody's immediate reaction. He talked with various publishers but found little interest in preparing books that could compete with the inexpensive literature on the secular market. The only way this could be accomplished was through major press runs, and no publisher was willing to take the risk without an obvious demand by readers.

Moody, however, decided to take that risk. Organized in 1894 and incorporated in 1899, BICA began to publish and disseminate inexpensive evangelical books and booklets, Scripture portions, and gospel leaflets.

Mass printings and paperback covers helped to cut book costs. *The Way to God*, the second book printed in the Colportage Library, totaled 100,000 copies in its first edition (Moody Press still prints *The Way to God*; more than 750,000 have been circulated.) The Colportage Library established new requirements for evangelical literature. Books had to be written in a popular, readable style by well-known authors; they would also have to be strictly evangelical and undenominational, well printed but inexpensive. The books had a uniform size and binding.

1. *A Brief Story of the Bible Institute Colportage Association of Chicago* (pamphlet), p. 3.
2. A. P. Fitt, *Preaching the Gospel in Print* (pamphlet), p. 2.
3. L. M. Aldridge, "Moody Press Distributes 1,500,000 Bible Portions in Many Lands During Year," *Chicago Daily News* (27 June 1936).

Beginning in June 1897, William Norton directed the operation for more than fifty years, until his death in 1948.

Fleming H. Revell, Moody's brother-in-law, whom Moody had encouraged to go into the printing business in the fall of 1869, published the first books. The retail price was fixed at ten cents a copy, one-third the price that was being asked for similar religious books, although the price was later raised to fifteen cents so that the colporteurs could make an adequate profit.

Seven out of the first eleven books published were by D. L. Moody (primarily edited collections of his best sermons). C. H. Spurgeon wrote the first book, however, entitled *All of Grace*. Moody wrote the second book, *The Way to God and How to Find It*, containing such chapter titles as "Love that Passeth Knowledge," "The Gateway into the Kingdom," and "Words of Counsel." This book was soon printed in German, Swedish, Spanish, and Bohemian.

Other books written by the famed evangelist and published in those early days were *Pleasure and Profit in Bible Study, Heaven and How to Get There, Prevailing Prayer, To the Work*, and *Bible Characters*. These books were well received by the Christian public; by 1903 about 1.5 million copies had been published.[4]

By 1939 the Colportage Library included 178 titles. Moody Press, when it took over the association's printing work in 1941, continued to publish the Colportage Library, and by 1966 the books published in this series had reached 515 titles.

The Colportage Library became a success story almost immediately. It is easy to understand why. The inexpensive price was the primary reason, but readers also like the uniform pocket book size, an innovation in religious publishing. People often purchased a set instead of one book. In addition, these books had a ready market created by Moody himself. He promoted them at every juncture. One of his ideas involved what might be termed the first "Book-of-the-Month Club." Moody encouraged people in his evangelistic meetings to sign up for the books so that they would automatically receive them as they came off the press each month. The first year books were issued two per month and the following year, one each month. Thus Moody was far ahead of his time, since the first secular Book-of-the-Month Club was not founded until April 1926, in New York City by Harry Scherman.[5]

Besides the colportage series, the association also printed a number of other publications on a periodic basis. A series of thirty-two-page Evangel Booklets with seventy-six titles had been published by 1940, for a total of nearly four hundred different books and booklets. The Evangel series later became the Moody Compacts. In addition to these four hundred titles, the association also printed and distributed copies of the New Testament and various Scripture portions.

The Bible Institute Colportage Association began with four major goals:

> First, to help stem the awful tide of impure reading matter that is annually being scattered broadcast, which is poisoning the minds and undermining the characters of all who read it; second, to reach the non-churchgoer; third, to get the

4. *Annual Report of the Moody Bible Institute for the Year 1903*, p. 17.
5. Joseph N. Kane, *Famous First Facts*, p. 119.

> printed page into the hands of every criminal behind the prison bars in the United States; fourth, to give an opportunity to godly men or women to do more effective service for the Master, in dealing with individuals in their homes about their soul's salvation.[6]

The first two goals reflect the zeal of the BICA founder. Moody had a passion for purity and bemoaned "impure reading matter." He believed that wholesome, inexpensive Christian literature would provide the reading public with an alternative to pulp fiction that focused on man's baser motives. In addition, Moody concentrated on reaching the "unchurched" and the "untaught" with the message of the gospel. This concern was demonstrated in his mission Sunday school work, in his evangelistic campaigns, in his involvement in the Chicago Bible Work and later in the formation of the Chicago Evangelization Society to reach the lower classes in Chicago. Moody's literature vision was a direct corollary to all of these other efforts. He saw in this medium one more way to "reach the non-churchgoer."

The third objective, to get the printed page behind prison bars, became a concern to Moody shortly after he inaugurated the association. He immediately started a book fund, and personally raised most of the money. As a result, colportage books, Scripture portions, and gospel tracts were sent free of charge to chaplains and religious workers for distribution in penitentiaries, prison, jails, and reform schools throughout the United States and Canada. This original effort to raise money to provide religious literature for prisoners encouraged other benefactors to start book funds that provided free literature to other specialized groups, including the Fire Station Book Fund, the India Book Fund, the Latin America Book Fund, and the Seaman's Book Fund.

In order to accomplish the fourth BICA goal—"To give an opportunity for godly men and women . . . [to deal] with individuals in their homes about their soul's salvation"—BICA organized a door-to-door team. Eventually known as "book missionaries," these men and women went door to door and church to church selling books. These individuals earned a commission in lieu of a salary, and by 1940, more than one thousand people were involved in this work.

Many young people who wished to train for Christian work became book missionaries to finance their way through school. Already by 1900, young men and women in all parts of the country had mailed letters to the Institute expressing their desire to enter school, but also their dilemma of having "no means to defray their expenses while training." Special arrangements were made to help students with their particular needs. The sale of books by the association had never been intended to be a money-making venture; instead, "all profits accruing from the work" were invested in more literature production and distribution and in other Christian ministries.

In addition to the direct sale of literature to the public, eventually MBI operated

---

6. *Annual Catalog of the Bible Institute for Home and Foreign Missions of the Chicago Evangelization Society* (1897), p. 25.

a bookstore to sell the publications of the BICA, as well as other Christian literature. This store served people in the greater Chicago area, while the colporteurs, or
book missionaries, continued in areas throughout the United States and in foreign
countries.

D. L. Moody's motto for BICA was to "do all the good you can, to all the people you can, in all the ways you can, as long as ever you can." Shortly after the
turn of the century, over 4 million colportage books had been published, including
104 different titles. Already one hundred colporteurs were at work in different
parts of the country, and the association was shipping materials to twenty-four different supply depots. In addition, they had printed nearly 425,000 Bibles, Testaments, and gospels, and nearly 700,000 gospel leaflets.

The prison fund had also been operating extensively. More than 500,000 colportage books, Bibles, Testaments, gospels, and tracts had already been distributed free to prisoners in both the United States and Canada. Other mission funds also
were being used to distribute free literature. More than 52,000 colportage books
had been sent to India; 3,000 to South America; almost 34,000 to men in the
armed services. Religious books reached into the most remote regions of America:
lumbermen in the northwoods received them, as did workers in Alaskan mining
camps and fishing stations.

This was merely the beginning of an extensive literature outreach. By 1930, the
number of colportage books published totaled more than 10 million copies, and the
number of gospels of John totaled over 6 million. When BICA became an organic
part of the Institute in the early 1940s, the number of colportage books published
had reached almost 13 million.

From this large supply of published materials, numerous pieces of literature had
already been distributed at no charge. By 1940 the number of pieces circulated annually by means of the 24 mission funds averaged above 2.5 million pieces. For
example, in 1938, 2,580,000 pieces of literature were sent in 22,000 shipments to
every state in the United States, as well as to the District of Columbia, Alaska, the
Canal Zone, the Hawaiian Islands, Puerto Rico, the Philippine Islands, Samoa, the
Virgin Islands, Canada, Newfoundland, and to 43 other countries.

BICA distributed books many ways. Perhaps the most unorthodox was via the
"gospel car" —really a truck or "house on wheels." In 1931 a New York businessman presented this car to BICA to be used in distributing literature. By 1939
colportage workers had driven 45,000 miles in the central states, made 20,500
calls in homes. During their visits they talked with 4,250 people about spiritual
matters and distributed 67,400 gospel tracts. As a result of the gospel car, 917 professed to accept Jesus Christ as Lord and Savior.

Forty years and 17 million New Testaments and Scripture portions after BICA
began, the Colportage Association became an integrated part of the Institute. In
1941 BICA changed from an outside branch of the Institute to a vital inner compo-
nent, as Moody Press took over the printing and sale of books. Meanwhile Moody
Literature Ministries began printing BICA's missionary literature.

The Institute had succeeded in publishing inexpensive quality books for the

Christian public. Soon she expanded with Moody Press, now one of the largest publishers of religious books.

15

Books, Bibles, and the Printed Page

Surveying a recent Moody Press catalog will quickly reveal the scope of offerings from this leading evangelical publisher. Bibles, atlases, Bible commentaries, and practical-help books for the pastor mingle with missionary biographies and the Moody Youth Library series.

Moody Press maintains the tradition started by the Bible Institute Colportage Association at the turn of the century, while updating its packaging and subject selection for the needs of the modern reader. Paperback books, the invention of D. L. Moody, are a mainstay of the line; they remain reasonably priced but are much more attractively produced than in earlier years. However, Moody Press has also enlarged its offerings in larger and more expensive cloth and trade paperbacks.

MISSIONARY BOOKS

Among the most exciting reading are the biographical stories of missionaries proving God's faithfulness as they serve in other cultures. *Mission: Venezuela* recounts the struggles of Wally and Margaret Jank to win a warring tribe of South American Indians to Christ, while *The People Time Forgot* traces the gospel's impact on villagers in a primitive valley in New Guinea.

Still a favorite more than forty years after its initial publication, *Hudson Taylor's Spiritual Secret* recalls the spiritual odyssey of the first missionary to China and founder of the China Inland Mission. Many other titles could be mentioned, as Moody Press continues to publish notable missionary stories and biographies.

BIBLE PUBLISHING

Moody Press entered Bible publishing in the late 1940s with the Charles B. Williams translation of the New Testament, entitled *The New Testament in the Language of the People*. It became an immediate success. In one sense, this was a pioneering venture, since conservative people have been well known in the past for their veneration of the King James Version and their reluctance to read other translations.

When the Lockman Foundation produced its *New American Standard Bible* in the 1960s, Moody Press became one of five major publishers to print the Bible. One Moody Press version of this Bible, called the Thinline edition, features thin yet durable paper that makes the NASB lightweight and compact.

In 1978 Moody Press introduced the *Ryrie Study Bible*, with theological, historical, and cultural notes by Dr. Charles Ryrie, a noted theologian and former professor at Dallas Theological Seminary. With its thorough book outlines and numerous charts, the Ryrie Bible quickly became a best-seller. Published in King James, *New King James, New American Standard*, and *New International* versions, it has sold more than 1.1 million copies its first seven years in print.

Three other Bible reference books aid the Christian in his or her study of the Scriptures. The *Nave's Topical Bible* allows the Bible student to explore all the verses on a specific topic—there are more than 20,000 topics—while Christians can find help in presenting the plan of salvation with the *Christian Worker's New Testament*.

BIBLE STUDY AIDS

Bible study aids consist of commentaries on numerous books of the Bible as well as such well-known evangelical works as *The Wycliffe Bible Commentary* and *The Wycliffe Bible Encyclopedia*. The *Wycliffe Commentary* contains 1,500 pages of explanatory information on the whole Bible, and has been written and edited by a staff of forty-nine scholars representing twenty-five schools of higher Christian education and fifteen Protestant denominations.

Unger's Bible Dictionary, another large publication, contains over seven thousand definitions and five hundred photographs, and includes recent geographical changes in the Holy Land as well as up-to-date archaeological discoveries. A companion volume is *Unger's Bible Handbook*.

Additional Bible study aids include historical works and such theological studies as *Theological Wordbook of the Old Testament*. Moody Press offers the Jensen Bible self-study guides, and three series of Bible commentaries from which to choose, including the *Everyman's Bible Commentary*.

Reference books typically are hardcover, thick, and expensive. Wanting to place quality reference works in the hands of every reader, Moody Press remembered the methods of D. L. Moody and created an inexpensive reference line called The Affordables. The Affordables are paperback versions of best-selling reference materials, simply packaged to keep prices low. As a result, the Unger and Wycliffe series cost half the amount of the original hardback books, making these reference tools available to everyone.

PRACTICAL-HELP BOOKS

The major lines of Moody Press books stress practical help for the believer, reflecting Moody's own focus when he started BICA almost one hundred years ago. There are helps for the pastor and the Christian worker, and books designed to deepen the spiritual life. Popular volumes for the pastor include *Making Sense of the Ministry, The Minister's Library,* and *Speaking to Life's Problems.* For adults, books such as *Promised-Land Living* and *The God You Can Know* guide the reader into a closer walk with God. More than one hundred books are available to children. Two children's books, *Read-Aloud Bible Stories* and *What Happens When We Die?* have received Gold Medallions signifying outstanding achievement in publishing.

Among Christian publishers, Moody Press has been a leader in dealing with social issues. *A Legacy of Hatred* recounts the horrors of the Jewish Holocaust and the Holocaust's effects on Christian and Jews. The highly acclaimed *The Least of These* has received a Gold Medallion for its comprehensive examination of the abortion issue and call for Christian opposition to abortion. Other books have dealt with issues of homosexuality, family life, and capital punishment.

The Sensitive Issues series is designed especially for teenagers. In this four-book series, fictional stories dramatize such issues as suicide, divorce, and drug addiction, helping young readers understand the problems while providing hope and guidance.

TEXTBOOKS

Moody Press began its textbook program in 1955. Under the direction of an editorial and textbook committee and a textbook editor, the program has expanded rapidly. Written from an evangelical perspective, more than 150 titles appear in the textbook list, covering Bible study, comparative religions, theology, Christian education, church music, church history, missions, archaeology, psychology, biblical languages, and homiletics.

Out of this impressive list of textbook materials, more than fifty have been written by current or former teachers at Moody Bible Institute.

C. Fred Dickason, chairman of the Department of Theology, has written *Angels: Elect and Evil*, a biblical study of angels, demons, and Satan. In the area of Bible, professor Edgar James has written commentaries on the epistles of Peter and 2 Corinthians.

Two professors in the Department of Christian Education have written several books on Christian training of children. In *Children's Church: A Comprehensive How-To*, Dr. Doris Freese explains how to design a program, create a curriculum, and, perhaps most importantly, how to understand children. Dr. Robert Clark is coeditor of *Childhood Education in the Church*, which includes essays by several Moody faculty members.

Several former teachers at MBI have been active authors while at the school and later at other institutions, including Harold Cook, Charles F. Pfeiffer, and Howard F. Vos. Former dean of education and faculty member, Alfred Martin, has published two Moody Press commentaries on Isaiah.

THE IMPACT OF MOODY PRESS

Moody Press sales involve both retail and wholesale distribution. The retail bookstore, which was formerly operated by the BICA and then Moody Press, is now part of Moody Retail, a separate department of the Publishing Branch. The original store continues to operate on the campus of Moody Bible Institute. In addition, MBI owns a second store on the south side of Chicago. A third store in the heart of the Chicago Loop drew major lunch-hour crowds during its twenty-one years in the downtown business district. Rising overhead finally forced the store to close in 1980.[1] In 1984 MBI also acquired three bookstores in Charleston, West Virginia.

Moody Press publications are sold in every state in the U.S. and in many foreign countries. Approximately 10,000 Christian bookstores, dealers, and libraries handle its supplies, and among many of these distributors, the name Moody Press and evangelicalism are synonymous.

One sign of the confidence book dealers place in Moody Press became obvious when a Book-O-Matic plan began in 1955. Organized so that stores who joined would automatically receive at a special discount a copy of every new Moody Press book, the plan has been well received for more than thirty years.

Demand for Moody Press generally has followed an upward course. In 1953 the number of units sold totaled nearly 7 million. This was the beginning of a rapid sales boon. During the next ten years, Moody Press more than doubled its sales. By 1959 the total number of pieces published in a single year totaled over eighteen million. Since 1959 an average of 95 new books have come off the press each year (in 1961 the number reached almost 140).

CHRISTIAN BOOKSELLERS ASSOCIATION

The idea for a Christian Booksellers Association began at Moody Bible Institute.[2] For many years prospective owners had contacted Moody Press almost daily for advice and information on how to open and operate Christian bookstores. William F. Moore, a Moody Press employee, and Kenneth Taylor, then director of Moody Press, discussed the need. Eventually they arranged several meetings with their Chicago area dealers to determine the level of interest in a Christian booksellers trade association.

As a result of these initial meetings, the first organizational convention was held at the LaSalle Hotel in Chicago in September 1950; two months later, on November 17, the Christian Booksellers Association (CBA) was incorporated as a nonprofit corporation in the state of Illinois. From its inception in 1950, CBA used the facilities of Moody Press in order to operate its office, paying its own salaries, postage, and other expenses. In February 1959, the association moved to its own

---

1. Flood and Jenkins, *Teaching the Word*, p. 216.
2. Letter from W. F. Moore, former president and executive secretary of the CBA from its inception in 1950 until September 1965.

office in suburban Chicago, where it remained until assuming its current headquarters in Colorado Springs in 1970.

Since 1950 the "entire Christian bookselling and publishing industry has multiplied many times over," and according to W. F. Moore, "this growth is a direct result of the Christian Booksellers Association," as well as an indirect contribution of Moody Bible Institute. The association not only came into being as a result of the vision of Institute leaders, but its growth and progress have been directly related to the interest shown by Moody Press.

REVENUE FROM MOODY PRESS

Since the Institute is a nonprofit organization that exists to serve the public, revenue from sales of Moody Press books is continually rechanneled into other MBI ministries. Some of the profits from Moody Press help to fund the educational branch, providing students with a tuition-free education. For more than one hundred years, Moody Bible Institute has never charged students for instructional costs, thanks to grateful alumni, interested friends, and affiliated programs such as Moody Press and *Moody Monthly* magazine (see chapter 16).

Moody Press also funnels part of its profits into Moody Literature Ministries. MLM distributes volumes of free literature annually, grants large sums of money for major special literature projects, and provides financial help to international students in the United States who are training for literature production or distribution. Indirectly, much of the outreach of Moody Literature Ministries is the multiplied outreach of Moody Press.

MOODY LITERATURE MINISTRIES

Through the years MBI has distributed free of charge, millions of dollars' worth of literature. This has included books to lumbermen, railmen, ethnic groups, and public libraries. Today Moody Literature Ministries distributes to prisoners, servicemen, and hospital patients domestically, and to bookstores and individuals overseas.

MLM began as the Bible Institute Colportage Association in 1894. By 1947, BICA had distributed without charge 17 million books and 205 million gospel tracts.

After BICA became part of MBI and the Colportage Department assumed the distribution of free literature, the program expanded quickly. Increased profits from Moody Press aided in the success of the Colportage Department, as did contributions from special friends of the Institute. Between 1946-1955, approximately 100 million pieces of literature were distributed, or an average of 10 million pieces per year.

In 1957 the department was renamed Moody Literature Mission. However, the new name soon confused prospective and actual supporters. Because of the word "mission," some people began to assume MLM was an agency training and sending missionaries abroad. MLM leaders became concerned that their organizational name was inaccurate.[3] Therefore, MLM was designated Moody Literature Ministries in 1978.

The response to this literature ministry has been gratifying. The MLM files include testimonies received from individuals around the world who have written to express their appreciation for the help received. Former MLM director, Peter Gunther, notes, "Both written testimonies in the mail, and verbal testimonies from visitors constantly inspire us to greater effort and a greater outreach. Chaplains, school teachers, and librarians ask for more and tell of readers who consistently return to receive more."

MLM AND PUBLIC SCHOOLS

In 1921 a representative of BICA traveling through the mountain areas of southern United States discovered that teachers in the rural schools wanted books to build their school libraries. In 1922 BICA began to supply books free of charge and found a hungry audience.

The school books program continued through 1981, with an average of 1,300 sets of free books being placed in public schools each year. During the first 40 years, MLM placed approximately one-half million sets in public school libraries. Since each set contained approximately 15 books, this involved a distribution of almost 7.5 million books, or nearly 3 million dollars of retail merchandise.

With each set of books given to a school, MLM included sufficient copies of the gospel of John as personal gifts to the students. Every student who read the entire gospel and memorized eleven key verses received a free *Pocket Treasury*, a ninety-five-page booklet containing selected chapters from the Bible as well as twenty-five different Christian hymns. From 1950-1964, more than 3.5 million gospels of John were sent to public school pupils.

In many cases teachers reported that the book program improved the student's attitudes toward studies, other students, and teachers themselves. In some instances, discipline problems diminished, and tardiness and attendance problems were solved. For example, some children who constantly arrived late at school, or were frequently absent, now came early in order to spend time reading from the Moody books.

REVOLVING FUNDS AND OTHER GRANTS

BICA became interested in the distribution of literature in other countries almost from its inception. By the end of 1903, over 52,000 colportage books had been shipped to India, 3,000 to South Africa, and numerous books, Bibles and Testaments to Canada. Year by year, the foreign work has grown and expanded its outreach.

Since 1947, MLM has emphasized financial assistance for literature production occurring within foreign countries instead of merely sending literature from the

---

3. *MLM Focus Newsletter*, Summer 1978.

United States. These overseas projects often have been carried out in cooperation with an established mission. Each project is carefully screened, and the cooperating mission usually is asked to raise at least half the cost of the project, while MLM has matched this amount from its overseas fund. The mission board receiving the grant then sends a year-end report to Moody Bible Institute telling how the money has been invested.

Often the publishing costs borne by the Institute have been on a revolving-fund basis. The mission agrees to use the money received from the sale of books and other materials to produce more literature. Not all the money that has been invested in overseas projects has been issued on a revolving-fund basis. For example, in 1953, out of the 38 projects in 25 countries, 12 involved non-revolving funds; that is, money was given as an outright grant for special projects such as newspaper advertising, special publications, and so on.

The number of projects sponsored or partially sponsored has grown rapidly. By 1955, the number of such projects had increased to 66 in 43 different countries.

During the next thirty years, more than 1,300 projects were completed in almost every country in the free world, wherever the gospel message could penetrate. Recently MLM has helped in China. In 1984 MLM assisted with projects in India, Bangladesh, Sri Lanka, and the Middle East. MLM also ships reference books and Bibles to several seminaries, the most recent being the Jamaican Theological Seminary. In Sicily, an MLM grant helped World Team open a Christian bookstore.

Projects range from providing paper stock for printing to binderies to help construct a printing plant. The final page of every Moody Press book contains an invitation to write MLM for further information about the Christian life, and MLM gladly mails books on the Christian life and Bible study aids to all inquirers. As a result, individual Christians and non-converts are as likely to receive overseas literature as organizations are.

EVANGELICAL LITERATURE OVERSEAS

Moody Literature Ministries has almost a mother-daughter relationship with Evangelical Literature Overseas, for ELO was conceived largely by two Moody leaders. ELO coordinates and gives direction to worldwide literature distribution by mission agencies. Peter Gunther, then MLM assistant director, and Ken Taylor, then Moody Press director, endorsed having a clearinghouse for the production and distribution of literature among mission groups. They envisioned ELO as a service agency to all evangelical groups to foster inter-mission cooperation.

On September 3, 1953, ELO incorporated with the following purpose:

> To promote and encourage the writing, production, printing and distribution of Evangelical Christian literature around the world and primarily for use in foreign countries and in foreign languages; to coordinate efforts of publishers and missionary boards and societies in this endeavor; to provide a library of available manuscripts in pertinent subjects; and to provide funds for such purposes and to

assist in all ways possible the writing, translation, publishing, and distribution of such literature.[4]

The direction of ELO was vested in a board of nine mission and publishing leaders, but according to official records, the work was "immediately under the leadership of Kenneth Taylor, director of Moody Press, and Peter F. Gunther, assistant director of Moody Literature Mission." In a short time this new organization became the "recognized arm of the Evangelical Foreign Mission Association and the Interdenominational Foreign Missions Association, plus several other evangelical missions."[5]

Evangelical Literature Overseas has never been organically tied to Moody Bible Institute or any other organization. Nevertheless, the financial support and leadership of Institute personnel contributed greatly to the development of inter-mission cooperation in producing and distributing literature.

MOODY INSTITUTE OF SCIENCE FILMS

In addition to distributing books, MLM also is active in the distribution of motion pictures. MLM sends most of the Moody Institute of Science films for showings in jails and hospitals. Clearly this film service meets a need: When the program was launched, these films were booked six months in advance, and chaplains were enthusiastic about their use. In 1961 MIS films were shown 1,050 times in 31 states in 111 different institutions. Twenty-five years later interest remains high; 68 different films were shown in 28 states in 1984.

---

4. Articles of Incorporation of ELO, No. 5, entitled "The Purpose or Purposes for Which the Corporation Is Organized."
5. Harold B. Street, "For Such a Time as This," *Good News Broadcaster* (May 1962), p. 32.

16

Moody Monthly Magazine

Moody Monthly magazine, alias *The Christian Workers' Magazine* and *The Institute Tie*, is the little newspaper that grew into a magazine giant. With more than 210,000 copies circulated each month and an estimated one-half million readers, the magazine has an amazing history. It began as a twice-a-month newspaper that lasted slightly beyond one year, ceasing publication in February 1893 due to poor economic conditions. Seven years later, in September 1900, the *Institute Tie* returned with an intriguing new format: a copyrighted, monthly magazine.

During the next eighty-five years the magazine's format and writing style changed substantially. Block type, narrow columns and black and white photos have yielded to a modern, clean appearance featuring color pictures, glossy paper and white spaces that prevent eye fatigue. *Moody Monthly*'s cover photos have won several awards from the Evangelical Press Association. In fact, the magazine has been selected "Periodical of the Year" twice[1], and has received dozens of EPA categorical awards during the past decade.

It also has changed its audience. As *The Institute Tie*, the magazine offered news for MBI alumni and friends. As *Moody Monthly*, it has become a successful general interest magazine and one of the largest circulation evangelical periodicals. It still remains affiliated with the school, as President George Sweeting acts as editor-in-chief. Yet the magazine accepts advertising from rival Bible colleges and prints articles by free-lance writers each issue.

In spite of all these changes, one aspect of *Moody Monthly* has remained constant through the years. The editors remain committed to the same purpose: to print doctrinally-sound, practical articles that will help the Christian worker and the evangelical public at large. The fundamental truths of Christian doctrine still appear on the pages of *Moody Monthly*.

The monthly periodical has its roots in a small biweekly paper called *The Institute Tie* published for former students. General economic conditions had forced its demise after fifteen months, but the publication revived in September 1900, as a

---

1. Flood and Jenkins, *Teaching the Word*, p. 223.

copyrighted magazine, with A. P. Fitt as editor and William Norton as business manager. Since its beginnings this monthly magazine has been operated by the school.

The "new monthly" published in 1900 focused on interests and programs of MBI. It included "all the news about the Institute, including letters from students on home and foreign fields, lectures, and activities by the instructors, outlines, and suggestions for sermon and prayer meeting talks."

A CHANGING FOCUS

The focus of the periodical changed significantly beginning in July 1907, when James M. Gray and R. A. Torrey became coeditors. The contents of the magazine began to reflect more of an educational objective, rather than being only a tie between the Institute and its former students and friends. Though still a mirror of Moody Bible Institute, the magazine began to meet MBI objectives by providing opportunities for Bible study, practical helps, and inspiration leading to more effective Christian service. The new format meant articles and studies, anecdotes, outlines, book reviews, evangelistic and religious news appearing along with monthly news of the Institute.

Among the earliest educational features were "Practical and Perplexing Questions," "The Layman's Commentary," and weekly "Studies in the Life and Teachings of Our Lord." Torrey became responsible for answering "Practical and Perplexing Questions." Several questions that he answered in the first issue were: "What do you think of the institutional church? Is it not detrimental to the real work of the church as set forth in the New Testament?" and "What theory of atonement does the Bible teach?"

In the same issue, Gray, then top official at Moody Bible Institute, began "The Layman's Bible Commentary." He wrote a biblical exposition for each issue, beginning with Genesis, and moved month by month through the whole Bible. This section was planned for the average layman, not the Bible scholar, and consisted of a broad outline treatment of the Bible in order to help "the reader to see the real nature of the revelation of God" as it unfolded "from age to age through Moses, through Samuel, through David, through the earlier and later prophets, through Jesus Christ and the Apostles and evangelists of the New Testament."[2]

For almost ten years, Gray faithfully prepared this material and covered every book of the Bible except Revelation. Beginning with the June 1917 issue, rather than giving a brief synopsis of Revelation, he began a detailed month-by-month exegetical study of this often perplexing book for the average reader. He took four months to give a semi-analytical treatment of the Apocalypse.

R. A. Torrey also began his second regular feature with "Studies in the Life and Teachings of our Lord." This section was designed to be an inductive study guide and reflected Torrey's classroom procedure in teaching the Bible. His purpose for these lessons, which were arranged so they could be studied week by week, was

2. James M. Gray, "The Layman's Bible Commentary," *The Institute Tie* (July 1907), p. 490.

"not to save the student the necessity of personal thought and study, but to stimulate thought and Bible searching."[3] To accomplish this goal, he wrote a series of questions and numerous Bible references that the student could look up and study in order to arrive at personal answers.

One of the most practical ideas in the magazine, which was actually a carryover from the old format, was a section called "For Sermons and Scrapbook." Illustrations, Bible texts, and suggested sermon outlines were included so as to help the busy pastor in his Bible study and sermon preparation.

THE CHRISTIAN WORKER'S MAGAZINE

In October 1910, the magazine was retitled *The Christian Worker's Magazine* to reflect the change in purpose and format. No longer a periodical only for Moody graduates and former students, the magazine now focused on all Christian workers.

When the magazine turned to an educational thrust in 1907, the feature articles as well as the regular departments focused primarily on Bible study and Christian living. But as Christian worker features were added, practical helps for Sunday school teachers became common. When the periodical became *The Christian Worker's Magazine* in 1910, the magazine included the following regular departments: "Studies in Personal Soul Winning," "Object Lessons for Children," "The Layman's Commentary," "The International Sunday School Lesson," "The Gospel in the World," "The Sermon and Scrap Book," and "Notes and Suggestions." "The International Sunday School Lesson" remained a regular feature for sixty years.

A new title appeared on the cover in September 1920, *The Moody Bible Institute Monthly*. At the same time, the size increased from its original 6 1/2 by 9 1/2 inches to its present size, 8 1/2 by 11 1/2 inches. The content changed slightly.

Beginning in March 1917, "Young People's Society Topics," began as a regular department, with a commentary on practical biblical subjects for use in youth meetings. This addition was an innovation in the magazine that led eventually to a strong emphasis on youth and youth work.

The new *Moody Bible Institute Monthly* continued to carry out the objectives of *The Christian Worker's Magazine* in serving as a means for Bible study, Christian service, and fellowship.[4] The main differences were size, more features, a new name, and a new price — $2.00 per year.

James M. Gray became coeditor of *The Institute Tie* in 1907 and became editor-in-chief after Torrey left the Institute in 1910. Gray served in this editorial position until his death on September 21, 1935, more than twenty-eight years.

In November 1934, Will H. Houghton became president of Moody Bible Insti-

---

3. R. A. Torrey, "Studies in the Life and Teachings of Our Lord," *The Institute Tie* (July 1907), p. 496.
4. This objective first appeared in the *Moody Bible Institute Catalog* (1915-1916) and was repeated regularly in the catalog issues to follow.

tute, and Gray became president emeritus. Gray, however, maintained his position as editor of the magazine and even contributed articles up to the time of his death. Afterward, Houghton immediately became the new editor. Houghton continued to follow the same editorial policies and practices as his predecessor.

Two unique columns appeared under Houghton's editorship. "Greek Word Studies" helped readers to understand original meanings of the biblical text and to find appropriate applications. Greek scholar and MBI professor Kenneth Wuest wrote the popular column for twenty-three years. Houghton introduced a second column himself, called the "Youth Page." He wanted this column to belong to the teenage readers. The first time this new feature appeared, he wrote: "Young people, this is your page. It is for you to say how it should be used. We want it to be of genuine interest and spiritual profit."

Houghton asked these questions: "What problems are you facing? What questions would you like answered? What helpful experience have your had?"[5] He continued this column for a year, but subsequently turned the column over to his wife, probably because of heavy presidential responsibilities. The column continued until June 1942.

A four-year period passed without a regular youth department in the periodical. But in February 1946, what was termed a "new magazine" was added to the regular monthly and called the "Youth Supplement." The purpose of this new feature —the largest addition since the inception of the magazine—was "to provide as much help for Christian youth" as possible.[6]

MOODY MONTHLY

In March 1938, editors dropped the words "Bible Institute" from the title and the magazine became *Moody Monthly*. This change reflected what had already happened. Ever since the larger title had been introduced in 1920, various leaders began immediately to refer to the periodical as the *Moody Monthly*. This already shortened title in regular conversation became a formal change shortly after Houghton became editor.

MBI presidents had always had an active role in the magazine's daily operations, serving as editors-in-chief over the years. But as the school and the magazine expanded, the responsibilities of both the presidency and the editorship seemed to increase proportionately. Therefore, shortly after William Culbertson became president in 1947, MBI decided to hire a journalism professional to supervise editorial operations. The President continued to serve as editor-in-chief, reviewing editorial policy and manuscripts, but the executive editor would be a Christian journalist.

This key change would have a major positive impact on *Moody Monthly* format and quality. Previously, MBI administrators and educators performed editorial duties; their twin responsibilities with MBI and its magazine diluted their talents and

5. Will Houghton, "Youth's Page," *The Moody Bible Institute Monthly* (September 1935), p. 21.
6. S. Maxwell Coder, "Introduction to the Supplement," *Moody Monthly* (February 1946), p. 398.

cut into their time. For instance, Professor Clarence Benson served as associate editor of *Moody Monthly* for fifteen years (1926-1941) while simultaneously directing the Christian Education Course and carrying a full teaching load.

President William Culbertson recognized the problem and three months after he assumed his responsibilities, MBI appointed a full-time associate editor. Later MBI hired Wayne Christianson, a former newspaperman and graduate of the Iowa State School of Journalism, as its first full-time executive editor.

Under the editorship of Christianson during the next two decades, the magazine improved in its design and editing. Full-color covers appeared beginning in the 1960s, and heavy, closed-in type was "loosened up" for easier reading.[7] More practical articles appeared in each issue, though biblical and doctrinal teaching remained a major emphasis. The purposes of the magazine—sound doctrine and practical helps for living the Christian life—continued unchanged.

Paid circulation has increased steadily through the years. In 1921 about 19,000 subscribers received the magazine. When Will Houghton became president in 1934, *Moody Monthly* had about 40,000 subscribers. Houghton, a master promoter, vigorously endorsed the magazine and circulation climbed to almost 75,000 under his leadership. By the early 1960s it had exceeded 100,000. The most spectacular growth occurred in the early 1970s, as the magazine entered into a national direct marketing campaign. Within two years, by 1974, circulation was approaching 250,000.[8]

Today *Moody Monthly* has more than 210,000 subscribers; research suggests the average general magazine is read by 2.3 readers, so readership probably exceeds one-half million. In terms of readership, *Moody Monthly* is the nation's premier Christian family magazine and a leader among general-interest evangelical periodicals.

Various regular departments have been added to the magazine over the years. "In the Study," a column by MBI Bible Professor Wilbur M. Smith, first appeared in 1952. It quickly became very popular with ministers as well as serious Bible students. The feature encouraged a "systematic . . . deeper study" of the Bible, and intended "to guide ministers through the vast labyrinth" of biblical literature beginning to appear.

Today the department titled "Pastor to Pastor," offers not only information on books but practical helps on sermon preparation, pastoral counseling, and current theological issues, among other topics. The column is written by pastors for pastors, but the magazine's other readers often benefit as well. When the article "Doctrine Is Practical" appeared in one issue, Jerry Jenkins, then manager of publishing, advised readers: "Don't pass the article up just because it's in the Pastor to Pastor department. We'll let you read it regardless."[9]

The many departments in the 1985 issues of the magazine demonstrate the balance in content: "Digging Deeper" offers biblical exposition; "Opinion" offers

7. Flood and Jenkins, *Teaching the Word*, p. 222.
8. Ibid., p. 220.
9. Jerry B. Jenkins, "Background," *Moody Monthly*, April 1985, p. 5.

thoughtful arguments on current issues by evangelical leaders, while "Doctrine" explains, illustrates, and defends basic doctrines; "Parenting" provides helpful advice in rearing children. "First Person" contains first-person accounts of conversion, with an opportunity for readers to write for information on how to become a Christian. There also are reviews of new books, records, and motion pictures by Christian film companies.

Moody Monthly has tackled many contemporary issues with cover stories and related articles on important themes. Themes have included child abuse, religious freedom, persecution and the church, modern Israel and the Jew, and the fruit of the Spirit. In May 1980, *Moody Monthly* published its most circulated[10] and perhaps most talked-about issue ever, an analysis of the abortion controversy. The magazine featured an interview with C. Everett Koop, noted pediatric surgeon and U.S. Surgeon General. Dr. Koop defended the unborn's rights and attacked abortionists.

The magazine is a successful teaching tool. Surveys have shown that subscribers are active in local churches, with nearly one-half serving as Sunday school teachers. One survey by Audience Analysts indicated that almost three-fourths of readers are lay people. Thus the magazine particularly helps those who are not professionally trained by giving ideas, suggestions, and encouragement in their lay service to the church.

The once insignificant biweekly newspaper has become a leading evangelical magazine. No longer merely an Institute tie or a magazine for Christian workers, *Moody Monthly* helps readers to grow in their Christian faith and practice.

10. Flood and Jenkins, *Teaching the Word*, p. 218.

Part 5

PROCLAMATION THROUGH PREACHING AND ELECTRONIC MINISTRIES

17

For Pastors, Families, and Women Only

D. L. Moody broke down the campus walls. Never one to be confined in his evangelistic zeal, Moody would not permit the Institute walls to hem in his teachers' gospel message. In 1897, eight years after the permanent school opened, the Bible teaching of Moody's new school burst out of the classroom and into America's byways. The Extension Department has sent MBI professors, leaders, and other full-time Bible expositors to Bible conferences ever since.

The Extension Department sprang from Moody's Northfield Conference, which in turn came from the Keswick Conferences in England. In fact, Moody wanted his conferences in Northfield, Massachusetts, to become the "American Keswick."[1] Camp meetings, with their evangelistic and revivalistic thrust, were common, yet Moody sensed another primary need among Christians.

> As [Moody] went from place to place, he found hundreds of believers anxiously asking after a fuller salvation, a higher knowledge of God's Word, and a deeper draught of the fullness of the Spirit; and it occurred to him to call together at Northfield [his birthplace and home], for a few weeks, those who yearned for closer fellowship with God, and greater power in service.[2]

Yearly conferences were held in the 1880s, with a temporary recess from 1882-1884 when Moody led evangelistic crusades in Great Britain. In 1896 Moody organized "union" classes, so-called because of their interdenominational nature. Bible and music were taught in these special classes, which were an extension to Chicago residents of the permanent school.

The Extension Department, organized a year later as part of the Bible Institute, grew out of these union classes. This ministry, now bearing a definite relationship to the school, began to grow and expand. By 1900 classes met in Detroit, St. Louis, and three locations in Chicago. By 1905, five weekly Bible classes met in Chicago, and six more in other cities.

1. Teunis Hamlin, "The Evolution of Northfield," *Northfield Echoes*, III, 23.
2. A. T. Pierson, "The Story of Northfield Conferences," *Northfield Echoes*, I, 2.

Within a few years classes had spread to fifteen centers, affecting 75,000 or more people. MBI was extending its Bible teaching ministry to include many who otherwise would have been unable to attend the school in person.

A BIBLE INSTITUTE EXTENSION MINISTRY

As the work developed, a new type of Bible Institute Extension[3] ministry soon came into being. In addition to the union classes, the regular instructors at the Institute and full-time traveling Bible teachers and evangelists conducted special meetings and Bible conferences for several days at a time in various parts of the country. In 1904 the following paragraph appeared in the school catalog to describe the department's activities:

> In addition to the teaching and training given at the Institute, and by correspondence, conferences, and classes are arranged for instruction in the Bible and in music in different parts of Chicago and throughout the land. Evangelistic services and campaigns are also planned and carried out with members of the Institute staff. Supplies are furnished for pulpits, pastorates, pastors, assistants, Bible teachers, superintendents of Sunday schools and missions, church visitors, singers, choir leaders, and almost every form of practical Christian work. The regular instructors frequently lecture and teach at conventions.[4]

By 1915 the Extension Department consisted of two main areas of work: the Bible teaching and evangelistic ministry and the Christian Workers' Bureau.

The general outreach increased each year until classes met in most states of the U.S. During the twenty years, 1928-1947, meetings were conducted in an average of twenty-eight states per year; during 1927 forty states held meetings. On the basis of department records, the MBI Extension has conducted more than 215,000 different conferences and meetings since 1900.

Since the turn of the century, at least 36.2 million people have attended these meetings, receiving spiritual encouragement and biblical teaching.

BIBLE CONFERENCE MINISTRY

For many years the Bible Conference remained one of the most far-reaching ministries of the Extension Department. This was especially true as religious liberalism began to penetrate deeply into the churches of America. As the Bible was being relegated increasingly to a place of secondary importance, people everywhere began to develop a hunger for direct Bible teaching.

The leaders at MBI were quick to sense this need. By 1928 the Extension Department was sponsoring three types of conferences in key locations throughout the country. Metropolitan Bible Conferences were held in such cities as New York

---

3. This was the term used at the turn of the century to describe the expanded ministry of the Extension Department.
4. *Catalog of the Moody Bible Institute* (1904), p. 35.

City, Boston, Philadelphia, and Baltimore. Summer Bible Conferences in well-known resort areas allowed people to spend several days or weeks combining a summer vacation with a spiritual experience. The Southeastern Bible Conferences conducted in Florida attracted vacationers as well as to those who were retired.

The best known Bible conference—and one of the most popular in America—is actually a birthday celebration. Founder's Week Conference celebrates D. L. Moody's February 5 birthday each year with week-long meetings featuring biblical exposition and challenge. The Christian public, including pastors and Moody alumni, join students for a week of spiritual renewal. They fill all 2,000 seats of Torrey-Gray Auditorium for each meeting; occasionally overflow crowds spill into other buildings to watch the proceedings on closed-circuit television.

Founder's Week began as Founder's Day. In 1901, shortly after Moody's death, the school commemorated Moody's birthday with day-long services. In 1919, Institute leaders extended the annual observance to one week, calling for a special five-day conference on the impact and meaning of World War I. With the theme "Evangelism and Vital Christianity After the War," MBI began to observe their founder's birthday as part of a week-long series.

The following year this special conference was, for the first time, published as the Founder's Week Conference. The sessions were canceled, however, because of a flu epidemic, but in 1921 the first Founder's Week Conference was actually held from February 1-5. Since then, Founder's Week has been a regular event each year at Moody Bible Institute.

In recent years Founder's Week has attracted growing audiences. Beginning in the 1970s, weekend sessions often moved to nearby Medinah Temple and Moody Memorial Church to accommodate crowds.

More recently the closing rally has been held in the Rosemont Horizon, the largest arena in the Chicago area. Here 17,000 people participate in the "Festival of Praise," featuring MBI's three choral groups, the Concert band, and a key evangelical speaker, such as Dr. James Dobson (1984) and Charles Colson (1985). In 1982 the audience became national, as the Moody Broadcasting Network began broadcasting the conference live to twelve stations from coast to coast. By 1985, MBI made the live broadcast available to more than one hundred stations in thirty-seven states. Clearly, Founder's Week is a grand birthday party for the grand evangelist, D. L Moody.

Bible conferences conducted during the summer months have played a distinctive role in evangelical education. Usually held for one week, they were designed to give participants a full program of Bible study, practical instruction, prayer opportunities, and fellowship, combined with a vacation away from work and home.

Leaders at MBI had clear objectives in mind while conducting these special summer sessions. For instance, President James Gray described a 1928 summer conference in Mountain Lake Park, Maryland, this way:

> The Bible conference . . . will have upon its platform from day to day preachers, teachers, and other Christian workers who are a unit in their testimony to the

authority and inspiration of the Holy Scriptures, who know the life and power of the Holy Spirit, and who have been trained in the school of experience in the various forms of Christian work.[5]

Bible conferences also helped audiences to understand and apply Scripture to their lives. President Gray noted the practical nature of Scripture when he invited the public to the Eagles Mere Bible Camp in 1928.

> If you would like to learn how the Bible may become to you the most interesting book, as it is in fact the most important book in the world, this is an opportunity. Pains will be taken to demonstrate a method by which you may immediately begin to study the Bible with relish and dig out its treasures for yourself. Even those who are inexperienced will find the instructions adapted to their needs.
>
> The aim will be to quicken and deepen the spiritual life and promote efficiency in Christian service to increase knowledge of the Word and of how to use it in everyday life.[6]

SPECIALIZED AUDIENCES

Specialization has struck America in the 1980s. From magazines to cars, consumers are able to choose a particular item that meets their own needs. Even television now offers programming for select audiences: cable television systems offer stations that are all sports, news, religion, movies, and all family content. To meet needs within the body of Christ, the Extension Department has begun to specialize as well. Extension now directs conferences for women, family, teenagers, and pastors.

Women's seminars unite Christian women for a day of fellowship and challenge from well-known Christian spokeswomen, such as Jill Briscoe and Evelyn Christensen. They focus on biblical teaching and encouragement, while offering spiritual counsel to individuals. In addition, Family Life Conferences help Christian couples. Experts in marriage counseling, family life, and teen work rotate round-robin to several churches during one week.

Many Christians invite couples with marital problems to the conferences. Extension Director James Gwinn reports that some divorced couples and separated couples have reconciled after attending the conference; other couples with weak marriages have received strength.

Sonlife Ministries offers direction for teenagers and youth pastors. Led by Dann Spader, Sonlife sponsors a three-day conference for high school students each Christmas, and his staff lead training institutes year round to aid youth pastors and workers in reaching teens. In 1984, the Basic Strategies Institute met in twenty-four cities to train youth leaders in strategies of love and discipleship of youth. For many youth workers, Sonlife renews the vision. One youth pastor in Wisconsin re-

5. *The Moody Bible Institute Bulletin* (June 1918), p. 2.
6. Ibid., p. 1.

ported, Sonlife helped him "dream big dreams" and "set definite goals."[7]

When President Sweeting announced plans for a national Pastors Conference in 1973, the Extension Department expected about three hundred. Instead six hundred pastors from thirty-seven states showed[8] and the word quickly spread. Now a capacity crowd of 1,350 pastors meet each spring. The Pastors Conference fulfilled the dream of Sweeting to establish a national evangelical conference for ministers. The pastors hear expository and inspirational sermons and receive advice on the how-to's of ministry in daily seminars.

The Extension Department also spreads the conference word through audio cassette tapes. About 20,000 cassette messages from the various conferences are distributed annually. The tape library, drawing on all major conferences, contains over five hundred titles featuring more than one hundred speakers. The speakers' list reads like a Who's Who of Evangelical Spokesmen.

D. L. Moody broke down the campus walls to send his teachers and other Bible expositors into the nation's byways because he suspected Christians throughout the country hungered for biblical nourishment. Obviously he was right, and today through conferences, seminars, institutes, and taped messages the Extension Department continues the feeding.

7. Flood and Jenkins, *Teaching the Word*, p. 130.
8. Ibid., p. 92.

18

Radio Messages

President James Gray clearly was a progressive. During his tenure he merged the men's and women's departments, and required English as part of the curriculum. He raised entrance requirements to include having a high school diploma, despite a storm of protest that the action would exclude many for whom the school had been intended. But on some issues Gray remained the traditionalist. He could not support radio broadcasting, for example. Like many other Christian leaders, he regarded the airwaves as mysterious, even sinister. After all, the New Testament had defined Satan as "the prince of the power of the air."

But shortly before MBI broadcasted its first program from its own studio, Gray had a change of heart. When a North Dakota resident wrote the school in 1926 and asked, "Is radio of God or the devil?" President Gray answered, "We think it is of God."[1] Once convinced of the right position, Gray embraced the medium fully. Gray delivered the first message, along with Reverend J. C. Page of the faculty.

Since that time, the radio voice of Moody Bible Institute, WMBI, has grown, adding an FM frequency, producing its own programs and launching a new Christian radio network in 1981. The first religious radio station remains at the forefront of broadcasting, according to the editor and publisher of "American Radio Research Reports." In 1983 Duncan described WMBI as "the leading non-commercial station in America in average listeners."[2] However, WMBI weathered a series of challenges, including changes of frequency, signal station interference, and political opposition before her success would become assured. At points during her first fifteen years, WMBI would fight for her survival.

The year Moody died, 1898, a young, creative Italian, Guglielmo Marconi, had managed to make practical use of the radio waves of Heinrich Hertz. Marconi succeeded in beaming the hertzian waves all the way across the Atlantic. The earliest American stations served primarily as a means of sending messages in radio telegraphic code. Finally, on November 2, 1920, a permanent licensed radio station,

1. James M. Gray, "Radio," *Moody Bible Institute Monthly* (March 1926), p. 309.
2. Phoebe Millis, "Broadcast Division History, 1926-1983" (Moody Bible Institute: August 1983), p. 46.

KDKA, began to broadcast a regular schedule of music, news, and entertainment in East Pittsburgh.[3]

Though President Gray was skeptical of the relevance of radio to the school, other Institute leaders recognized a unique opportunity to advance the gospel. As early as 1921, shortly after KDKA went on the air, several men began discussing the possibilities of radio broadcasting.

Some credit S. A. Woodruff with the original idea, but the man who played the most important role was young Henry Coleman Crowell. An engineering graduate from Yale, Crowell became assistant to the president in 1925 and was given charge of developing the radio work. Although the Institute was hesitant at first to venture into the field of broadcasting, during the early part of 1925 donations started to come in designated for this purpose. The possibilities were reevaluated, and eventually the board of trustees approved the construction of a radio station.

Even before the five-hundred-watt Western Electric transmitter and the broadcasting studio had been completed, MBI went on the air in dramatic fashion. A violent thunderstorm in downtown Chicago delayed the arrival of musical talent for a live broadcast on station WGES. The frantic program director for WGES noticed two young Moody men playing their cornets at an exposition in the Chicago Furniture Mart. He liked what he heard and quickly invited the young men to fill in for the missing talent. Crowell, who was at the Institute exhibit booth, gave his approval, and the first gospel music by students at Moody Bible Institute went out over the air.

As a result, a few days later officials from WGES asked Moody to broadcast at no charge from their studios each Sunday evening on a special Institute broadcast. Thus for several months a gospel program was aired from the WGES studios.

First Broadcasts over WENR

Early in 1926, the Moody station was ready to go on the air from its own studios. Although a license had been applied for, it had not been obtained because of a serious problem that had developed on the national scene. Numerous stations were coming into being. By the year 1925, there were almost six hundred radio stations already in operation in the country.[4] Giraud, Garrison, and Willis call this time the period of chaos in American radio history. From July 1926, to February 1927, while Congress was enacting new radio legislation, nearly two hundred stations went on the air. They "used any frequencies they desired, regardless of the interference thereby caused to others. . . .The result was confusion and chaos. With everybody on the air, nobody could be heard."[5]

---

3. Martin Codel, ed., *Radio and Its Future*, p. 7. Although there are several radio stations that date their beginnings from 1920 or even earlier, "KDKA was the first commercially-licensed standard broadcast station listed in the Department of Commerce records." KWQ in San Jose, California, dates from 1912, and ZK, in New Rochelle, New York, broadcast music beginning in 1916 (Head, p. 109).
4. C. Giraud, G. R. Garrison, and E. E. Willis, *Television and Radio*, p. 30.
5. Ibid., p. 31.

Although many stations were evidently very careless in complying with government regulations, the Institute took no steps to violate its long-standing ethical practices. On the other hand, neither were the leaders at the Moody school content to stand by without in some way legitimately going on the air. Consequently, they made an arrangement with the Chicago radio station WENR to broadcast six times a week, while using the Institute's newly constructed studio.

Their first broadcast, on March 3, 1926 from 8 to 10 P.M., evidently made President Gray a believer in the benefits of radio. After Gray had somewhat skeptically delivered his message, he walked from the studio across Institute place to his office in the 153 building. No sooner had he entered the office than the phone rang. The voice on the other end of the line, to Gray's astonishment, came from Florida reporting that his message had just been received. Other calls and correspondence followed, dispelling any doubt in Gray's mind as to the value of radio.

WMBI GOES ON THE AIR

After this initial broadcast, the Institute went on the air regularly six hours a week. Only five months after the first broadcast over WENR, the commission granted a license with the call letters WMBI, and assigned a wavelength of 288.3 meters. Yet major problems lay ahead.

The morning after WMBI's maiden broadcast on July 28, 1926, Institute leaders discovered that WKBA had also been granted a license and had gone on the air the same evening as WMBI on the same wavelength. Fortunately, the two stations were able to work out a satisfactory division of time.

Interference with other stations became the second major problem. Most of the interference was caused by the imperfect broadcasting facilities as well as the radio receivers of those early days. WMBI attempted to solve these problems as cordially as possible, and even offered to send an engineer to adjust the radio receivers owned by those people who reported interference from the Moody station.

In spite of these problems, WMBI stayed on the air, and on August 22, the Institute terminated its arrangements with WENR and initiated its first complete schedule of broadcasting over WMBI. By June of 1927 there were five main time periods consisting of thirty-three separate programs.

WMBI faced its third major problem the following year when the Radio Act of 1927 became law. The legislation created the Federal Radio Commission, composed of five members, to control U.S. radio. They were given power to issue licenses and to designate the wavelength to be used, the power, and the hours of operation of the station.

All broadcasting stations were allowed to continue on their frequency assignments for a period of two months while public hearings were held in Washington to consider ways in which broadcasting problems might be solved. The major difficulty facing the commission was that there were 733 stations licensed under the old law, and these stations had to be accommodated on 89 wave channels. To make the problem more complex, several hundred applications were on file to erect new stations.

Institute leaders were well aware of what this radio act could mean to many stations on the air. Crowell had been closely watching developments and the day following the passage of the 1927 Radio Act, President Gray addressed a letter to every person on the Institute mailing list, asking each to write officials in Washington. A postcard was also enclosed for immediate return that supported granting WMBI a new license. Almost 50,000 cards were returned.

On the dates set for the hearing, H. C. Crowell made what was destined to be the first in a series of ten trips to Washington during the next three years. Defending the need for station WMBI specifically and religious stations generally, he asked the FRC:

> Would it not be possible to allocate a small number of wave channels to be used jointly by educational and religious stations? This channel [could] be suitably located, not at the remote ends of the present band, but where they would be of service to the average listener with their present receiving sets. I think it will be found that such Institutions are fairly well scattered throughout the country and that each, with its limited schedule of hours would have small difficulty in agreeing to a division of time. Thus it would be possible to relinquish many present wave channels now devoted to this type of service and greatly consolidate the number of stations into a few channels. This would result in the releasing of many channels now used for such a service for the use of commercial stations.[6]

On April 22, an announcement came granting WMBI a special permit to continue broadcasting beyond the previously specified sixty days following the Radio Act.

But this permit was only temporary and the problem of being allowed to continue indefinitely was far from being solved. The FRC urged the Moody station to share time with other local Chicago stations. In a telegraph message the FRC noted that WMBI had created signal interference for other stations and issued an ominous warning: "Power increase absolutely out of question and cut in power may be necessary. Please consider this situation carefully before making final conclusion."

It would have been easy to panic. In order to keep from losing all opportunity for broadcasting, it would seem logical to follow the commissions' warning. However, upon receipt of the telegram, a delegation immediately left for Washington to seek an audience with the commission. H. P. Crowell, chairman of the Institute's board of trustees, H. C. Crowell, and an Institute attorney were cordially received and given a private hearing. During this conference, FRC members showed definite interest in WMBI and, after considerable deliberation, the Washington officials stated that they felt the Moody station was "operating in the interests of public convenience, interest and necessity." As a result, the commission did not push for consolidation with station WBBM as planned. Instead the FRC gave tentative approval for a new wavelength assignment.

6. Annual Report (1927), p. 7.

On May 23, the assignments for all Chicago stations were announced, and WMBI was placed at 1140 kilocycles, 263 meters, and was to divide time with WJAZ, the Zenith station. A new sixty-day license was soon issued, becoming operative as of June 15. Thus ended major problem number three.

Transmitter at Addison

The future seemed favorable for WMBI following this assignment. Soon MBI purchased property in Addison, Illinois, and received a building permit for a transmitter on the site. The 5,000-watt transmitter began operation on January 20, 1928. WMBI was now on the air operating on five thousand watts, continuing to share time with WJAZ.

Quickly, however, WMBI confronted problem number four: The Davis Amendment to the Radio Act. The amendment divided the United States into several zones, allowing a limited number of stations per zone.

Two months later, 164 stations were warned to show cause on July 9 as to why their licenses should not be revoked on August 1. Out of 164 stations, twenty-two were in the immediate Chicago area. Fortunately the Institute was not told to appear for this hearing, which again was evidence that WMBI's programming and purpose for being on the air were respected by the commission.

However, this reduction in the number of radio stations did not solve the problem. Two members of the commission came to Chicago in June to address all of the radio broadcasters. They strongly urged consolidation since there were three times as many stations in the fourth zone, which included Chicago, as could be licensed under the new law.

On August 31 of the same year, another plan went into effect, and the total allocation for Illinois again made the future for WMBI look "extremely serious." But surprisingly, on September 8, WMBI was assigned to one of eight clear channels in the fourth zone to share with three other stations. But before the Institute was actually able to shift to the new frequency, the FRC reassigned stations WMBI and WCBD to another frequency, 1180 kilocycles. This was actually a cleared channel in the third zone. However, both stations were classified as "limited time" stations, obligated to give way during the evening hours to WBT at Charlotte, North Carolina, a station formerly assigned full-time to this frequency.

To the leaders at the Institute, this situation was quite unsatisfactory. WBT had full power to make use of any evening hours it pleased, and WMBI was "only allowed to use together with WCBD the channel when it was not being used in the third zone." Ten days following this new assignment, Institute officials appeared in Washington to plead their case. They were cordially received, but the FRC could offer no solution to the ever-growing problem of allocating frequencies without creating interference.

Matters seemed to go from bad to worse. WBT revised its schedule and cut out all evening time for WMBI, except very late hours. On November 8, the Carolina station protested that the Institute had been assigned to its frequency.

WMBI APPLIES FOR A NEW FREQUENCY

The next major event involved a rather aggressive and dramatic step on the part of Institute leaders. On January 4, 1929, WMBI and WCBD of Zion were each advised by Washington officials to apply for one-seventh time on 870 kilocycles, which was then being used by WENR, a station that shared time with WLS. It was the commission's opinion that WENR could, without too much difficulty, be shifted to another frequency.

All went smoothly until WCBD was disqualified from applying for the one-seventh time based on a negative ruling from an earlier appeal. To complicate the picture further, the Federal Radio Commission went on record as saying that all religious stations like WCBD should be classified as propaganda stations since their broadcasts were only of interest to a small section of the public and that they must, therefore, be given inferior assignments in wavelengths and hours.

Institute leaders were now faced with two questions. First, should they proceed to seek one-seventh time on 870 since WCBD was disqualified? Second, would the commission's negative opinion regarding religious stations militate against WMBI in the forthcoming hearing involving WENR?

The Institute attorney advised to proceed with the hearing since he felt it could be shown that WMBI was not a "propaganda" station, but rather an interdenominational, educational station, appealing to all segments of the religious and nonreligious community.

The Moody leaders prepared their case carefully and thoroughly. The witnesses each testified as to the value of WMBI, followed by Gray, the Institute president, who spoke for forty minutes before the commission on why he felt the Washington officials should act positively regarding the Institute's application.

Here stood a very conservative man—theologically, administratively, and in every other way—pleading with the Federal Radio Commission in Washington to assign WMBI a new wavelength so that Moody Bible Institute could continue to extend its ministries. This is significant, as four or five years previously he had shown real skepticism about the place of radio in the home, let alone as a part of the total ministries of Moody Bible Institute.

It was not surprising that the FRB informed the school on April 14, 1930, that the Institute had lost its case. In fact, the commission had little choice in the matter since the Court of Appeals had ruled earlier on another case allowing WENR half time on 870, the other half to be used by WLS. In spite of this failure, WMBI scored another important point in Washington in making itself known as a significant radio station worthy of consideration. Certain FRB members told H. C. Crowell that WMBI's case was the most organized and best presented they had witnessed.

The years between 1926 and 1930 were critical for WMBI, but following the Washington hearing, the road became relatively smooth by comparison.

Both in 1930 and 1931, Crowell decided to visit Washington to maintain a first-hand contact with the commission and to keep the members informed as to the status of WMBI. FRB members in 1931 unanimously expressed their belief that WMBI was operating in the public interest. They assured Crowell that the station was secure as long as it was not directly attacked by another station in an under-quota state.

These were reassuring words during a time when several religious stations were being forced off the air because they were "not serving the general public." Nonetheless, more and more stations were coming into existence, power was being increased, and the overcrowding of stations on the air persisted. This continued to cause concern even in view of the reassuring words from the commission.

THE FEDERAL COMMUNICATIONS COMMISSION

On June 19, 1934, the Federal Communications Commission (FCC) came into being with a mandate to oversee all areas of telecommunication in the United States: telephone, telegraph, and broadcasting. This administrative change had no serious effect on WMBI. When a representative from the FCC stopped at the Institute to make a routine check early the next year, he told MBI officials that their station was in very good standing with the new commission members and that they had appreciated the care that had been exercised from the beginning in making financial appeals. He also reported that very few letters of protest had been received by the commission concerning the Moody programs.

WMBI's policy of avoiding offense to fellow broadcasters and listeners now began to yield rewards. Since its inception WMBI took utmost precautions to avoid offending listeners through strong propaganda, financial appeals, and slanderous remarks against other religious viewpoints. Outside speakers were chosen carefully and forewarned against careless speech. The station was not above criticism, to be sure, but the commission records, as reported, revealed an unusual silence, and later research among listeners also revealed a general hesitancy to criticize the station's programs.

When WCBD was granted a new frequency in 1939, WMBI suddenly found itself sharing 1080 on the dial only with WCBD. The Institute immediately filed an application for full limited-time operation in Chicago, and subsequently received approval. On July 6, 1941, WMBI began expanded broadcasting. This new schedule permitted fourteen and one-half hours of daily programming during the long daylight hours in June and July. Immediate steps were taken to secure an adequate program and to increase technical staff.

A SETTLED FREQUENCY

The Havana Treaty, known as the North American Regional Broadcast Agreement, was originally adopted in Havana on December 17, 1937, by representatives of Canada, Cuba, the Dominican Republic, Haiti, Mexico, and the United States. The major purpose of the treaty was to avoid international interference in broadcasting. On March 29, 1939, it was finally signed by all countries involved and most of the United States stations were soon shifted in frequency. In 1941, the Institute moved to an operation frequency of 1110 kilocycles. WMBI-AM began broadcasting on full limited time on its new frequency and has continued this schedule ever since. The "sign on" and "sign off" periods are determined by "sunrise" and "sunset" and fluctuate from twelve hours during the winter months to fifteen during the summer.

The advent of FM for educational use in 1936 intrigued officials at Moody. They saw in its development the answer to the problem of "limited time." Their application for a new high-frequency educational broadcast station was initially rejected by the FCC. Later approval came, but a ban on station construction during World War II postponed further work. Finally the station began operation on October 1, 1943, when the FM station joined WMBI at approximately 10 A.M. and operated simultaneously until sunset. After WMBI signed off, the Institute continued its programs until 9 P.M., over WDLM-FM — the last three letters standing for Dwight Lyman Moody's initials.

The Institute continued to broadcast on both WMBI and WDLM for nearly ten years. However, after careful investigation, it was discovered that the FM station seemingly was reaching a relatively small audience. Though serving a very useful purpose, FM had not caught on as was hoped, and consequently the Institute officials decided to cease broadcasting on WDLM. The termination of FM broadcasting from the Chicago studios in December, 1952, turned out to be only temporary. FM broadcasting, though lagging in the early fifties, soon developed into the fastest growing entertainment medium in the country. By 1960 the trend was going only one direction—upward. FM frequencies were becoming scarce in top markets, and in some localities none were available.

Fortunately, the Board of Trustees recognized this new trend early. On October 15, 1958, they asked permission to erect a noncommercial, educational FM station on channel 211, 90.1 megacycles. By July 1960, the station began broadcasting with a power of 47,000 watts, the fourth strongest FM station in Chicago. On July 28, 1965, the FM power was increased to 100,000 watts, enabling the signal to reach as far as the signal of WMBI-AM.

THE MOODY RADIO NETWORK

The story of Moody Bible Institute and FM extends beyond Chicago. It begins in Cleveland. When a group of Christian businessmen began planning a religious radio station in Cleveland, they decided to ask the Institute whether it would be interested in operating the station.

This was an unanticipated event that called for careful deliberation. As early as 1954, Robert Parsons, then director of the Radio Department, had urged the administration to buy or construct a station in another area. At that time it did not seem feasible. After careful thought, however, Institute officials agreed it was time to act and accepted the Cleveland proposition, providing the station would be supported locally. The FCC readily approved the application, and the following year Moody was given title to the station and began broadcasting November 23,

1958, on 103.3 megacycles at 21,500 watts.

By 1964 the total hours each day increased to sixteen, from 7 A.M. to 11 P.M. WCRF is currently operating twenty-four hours a day. Since a large portion of the programs used at WCRF are prepared in the Chicago studios, a minimum staff is needed in Cleveland to keep the station operating smoothly.

One year after the Cleveland group had contacted the school asking for assistance, MBI officials decided to expand within Illinois. For some time, what had been an extended outreach by WMBI west of Chicago had gradually decreased due to interference from other stations operating on or near 1110 kilocycles. Consequently MBI petitioned the FCC in 1958 for a permit to build an AM station to operate in East Moline, Illinois. The call letters WDLM, which had previously been used for the Chicago station, were approved by the FCC for the Moline station, and on April 3, 1960, the third Moody station went on the air operating at one thousand watts from sunup to sundown. The station originally received programs by direct wire from Chicago and largely duplicated the WMBI broadcast schedule. Today the station is locally operated for superior audio signal and to localize programming.

The addition of WDLM created what became the Moody Radio Network. In subsequent years, other individuals and Christian broadcasting groups have asked the Institute to start new stations or assume management of existing ones. Today eleven stations across the U.S. are owned and operated by MBI. In Spokane, KMBI and KMBI-FM (acquired in 1974) broadcast the good news. The FM signal radiates in all directions for wider coverage and nighttime reception.

In Florida, two stations broadcast from St. Petersburg, WGNB and WKES-FM (1978), and one from Boynton Beach, WRMB-FM (1979). In between are stations in Chattanooga, WMBW-FM (1973), Cleveland, East Moline, and the two flagship stations in Chicago. In 1980 a sister station to WDLM in East Moline began operation, WDLM-FM.

But the extent of broadcasting by owned-and-operated stations had reached the limit in 1980. The Institute operated seven stations on the FM band, the maximum then allowed by the FCC. With this limit, MBI could reach only 11 percent of the American radio audience.

In spite of this barrier, the Institute had a strong desire to reach as many listeners as possible. With five of its stations, MBI was able to extend the coverage by using a series of repeater stations, or FM translators.

WMBW has extended its signal beyond Chattanooga into eastern Tennessee as far as Elizabethton, home of the Moody Aviation School. Translators also beam WMBW's signal into parts of Virginia, Alabama, and Georgia. In Spokane, twelve translators send KMBI's signal to Idaho, Montana, and Oregon. In addition, several Canadian cable systems had added KMBI's signal to their service, so that KMBI reaches into Western Canada, including Calgary, Alberta. WMBI, WDLM, and WCRF also use translators to reach distant cities in Illinois, Iowa, and Ohio.

SATELLITE BROADCASTING

When broadcast officials created a network development section in 1979, they planned to add more translators in remote communities to extend the broadcast signal of owned-and-operated stations. However, network officials soon were deluged with requests for Christian radio in regions far remote from the original stations.

The answer was satellite technology. One communication satellite could relay a radio signal across much of North America, where satellators (satellite-fed translators) could pick up the message. In addition, existing stations and cable systems could catch the signal by using a satellite-receive dish. Satellite transmission offered many advantages: almost instantaneous live broadcasting, reduced costs, and quick start-up time. These final two advantages have made Christian radio more available to the country.

The project began in 1981 and received strong public support. During five "satellite awareness days" over a two-year period, officials and radio hosts on the newly-established Moody Broadcasting Network explained satellite programming and the vision behind the larger national network of news, commentary, music, and spiritual challenge. Callers showed their interest in MBN by contributing over $1 million to help with operational expenses of the new network and construction of much-needed new studios.

Soon satellite service began in North Pole, Alaska, with five satellators transmitting the MBN signal across parts of Alaska.

After this notable beginning, the FCC in 1984 turned down MBI's petition for a rule change that would allow satellite-fed FM translators in the forty-eight contiguous states. The five satellators in Alaska could continue, but the FCC ruled that no additional ones could be constructed at present. Network officials have again petitioned the FCC to allow the satellator program. This matter is still pending.

GROWTH OF MBN

This temporary setback caused network officials to concentrate on offering satellite programming to full-power stations and cable radio systems, with immediate success. Because of this growth, in 1983 the Department of Broadcasting was designated the Broadcasting Division of the Institute.

The Moody Broadcasting Network meant Christian radio was now available to cities and towns that had none. Would-be listeners quickly realized this. Cable subscribers approached their local company requesting that MBN be added to their service. Local church groups banded together to raise funds and apply for construction permits to build their own stations to rebroadcast MBN programs. At established stations, radio managers realized they could add to the variety and quality of their programming by broadcasting all or part of MBN's signal.

By 1985, the potential listening audience from all affiliates—stations receiving at least one MBN program—was at least 120 million, or 50 percent of the total potential American radio audience, according to a network spokesman. With 136 affiliates in thirty-seven states, fifty-seven cable systems, and ten satellators, network programs reached thirty-eight of the top fifty metropolitan areas in the U.S.

MBN has developed programs for Christian radio stations nationwide, now offering such programs as Prime Time America, Christian Perspective on the News, and two call-in programs, Open Line and The Minirth-Meier Clinic. As the newest network program, the Clinic features two psychiatrists answering questions about physical and mental health by drawing on their training as well as principles of the Christian faith. MBN also broadcasts news from the International Media Service. IMS offers national, international, and significant religious news reported by objective Christian journalists.

"We have been able to tie the Christian community together through radio, doing things that would be impossible for any one station to do," noted Robert Neff, manager of the Broadcasting Division. MBN is the pioneer. Other networks have followed, and Neff called them friendly competitors. He expects MBN to develop more unique programs, including original dramas and music programs. New studios opened in 1985, replacing forty-five-year-old facilities that spanned three floors. By linking the staffs of the network and stations WMBI and WMBI FM on one floor (eighth floor of Crowell Hall), coordination of local and network programming is easier. The studios feature state-of-the-art broadcast technology.

The division continues to expand. "The Moody name adds confidence," Neff explained. And it adds hope, as MBN spreads the teaching and edifying ministries of the school across the United States.

THE AUDIENCE

Through the years Moody broadcasters have redefined and specified its audience. Originally WMBI, the flagship station for the network, aimed its broadcasts at ". . . the spiritual needs of its actual and potential listener in all age brackets." Later station management decided to direct programming at "the Christian family unit, zeroing in on the parents, with supplemental programming to reach all members of the family." In 1983 the Broadcasting Division adopted its present focus: "The growing Christian, with primary emphasis on the 25-55 age group."[7] Both the network and the Chicago stations program to reach this age segment.

Leaders in MBI broadcasting have always had an interest in reaching the immigrant and ethnic America with the good news. Of course, this meant broadcasting in foreign languages. Programs in Yiddish, German, and Swedish all originated in 1927. Later, other foreign language programs were added, including those in Dutch, Italian, Greek, French, Polish, Russian, and Spanish. These programs continued until World War II.

Broadcasts to the American immigrant resumed in 1974 with two hours of Spanish programs targeted weekly to the 1.2 million Hispanic people living in Chicago (34 percent of the city's population). Today WMBI-AM broadcasts its Saturday

---

7. Millis, "Broadcast Division History," p. 43.

programs exclusively in Spanish. As a result, Hispanic listeners call and write the station for counsel, prayer, and church referrals. Scores of listeners have been led to faith in Christ.[8]

WMBI's earliest children's programs, Early Bird and KYB (Know Your Bible) Club, have led to a variety of children's programs with a Christian emphasis. Today about five hours of programming is dedicated to children each week.

In its first days of broadcasting, when there were far fewer stations and atmospheric conditions were right, WMBI was an international station, its Chicago signal reaching New Zealand, Ecuador, and the Fiji Islands. The days of a global signal are past, but the radio outreach remains international. Program tapes produced by the Division of Broadcasting are distributed to more than 300 stations in more than a dozen foreign countries.

The outreach may be global, but leaders never forget that the results are intimate in the lives of listeners. The spiritual impact of the radio messages cannot be directly measured. Though most listeners are Christians, many broadcasts contain an evangelistic theme and have an impact. While vacationing in her summer home in Florida, Lita Kurtzer flipped the radio dial trying to locate a clear station. Her fingers finally stopped at WRMB, whose signal from Boynton Beach came through loud and clear. The frequent references to the Bible and the Old Testament impressed the Jewish woman. She became a regular listener.

"As I listened, I was being taught the Word of God. One day I realized that according to Scripture, I was separated from God by sin. I learned that Jesus was the Messiah of Israel promised in the Old Testament. He was the only way to God. As a result . . . I invited Jesus to come into my heart, to forgive my sins and to take charge of my life."[9]

Other broadcasters recognize the impact and integrity of Moody broadcasting. The president of WGN-TV and radio in Chicago once said, "These call letters WMBI not only stand for Moody Bible Institute, but for the finest principles inherent in responsible broadcasting." Social and political commentator Paul Harvey summarized the radio ministry of MBI effectively upon WMBI's fortieth birthday in 1966. Harvey noted during his national newscast that day: "Since 1926 . . . WMBI had amplified God's Word with dignity and effectiveness."[10]

8. Ibid, p. 31.
9. Eric Fellman, "Static-Free Witness," *Moody Monthly*, March 1983, p. 116.
10. Millis, "Broadcast Division History," p. 46.

19

God's World on Display: MIS

Some people living in San Francisco still remember the day Irwin Moon allowed one million volts of electricity to race through his body for several seconds. His sleeves rolled up, his back and arm muscles taunt, the former California pastor shouted "Now!" and a switch was thrown.

Miniature lighting bolts seemed to leap from the fingers of his hands, dancing in the air. The stunned audience gasped, but all sounds were lost as the incessant, crackling electricity echoed off the auditorium walls. A few seconds later Moon yelled a second time "Now!" and the power was out. The scientist-preacher stepped off the electrified platform unharmed.

Few people had expected anything like this when they entered the Sermons from Science pavilion at the San Francisco World's Fair in 1939. Word quickly got around, and for nine months Moon performed before packed audiences three times a day, often seven days a week. Some days, so many wanted to see these demonstrations of God's chemical and physical wonders that Moon presented his "sermons" eight times through the day and night.

That scene represents one of the earliest highlights of Moon's platform ministry with Moody Institute of Science. The dramatic one-million-volt surge demonstration continues today in performances where Dean Ortner, a former scientist and college teacher, sends the charge through his body and out his hands, engulfing a pine board in flames.

For some supporters, MIS is the Sermons from Science demonstrations, including the million-volt coil. Others think of the twenty-three science films that have won fifty-eight international film awards. Employees at MIS headquarters in Whittier, California, like to walk down "Oscar Alley," their name for the hallway holding the numerous awards. Three educational films also have won film accolades, and for students in public schools nationwide, Moody Institute of Science means funny and fantastic movies about the life cycle of the bee or animal eating patterns and the truth that the Creator who watches over animals can watch over them too.

MIS began when an enthusiastic preacher, positive that science would confirm

—not deny—God's presence, met the president of a school willing to try new forms of evangelism to reach the common man. Dr. Irwin Moon, experimenter, would-be physicist, and preacher; and Moody Bible Institute, innovative and practical like its founder, D. L. Moody. The union was ideal. In 1945 MBI opened the Moody Institute of Science, a science laboratory to study natural phenomena and to record the findings on film and present them in live demonstrations.

Moon had first presented what he called his "sermons from science" in 1931 at his Los Angeles church. Several of his sermons became illustrated lectures using scientific equipment and laws to convey spiritual and biblical concepts. Later he began to film simple scientific demonstrations to illustrate his sermons— "the recurrent theme being that the wonders of science are but the visible evidence of a Divine Plan of Creation."[1]

Other churches as well as civic groups heard about these unusual sermons and soon the demand to see the laboratory of faith pressed on Moon's schedule. In 1937 Moon resigned his pastorate to give full attention to Sermons from Science. Appearing in the largest civic auditoriums and on university campuses, he drew capacity crowds.

MOON JOINS MOODY

The same year Moon entered this full-time, specialized religious work, he met Will Houghton, president of Moody Bible Institute. Houghton watched a Sermons from Science demonstration in Los Angeles and recognized a new evangelistic and educational technique in action. He invited Moon to join the Institute extension staff. Moon hesitated, thinking such an association might limit his contact with unchurched people. His special interest was to reach high school and college youth whom he felt could be convinced of the truth of the evangelical message through this new medium. He was reassured that MBI had similar goals and joined the MBI Extension Department in 1938.

The Moody Institute of Science and MIS films were still seven years away, as Moon concentrated on live demonstrations. In 1939 Moon transported two tons of scientific equipment to San Francisco. With the help of local businessmen, Moon built a Sermons from Science pavilion at the World's Fair.

The show was a solid success. Often the demonstrations began hours ahead of the scheduled time because early arrivals had filled up the auditorium, and more people were waiting outside. Crowds listened quietly to his thought-provoking questions repeated after each experiment: "Can you believe these miracles are the result of chance or accident? Or are they a part of a divine pattern. What do you think?"[2]

After the World's Fair, Moon traveled across the country holding meetings in major auditoriums. When war broke out in 1941, he turned toward the servicemen on military bases. For five years he ministered to young GIs, giving them an op-

1. Darrin Scot, "World's Biggest Little Studio," *American Cinematographer* (August 1961), p. 4.
2. Flood and Jenkins, *Teaching the Word*, p. 199.

portunity to receive Christ as Savior before going into combat overseas.

During the war, Moon produced his own film entitled *They Live Forever* and completed the photography for what became the first science film produced by MIS, *God of Creation.*

The inventive and ambitious Moon turned his own home into a combination film laboratory and movie studio to produce these two films. His bathroom became the film lab, his bedroom the studio.

Moon became one of the first filmmakers to use time-lapse photography, developing his own intervalometer.[3] This electrical timing device could turn both floodlights and camera on and off at preset intervals. With his camera lens trained on a small camellia, Moon photographed a spectacular sequence in which the flower grows and blooms in minutes. Viewers unaccustomed to this camera technique asked the creative film producer to explain his "secret" to rapid plant growth.

Moon quickly recognized the potential for this new medium. By featuring scientific demonstrations in films, he could multiply his ministry many times, channeling his time and physical energy to new scientific-evangelistic projects. His tour of U.S. military bases had demonstrated the practicality of film as a teaching tool. Educational historians recognize the war years as the period when educational films became an acceptable, practical teaching instrument.[4] Watching GIs view military training films and seeing the success of his own amateur productions (though skillfully conceived), Moon approached MBI to create a unique laboratory.

FOUNDING OF MIS

Along with F. Alton Everest, a friend and electrical engineer, Moon proposed that a Christian laboratory be formed as a part of the Moody Bible Institute. The man argued that the gap between evangelical Christians and the scientific world was continuing to widen. A Christian laboratory could help to bridge this gap, particularly among young people. The laboratory would perform scientific studies and develop photographic equipment and technique for its live and filmed demonstrations of God's creative power in nature. As a result, Moody Institute of Science came into being in 1945.

Everest became the first director of research and later executive director of MIS. When he met Moon in 1941, both men were interested in starting an evangelical organization for science educators. Along with MBI President Houghton, these men were catalysts in forming the America Scientific Affiliation. Houghton explained the objective of the group in a letter to Everest.

Some of us believe the time has come for a meeting of science teachers who are

---

3. "Eastman Kodak Gold Medal Award," 1980 Awards Program of the Society of Motion Picture and Television Engineers, 10 November 1980.
4. Godfrey M. Elliott, ed., *Film and Education*, p. 17.

Christians and who feel that some scientific facts are not bearing proper recognition, while some hypotheses are being presented as laboratory truth. It might be that eventually an organization will come into being, but this is not the immediate plan of the two or three in back of this letter. Our thought is of an annual meeting which could be a kind of clearing house for ideas. There should be the presentation of papers, and from discussion of those papers.[5]

The American Scientific Affiliation was founded in 1941, with Everest as its first president and the organization remains active today. Its members are scientists and educators who "investigate the philosophy and findings of science as they are related to Christianity and the holy Scriptures," and "disseminate the results of such studies to both the Christian and secular worlds."[6]

Moon and Everest soon turned their energies to expanding MIS, but a strong relationship was maintained between the two groups through the years.

FILM CONTENT

The emphasis on live Sermons from Science demonstrations have continued. But the greatest multiplication of effort has been in filming these Sermons from Science.

The first film, *God of Creation*, was released in 1946 and caused an immediate sensation. It included a number of "firsts" in cinematography, and its technical innovations would typify the MIS films to come. Moon used his own time-lapse technique with many natural phenomena to document the way plants grow—their movement in the direction of light, and the way food is synthesized from sunlight. His cameras produced the first color film of the metamorphosis of a caterpillar into swallowtail butterfly. He placed a specially-adapted lens onto a telescope to explore stars and planets, and then mounted other lenses onto microscopes to record the living cellular world.

Throughout the film, the facts of science are portrayed in a visually clear and undistorted fashion. During the final two minutes, Moon concludes that the facts of science just portrayed reveal "evidences of a Divine plan in the universe." This conclusion is neither preachy nor fervent, for Moon believes the facts of nature so portrayed will speak for themselves regarding the relationship between science and religion.

Felix Streyckmans described the tone and purposes of Sermons from Science films this way:

> Without asking you to have faith, without asking you to believe in the Bible, without appealing to your idealism, and only regarding that you have an open mind, Moody shows you these photographs of animal, vegetable, insect, plant and bird life, without argument, without quotations from Scripture, and lets you decide at the end of each film whether what is taking place right here on earth

5. Wilbur M. Smith, *An Annotated Bibliography of D. L. Moody*, p. 142.
6. Constitution of the American Scientific Association.

now, before your own eyes, is a grand coincidence, an evolution of survival, or the Plan of a Master, who not only has created according to His own design, the world in which we live, but most obviously has a direct interest in every one of the creatures.[7]

God of Creation set the tone for the science films to follow. In its first forty years, MIS has produced twenty-three such films, ranging from thirty minutes to an hour in length. Some of the scientific subjects that have been treated are atomic energy, sea life, animal instincts, the human heart and bloodstream, the senses, and seed dispersal.

Sound motion picture production has not been limited to Sermons from Science films. In addition, MIS has distributed sixty-two educational films, ten missionary/ Christian life films, and twenty-eight children's films.

During the 1980s, MIS began distributing films about practical Christian living. Two film series discuss the role of the family and disciple-making, and feature pastor-teacher John MacArthur, Jr. *The Family: God's Pattern for Living* has been shown to more than 1.5 million people during its first four years and has been translated into Japanese with great success.

MIS also produces filmstrips with audio cassettes. About one hundred filmstrips, including Bible stories, Bible background, and leadership training filmstrips, are used in the local church.

Although most of the material has a strong evangelical emphasis, an entirely different objective exists for the educational science films produced for public school system. Designed to fit into the science curriculum, these films challenge the minds of almost 40 million school children each year with the concept that God is Creator. These films are non-sectarian and have acceptance in 75 percent of the public school systems. By 1985 more than 100 educational films and filmstrips were in circulation, with 55,000 prints in university media libraries.

FACILITIES AND EQUIPMENT

Classified by Darrin Scot as the "World's Biggest Little Studio," Moody Institute of Science is a self-contained unit including facilities for field exploration, laboratory research, sine-radiography, photomicroscopy, and many other types of photography, as well as complete motion picture production. Since opening its doors in the mid-forties, the technicians at the Institute have collected and built sound equipment and cameras to perform numerous technical tasks. Some of the processes performed with their own equipment are animated photography, time-lapse sequences, and microscopic work. Separate departments produce photomicrographic sequences, art work, titles, and animations. Lip-sync shooting is done on a well-equipped sound stage, consisting of two permanent sets. Dubbing facilities are also available.

---

7. Felix B. Streyckmans, "Sermons from Science," *Kiwanis Magazine* (March 1951), p. 12.

Included in the MIS headquarters is a machine shop that is used for numerous purposes, and a processing laboratory in which all of the release prints are made. The total output averages 2.5 million feet of film per year. As MIS moves into its fifty decade, its commitment to state-of-the-art technology remains unchanged. Future plans include construction of a complete video studio, editing facility, and a computer graphics system.

FILM INNOVATIONS

Creative minds recognize creative talent. Therefore it's not surprising that Albert Einstein, Lowell Thomas, Walt Disney, and Captain Eddie Rickenbacker all have applauded the technique and content of MIS science films. Einstein attended a showing at Princeton University of *God of the Atom* and went away impressed like everyone else. *God of the Atom* was only the second MIS film, yet even the normally cynical *London Times* praised the work. The tradition of technical excellence has continued since then, earning MIS films and their makers major recognition.

In *Red River of Life*, MIS cameras filmed the inner workings of the human heart. A writer in *Look* magazine noted:

> For the first time in medical history, doctors can look into a human heart and watch it work. With a motion-picture camera, they can record how the important valves of the heart normally open and close, allowing the blood to pass through the heart's four chambers. They can even force the heart to act as it would with high or low blood pressure and with a fast or slow beat. By seeing normal as well as diseased action of heart valves, surgeons now will be able to devise better surgical methods for the repair of diseased valves that are functioning poorly.
>
> The hearts used in these studies were removed from dead bodies, but they function as if they were still beating within the human breast. This is made possible by an apparatus known as the cardiac pulse duplicator.[8]

MIS achieved another technical breakthrough in the 1960s. Existing bellows and extension tubes used in macrophotography required strong lighting. Trying to film bees at work in a honeycomb seemed impossible, as the hot lights melted the honeycomb and began frying the bees. Moon and his staff wondered if they really could finish *City of the Bees*.

Finally they found a solution, a system of supplemental lens and the use of electronic flash (strobe unit) synchronized with the camera shutter. The shutter opened a brief one-millionth of a second and the flash quickly triggered. The result was maximum exposure with minimum heat. The hive and bees were safe, and MIS technical creativity again had triumphed.

The impact of the MIS cardiac pulse duplicator, and new techniques in macrophotography, as well as technical innovations in other areas earned Dr. Moon the

---

8. Roland H. Berg, "First Pictures Ever Taken Inside the Beating Heart," *Look* (October 1957), pp. 66-67.

Eastman Kodak Gold Medal Award in 1980. The society of Motion Picture and Television Engineers presented Moon with the Gold Medal to recognize "outstanding contributions which lead to new or unique educational programs utilizing motion pictures, television, high-speed and instrumentation photography."

City of Bees earned MIS its first international film award, and many have followed. In May 1985 MIS released *Journey of Life*, which continued the tradition of technical innovation. MIS technicians converted a borescope fiber optic system from a medical instrument into a filmmaker's eyepiece. Designed to allow physicians to peer into the throats of patients, the optical system was adapted to the camera. In *Journey of Life* the viewers could be "inside" a plant. They looked up at a dandelion puff from the head of the plant and gazed inside the Iceland poppy.

The technological advancements have earned MIS scientists publication in major academic journals. For example, in 1947, the *Journal of the Society of Motion Picture Engineers*, published an article by Moon entitled "A Photo-electric Film Cuing System." In 1957, Moon and Everest wrote for the same journal another article, entitled "Multiple-Camera Control," which presented a "simplified" system by which four or more standard blimped cameras could be started and stopped at will during sound takes with automatic head and tail sync marks.

The first color motion pictures from inside the human heart appeared in *Red River of Life*, and the medical community took notice. Three scholarly journals published articles, including the *Journal of the Biological Photographic Association*. The journal published the manuscript by Everest and G. Keith Hargett entitled "Photography of the Heart Valves with the Cardiac Pulse Duplicator."

Numerous other articles by MIS personnel suggest MIS has had a strong impact on the world of science. The MIS philosophy always has been that any public presentation must be thorough, scientifically accurate, and as technically perfect as possible.

However, more important to MIS leaders than the scientific impact are the specific contributions to evangelism and evangelical education. The scientific method and the resulting knowledge are considered only a means to a goal — the presentation of the evangelical message wherever possible. Without doubt, careful research, adequate conclusions, and technical proficiency have opened many doors to present this message.

FILM AS MINISTRY

James Adams became manager of Moody Institute of Science in 1973 as Moon retired, and MBI President George Sweeting became the on-camera host of the film series. Sweeting appears in six MIS films, his strong voice and personality adding credibility to the series.

With the 1985 release of *Journey of Life*, the visible narrator disappeared. By eliminating an on-camera personality, the science films had easier international applications. With background narration, the film could be more easily translated and visible Western dress would be eliminated. MIS Science films have always drawn large crowds in showings overseas; the new format will make the movies even more culturally relevant.

By mid-1985, MIS had produced 350 foreign language versions of the science films, involving 27 languages. Sound tracks included such languages as Armenian, Cantonese, Danish, Dutch, Finnish, German, Greek, Italian, Japanese, Korean, Mandarin, Norwegian, Spanish, and Swedish.

During the first forty years of MIS, films have been shown in more than 130 countries. An ever-growing ministry, these films are used extensively by missionaries in churches, schools, public auditoriums, and on television.

The Moody films are popular for two reasons: the respect for science and technology in Third World countries, and the culturally neutral content of the films.[9] Missionaries request films frequently and report positive effects. "The gospel/science film is the best tool we have to penetrate non-Christian institutions . . . no other type of ministry . . . draws the unsaved together for a hearing of the gospel," says one missionary. Another adds, "Moody films . . . are like a master key to open all the doors."[10]

Recently MIS has shipped films behind the Iron Curtain, with showings even in China and the Soviet Union. At one showing, more than 3,000 people jammed a Russian church. At the film's conclusion, more than one hundred came down the aisles to receive Christ as their Savior.[11] Notes one missionary, "When [the Soviet people] first viewed the films, they were amazed that anything [with a scientific] apologetic could be presented in such a way."[12]

The Sermons from Science films are welcomed on military bases as well as at major corporations. Moon had an extensive ministry in the armed services during World War II presenting Sermons from Science demonstrations on military bases. After MIS was officially organized and began to turn out science films, the Institute found a ready market among this same United States constituency, as well as among the Canadian, British, and Australian military. Copies of these films are currently provided for every branch of the armed services.

The U.S. Air Force has been the greatest user of the movies. Nearly 3,000 prints have been supplied to the USAF. The Air Force made the viewing of MIS films compulsory for all recruits as part of a character guidance program. On nuclear submarines, where Navy personnel live months at sea and are without chaplains, officers and sailors can watch several of the MIS films.

One Army general has written MIS: "Ordinarily, religious films do not receive universal acclamation. . . . In this case, however, we have repeated requests for further films of a similar nature."

More than fifty industrial and business organizations have screened MIS films. The companies include Aluminum Company of America (Alcoa), Eastern Airlines, Goodyear Tire and Rubber Company, General Foods Corporation, Interna-

9. "A Story of God at Work," p. 10.
10. Ibid.
11. Flood and Jenkins, *Teaching the Word*, p. 203.
12. "A Story of God at Work," p. 10.

tional Business Machines (IBM), McDonnel Douglas, RCA, United States Steel, and Westinghouse.

SERMONS FROM SCIENCE DEMONSTRATIONS

The live Sermons from Science demonstrations that launched the unique evangelistic ministry of Irwin Moon and later the Moody Institute of Science remain a vital part of MIS today. Performances are as popular at military bases and university campuses as they were decades ago, and the electrical sparks still fly from the man on the million-volt coil. Live demonstrations depend on audience participation and generous doses of humor, and they continue to include a call to know the Creator.

George Speakes took over the live science demonstrations one year after MIS began, in order to free Moon to manage the science institute. For twenty-nine years Speakes, a former mechnical engineer and Navy pilot, challenged military audiences around the world and millions at World's Fairs of their need for Christ.

More than 4 million people have viewed Sermons from Science demonstrations at 6 World's Fairs, including 1.4 million at the 1964 New York Fair and another 1.2 million at the 1967 Montreal Fair. Almost three-quarters of a million people attending the expositions responded for spiritual counseling after watching a live MIS demonstration or film.

MIS also has gone to the Olympics. Both athletes and spectators attended the science demonstrations and MIS films during the 1972 and 1976 Summer Olympic Games. MBI students acted as counselors and recorded decisions by inquirers from thirty-five nations.

The popularity of Sermons from Science continues today. Dean Ortner assumed the M.C. role at these demonstrations in 1976. Ortner's science demonstrations are always in big demand. An Air Force Lieutenant colonel wrote in 1984:

> I have personally watched Dean Ortner capture the total interest of not only those who came to see the program, but those sometimes bored, sometimes unmotivated, sometimes sullen troops who have stayed on after the evening movie to "catch the action." I've seen the light of spiritual curiosity coming on those same folks as they've had lively no-nonsense discussions with Dean after the programs, sometimes until the early morning hours. And, as the bottom line, I've seen lives permanently changed as a result."[13]

Like the MIS films, Sermons from Science are also presented to students in public schools. School administrators and teachers in Seattle gave the program high marks during several 1984 presentations. "My students are 'glued' to their chairs, eyes fixed on Dean Ortner and his science demonstrations as he presented clear, logical evidence for a Creator who is involved in our daily lives," wrote one Seattle teacher.[14]

13. Letter from Robert L. Brotzman, Lt. Col., USAF, 28 June 1984.
14. Moody Institute of Science 1984 Annual Report, p. 6.

In addition to the million-volt climax (not performed every session), Sermons from Science features such unlikely events as metal floating in air, music played on a beam of light, and walls that talk. But the amazing occurrences are not magic, nor are they meant merely to entertain. Ortner explains: "This is not hocus-pocus; it is natural law, as discovered by science. I give a scientific demonstration, not a seance. My purpose is not to amuse people with parlor tricks but to show that eyes and ears are tragically feeble instruments in some realms of nature."

Ortner adds, "Natural and spiritual laws we cannot make. Neither can we alter them. We must discover, follow and obey them or suffer the consequences."

Nowhere is the need to heed nature's law clearer than when he stands on the electric coil. It generates a high-frequency field of 65,000 cycles. Because the human body responds to electrical current at sixty cycles, this ultra-high frequency charge surges through him without instant death. Still, Ortner admits his muscles ache and his body temperature is affected by the charge. But he continues to do it for one reason: to show the audience their need for a spiritual relationship with God.

"No other illustration shows so vividly how one can be in tune or out of tune with God's physical laws. If you are not in tune with God's spiritual laws, you cannot tap into His source of power."[15]

TELEVISION AND VIDEOTAPE CASSETTES

The latest MIS venture is the production of videotape cassettes for home viewing. With the phenomenal sales growth in video recorders, Christian families are looking for quality films, and MIS can supply a wide selection of award-winning science and religious films from its collection. Videocassettes for the U.S. market are expected soon.

In addition, MIS officials in 1985 signed distribution contracts for videocassette sales overseas. Initially cassettes will be sold in West Germany, Norway, Great Britain, Australia, South Africa, and Japan.

MIS films will also be shown on cable television. The science institute has contracts with the three major Christian networks, the Christian Broadcasting Network, Trinity Broadcasting Network, and ACTS (the Southern Baptist television network).

FOREIGN MISSIONS

By mid-1968, MIS had produced a hundred foreign language versions of the science films in sixteen languages. Many of these films were being used in over eighty-five different countries of the world. Part of an ever-growing ministry, today these films are used extensively by missionaries in churches, schools, public auditoriums, and on television.

MIS is currently putting forth effort to increase this foreign film ministry. Nu-

15. Gary L. Wall, "The Man on the Coil," *Moody Monthly*, March 1979.

merous problems are involved, such as maintaining professional standards in translation and synchronization, controlling the use of the Outreach Through Films and Science Demonstrations films, and financing such a program. But constant demand for such services from missionaries all over the world has convinced the leaders at MIS that this is a ministry worthy of their interest and continued efforts.

WORLD'S FAIR MINISTRY

From April 21 to October 21 in 1962, George Speake appeared at the Seattle World's Fair showing Sermons from Science films and conducting live demonstrations in a special pavilion. In one sense this was an extension of the type of ministry performed by Moon over twenty years before at the Golden Gate International Exposition, when he appeared for a nine-month period in 1939 and again for six months in 1940 under the auspices of the Christian Business Men's Committee.

The Sermons from Science exhibit at the Seattle Fair was actually a cooperative venture between MIS and a group of Seattle men, the Christ for the World Committee. During this six-month period, Speake gave three live demonstrations seven days a week for 184 consecutive days. In addition, eight or nine films were presented each day. Approximately 417,000 saw the live demonstrations.

A special counseling room was arranged in the exhibit hall and people who had further questions about the message of Christianity were invited to stay. Over 22,000 persons went into the counseling room to hear a seven-minute presentation of a message treating "God's Plan of Salvation." After the presentation, several counselors conversed with a number of people privately regarding spiritual matters. A number of commitments and decisions were recorded.

In 1964-1965, MIS appeared at the New York World's Fair for two 180-day series, and in 1967, at Expo in Montreal. The exhibits at both fairs drew capacity crowds and created unusual interest.

CHURCH USE

When the MIS program was launched in 1946, films were taken to churches by Moody Bible Institute Film Department representatives. This plan was continued until 1950, at which time the films were made available on a rental basis. By 1959 the total number of film rentals was averaging over fifteen thousand per year.[16]

One of the greatest contributions to churches has been the MIS filmstrip series. Prepared both for leadership training purposes as well as for Bible teaching, these materials are handled on a sales basis. The leadership training materials, which include the Successful Teaching Series, the Know Your Child Series, and the Building a Better Sunday School Series, have been designed especially for use in developing leadership in the church. As of August 1964, there were over sixty thousand prints in use from these three series.

16. Although church groups would be the largest users of these films, it should be noted that this figure also includes rentals by civic groups, industrial organizations, and others.

MIS also produced a number of Bible story, Bible background, and Bible survey filmstrips. These have been designed as Bible teaching aids for use in churches and, as with the training series, they have also had wide acceptance. As of August 1964, there were nearly seventy-four thousand prints in use.

PUBLIC SCHOOLS

Films for educational use are carefully prepared to present an emphasis that is non-sectarian, but one that presents moral and spiritual values. These films have had wide acceptance. Since 1954 the number of schools using MIS educational films climbed steadily so that by 1966, more than 40,000 schools had received MIS films.

These films have had endorsement from outstanding public figures. For example, this letter was received by Moon from Richard Nixon while he was vice-president:

> I was greatly interested to learn of your concept for motivating the youth of our country toward careers in scientific fields. We cannot develop scientific talent unless we first provide the inspiration which will give rise to a desire to learn more about this important body of knowledge.
>
> At the same time we cannot afford to place undue emphasis upon scientific materialism. We must develop the whole person, not just one side of the intellect. This requires that we continue to stress the underlying moral responsibility and strength of character which have always been a part of our heritage. Our students must develop into well rounded and responsible parents and citizens.

This excerpt was taken from a letter written by Thomas Gates, Secretary of the Navy, 1958:

> In your four major films, Living with the Atom, Mystery of Time, and Story of the Blood Stream (Parts I and II) you have succeeded in describing complex scientific phenomena in an outstanding manner, not overlooking the moral and spiritual values implicit in the wonders of nature. I recommend these films without reservation to all young people of any faith or denomination.

Part 6

PAST, PRESENT, AND FUTURE

20

In These Halls: MBI's Impact

A team of five administrators and academic experts visited the MBI campus in the early eighties to evaluate the school's various programs, offer recommendations for improvement, and to decide whether the school should continue as an accredited member of the American Association of Bible Colleges (AABC). When the accrediting team issued its report in 1982, it offered an unsolicited testimonial to the impact of Moody Bible Institute on the Bible school movement: "Moody Bible Institute has been in continuous operation for almost 100 years and has been a leader in the Bible college movement. Its outreach is worldwide. The continuity of leadership is demonstrated by the fact that during its history it has had only six presidents. . . . Enrollment has been on an incline."

Most historians of the Bible institute-college movement agree that Moody Bible Institute has been more influential than any other institute or college within the movement itself. Frequently called the mother of the Bible institute-college movement, the Chicago school established a tradition that has grown to include more than 250 schools in North America alone. This growth was gradual until after 1931, when the number of new schools spurted (see figure 8, p. 210). The largest increase in new schools occurred between 1941 and 1950, when eighty-two were founded.

The 1962 Witmer study revealed that about 25,000 students were enrolled in all Bible institutes and colleges that year. By 1985, among Bible schools in the AABC alone, 36,000 students attended 124 schools.

Perhaps MBI's greatest contribution to evangelical education has been how it has multiplied its own ministry, introducing a pattern of education other schools would copy. Witmer concludes, "the outstanding success of the Moody Bible Institute has influenced greatly the Bible institute-college movement. Certain features of its program, such as practical Christian training, have been copied by a number of other institutions."[1] In his book *Christian Education in a Democracy*, Frank Gaebelein writes: "Moody's contribution to the Bible-institute movement is incalculable. From MBI have come such commonly adopted features as Synthetic

---

1. S. A. Witmer, *The Bible College Story: Education With Dimension*, p. 34.

Bible Study, evangelical teacher training courses, and emphasis on personal evangelism. With its auxiliary divisions—radio, publication and film—it is recognized as a leading world force for the Gospel.''[2]

Its strategic metropolitan location and progressive facilities have been primary factors in the school's impact on the country and the world. After the Second World War, the board of trustees debated moving into the suburbs. Many new Bible schools were being constructed outside the city, and existing schools were resettling in rural and suburban communities in large numbers. The advantages were obvious: a quieter, secluded atmosphere, less expenses, and a substantial capital gain if they sold the site located on prime city real estate. The board prayed, discussed, and evaluated. Finally they confirmed the urban focus of the Moody ministry; the campus would remain on the corner of Chicago Avenue and LaSalle Street, in the heart of the city. As a mission field and training ground, central Chicago could not be ignored.[3]

City officials have confirmed the wisdom of the decision many times since then. Land has become available at reasonable rates, and the campus has gradually expanded. The city sold Institute Place, the street that snaked through the campus, to the school in 1947, and began a campus expansion that has stopped only occasionally for consolidation.

In 1951 a major woman's dormitory, Houghton Hall, was dedicated; today about 440 women students live there. Near them on the first floor is the flagship Moody bookstore. In 1955 officials dedicated Torrey-Gray Auditorium and Doane Memorial Music Building. A new, major academic building, Fitzwater Hall, welcomed students onto its four floors of classrooms and studios in 1962. The school purchased a former Masonic temple in 1968 and renamed it North Hall. Over the years it has been refurbished to provide rehearsal space for music groups, offices for the student publications, classrooms for Women's Guild, and a full-size basketball/volleyball court with spectator seating. Most of North Hall is devoted to recreational and intercollegiate sports. In recent years new flooring has been laid in both the large and small gymnasiums, and students have been able to sharpen their bodies with an indoor track, a universal gym, and weight training area.

A modern campus facility emerged in the early seventies. The nostalgic but worn 153 Building in the the center of campus was leveled; in its place came a beautiful subterranean student dining room, topped by a tree-lined upper plaza. In 1972 the new men's dormitory welcomed returning students. Towering nineteen stories over the campus, Culbertson Hall can lodge more than five hundred men. Though Crowell Hall no longer is the tallest campus building, as the main administrative building it remains a pillar of strength. The famous arch bids entry to this eleven-story structure named after Henry Parsons Crowell, founder of Quaker Oats and chairman of MBI's Board of Trustees for more than forty years.

With the completion of Culbertson Hall, the grounds underwent a major land-

2. Frank E. Gaebelein, *Christian Education in a Democracy*, p. 169.
3. Robert G. Flood and Jerry B. Jenkins, *Teaching the Word*, p. 81.

scaping, with benches, grass, trees, and flowers creating an urban oasis. The enlarged plaza was renamed Alumni Plaza. A few years later Chicago awarded the campus its City Beautiful award.

More than two hundred MBI employees work at the Norton Building, a beautiful five-story brick structure located about eight miles north of the main campus. A. C. Nielsen donated its headquarters to MBI when Nielsen moved into the suburbs. Mr. Nielsen, the founder of the television ratings and research firm, had been a neighbor of MBI trustee Henry C. Crowell. Clearly Nielsen was impressed by Crowell's integrity and manner, for when he decided to offer the building to a charitable organization, MBI was at the top of his list.[4]

Most recently the school has purchased Locust Street and land between Wells and Franklin extending north to Oak Street. As a result the school's soccer team has its first regulation-size field, and Institute staff and students have an outdoor track. The noise of jack hammers and heavy construction equipment has not been heard on campus since 1972, but that may soon change, as administrative leaders envision a new building program in the near future (see chapter 21).

The campus panorama cannot reveal fully the tradition of the first one hundred years. The arch facing LaSalle Street and extending toward the plaza hints at it, as do the dozen dioramas in the first floor of Smith Hall, which trace milestones in the life of the school and its founder. But her heritage has affected all of evangelical education, from first-grade Sunday school classes to the missionary enterprise, to the Bible institute movement itself. That heritage infuses strength into current ministries and offers direction for future endeavors.

As an Institute of higher learning, MBI's greatest legacy probably lies in evangelical education. MBI brought many innovations to evangelical curriculum. D. L. Moody introduced a program to train church musicians. No comparable program appeared until Northwestern University launched its church program in 1896. MBI was a leader in missions, being the first school to have a complete program in Jewish missions. The school also introduced a new type of specialized missionary education. In 1941 a Technical Course began to prepare men to be expert missionary pilots or to be qualified in missionary radio communications. This type of program was new in religious education, and the Missionary Aviation-Technology Department remains a leader in training missionary aviators.

In addition, MBI was the first undergraduate school of higher Christian education to offer a full program to prepare leaders of a Sunday school curriculum. First known as the Sunday School Course, the program became the Religious Education Course by 1924; MBI had become the first undergraduate school to offer a professional curriculum for directors of religious education.

Several of its schools were first-of-their-kind endeavors. Begun in 1901, the Moody Correspondence School was the first offered by an evangelical school. The Evening School paralleled the origin of the evening school movement in general education, while offering the first Bible-oriented evening school in 1903. First

4. Flood and Jenkins, *Teaching the Word*, p. 105.

broadcast in 1926, the Radio School of the Bible became the first and remains the longest running educational radio program in secular and religious broadcasting. Regular "schools of the air" did not come into prominence for several years. The Institute pioneered offering Bible subjects via radio, as well as sending course outlines to interested listeners and grading examinations for the radio students.

The Institute's Day School for full-time undergraduate students was not the first Bible school, yet religious historians regard its program as innovative. Unlike earlier Bible schools created primarily to train foreign missionaries, MBI began with the primary goal of preparing missionaries to serve in urban America.

MBI also has established a legacy for three evangelical movements: the Bible institute, Bible conference, and fundamental movements. D. L. Moody's school was not the first Bible institute founded in America, but it has become the best known, the "mother" of many other similar schools. Historians of the Bible institute-college movement agree that the Chicago school has been more influential than any other school within the movement.

Bible conferences did not begin with D. L. Moody, but his Northfield Conferences in the 1880's popularized the concept and spurred expansion of Bible conferences throughout the country. The MBI Extension Department soon became one of the main promoters of Bible conferences, and influenced the movement more than any other evangelical organization. The school sponsored and conducted Bible conferences across the nation, hosting as many as twenty-five different conferences in one year.

Moody Bible Institute has been a major, positive force in the movement to uphold the fundamentals of the Christian faith. MBI came into being several years before the fundamental-liberal controversy. However, soon after the publishing of the volumes entitled *The Fundamentals* in 1909, the Moody school earned a reputation as being a great center where fundamentalism was taught and practiced.

Particularly at the beginning of this movement, fundamentalism was primarily a reaffirmation of the fundamental doctrines of evangelicalism. Since its inception, MBI has held to these fundamental theological maxims. When liberalism began to penetrate the religious life of the country, Institute leaders, especially Torrey and Gray, spoke out openly without apology for an orthodox position. In fact, the MBI Bible Conferences became a primary way to teach a biblical orthodoxy and to make a strong plea for a return to orthodoxy. In this way MBI contributed significantly to the fundamentalist cause.

Though Institute leaders over the years have spoken out freely about their belief in the fundamentals of the faith originally set forth in *The Fundamentals*, they have normally tried to avoid the divisiveness of some of the fundamentalist leaders. Clearly MBI is a fundamentalist school in that it constantly reaffirms its belief in the fundamentals of faith that were part of evangelical theology long before a theological war broke out. Most historians of fundamentalism identify MBI as one of the leading schools that helped further the movement.

Through the years, various MBI ministries have given birth to new organizations that have become independent operations. These separate corporations have grown greatly and have multiplied the original efforts of MBI many times. Faculty member Clarence H. Benson and BICA employee Victor Cory teamed up to form Scripture Press to publish Sunday school curriculum material that Benson and his students formulated. Today Scripture Press distributes evangelical Christian education materials for the total church program, serving scores of denominational and nondenominational groups.

Benson was also instrumental in forming the Evangelical Teaching Training Association. As the first secretary of ETTA, Benson developed the ETTA training program. Its curriculum essentially was the Christian education curriculum that Benson had developed and taught at MBI. ETTA, with its Preliminary and Advanced Training courses for the local church and Standard Training Course for use in higher education, has influenced evangelical education widely.

The idea for a Christian Booksellers Association began at MBI after Moody Press had received numerous requests for advice and counsel on how to open and operate Christian bookstores. Growing out of Moody Press, CBA has expanded its operations noticeably, and today the CBA annual convention is among the ten largest trade shows in the United States.[5]

Evangelical Literature Overseas, like the CBA, owes its origin and much of its early development to Moody Bible Institute. Kenneth Taylor of Moody Press and Peter Gunther of Moody Literature Mission were key figures in establishing ELO to coordinate efforts among various mission boards and agencies in overseas literature production and distribution. Today ELO offices in Wheaton, Illinois, serve more than 150 evangelical missionary fellowships, mission boards, and agencies.

The legacy of Moody Bible Institute to the Bible institute-college movement and to evangelical education, to evangelical movements, and to other evangelical organizations would be a muted testimonial if the school's vigor and purpose had dwindled during the first one hundred years. But observers inside and outside the Institute insist that is not the case. An earlier accreditation team from AABC concluded after inspecting the school — its programs and its students — "One cannot look at Moody Bible Institute and fail to recognize its excellence as a specialized Bible college. . . . The highest quality of spiritual life, the administration, the faculty, and student body is immediately apparent."[6]

For one hundred years the school that D. L. Moody founded has sought to honor God through its many educational and evangelistic ministries. MBI enters Century II with a bold vision but a firm loyalty to her mission, as we shall see.

5. Flood and Jenkins, *Teaching the Word*, p. 213.
6. American Association of Bible Colleges, "1971 Evaluation Report of Moody Bible Institute," 8 December 1971, p. 2.

21

Entering Century II

Dwight L. Moody was a practical man; his school always has offered pragmatic programs. School administrators have never feared change or innovation when it would fulfill the needs for Christian ministry. After all, Moody had founded the school with a new program to train people to fill a gap that existing institutions and seminaries had overlooked. Today Moody Bible Institute enters her second century of service with innovative educational programs and a continual desire to address the spiritual needs of her city, country, and world.

THE GRADUATE SCHOOL

In June 1985 MBI welcomed eighty-one pastors, missionaries, and evangelists to her Graduate School. With graduate courses offered in one-week modules four times a year, the school represents a combining of the practical and the theoretical, a hallmark of the Moody educational tradition. Students earning thirty-six semester hours receive a master of arts in ministry, a professional degree. Most students will complete the program in three to four years. Students enter with a baccalaureate degree, thirty academic hours of Bible, and two years of ministry experience. They complete a core curriculum, while specializing in one of three tracks: preaching, management, or counseling.

"The program reflects the Moody tradition of providing people to stand in the gap," said B. Wayne Hopkins, dean of the school. That gap has developed as seminaries offer an increasingly academic curriculum, according to Hopkins. The master of theology (Th.M.) degree has emphasized research; the master of divinity (M.Div.) historically was designed to be a practical degree. "But it is becoming more academic. Therefore, students are coming away from seminary campuses with not a lot of preaching, little counseling, and probably no courses in management."

Two kinds of students enrolled in the inaugural classes. Many students were seminary graduates who enrolled "to receive training they did not receive on the seminary level," according to Hopkins. Other students had only a Bible college degree and were active in a Christian ministry. This type of student did not want seminary training since he already had completed several of the Bible and theology courses. Yet the student needed more training.

Instructors do not overlook the theoretical and historical framework, but they emphasize the practical application. Each course has two instructors, one an academician, the other a practitioner. "So the student has someone who is an expert in theory and someone who is an expert in the application of that theory," Hopkins explained. The instructors have included successful pastors, missionary leaders, authors, and management consultants. They have team-taught with professors from Dallas Theological Seminary, Trinity Evangelical Divinity School, and Moody Bible Institute.

The objectives of the school reflect a three-dimensional approach to graduate Christian education (see figure 9, p. 210). The first dimension is *skills*: communication (preaching), management, and counseling. Students learn these skills to apply them to *tasks*, the second dimension. The three tasks of Christian education are evangelism, equipping saints (all who believe in Jesus Christ as Savior), and training leaders. These tasks are fulfilled in four *areas*: rural, suburban, inner city, and cross-cultural ministry. Graduate students receive training in all three dimensions: skill, task, and area.

Courses are diverse to fit the three-dimensional educational model. Current offerings include a Biblical Approach to Counseling, Revitalization of the Twentieth Century Church, Church Growth, An Evangelical Theology in Practice (ethics), Excellence in Leadership, and How to Minister as a Woman with Confidence. More courses are being added for women, who comprise two-thirds of all Protestant missionaries, and several courses will address unique ministry opportunities and needs of women. In 1987 the Graduate School will offer workshops for wives of enrolled students. Noncredit in nature, the workshops will aid in the wife's spiritual growth and help her understand her husband's ministry.

Students pay travel costs and a nominal tuition charge that covers some of their education. Institute alumni and friends help cover the rest of the educational cost. "This allows more students to attend. Many ministers fall into the low income level according to current government's statistics," Hopkins said. "We want to make education available for pastors and missionaries [who have low salaries]." Like those in the undergraduate school, students in the Graduate School see the blessings of God's provision through Christian friends who contribute to the training of church leaders at Moody Bible Institute.

Student response indicates that the Graduate School is indeed filling a gap in graduate training. A pastor from Ohio writes: "This program is exactly what I need. The people you have placed in the classroom to teach are outstanding. The guest professors gave great insight into the ministry too. What an innovative program!" Another student described his course as "a rewarding week of studies in terms of knowledge gained, skills developed, and friends made."

A FOUR-YEAR BACHELOR'S DEGREE

"Historically, when programs outlive their usefulness, they are no longer offered at MBI." Academic Dean Howard Whaley describes the new baccalaureate program, effective August 1986, as a case of replacing an outdated five-year program with a practical four-year one. He cites the dentistry program, missionary radio technology program, the Swedish-English Course, and missionary nursing program as examples of former curricula no longer offered or needed.

The four-year baccalaureate seems to be needed. Under the five-year program students finishing the diploma program had to complete two years at a college for a bachelor of arts degree. If a student already had two additional years training at a college or university, he still needed three more for a bachelor's degree. In effect this represented an extra year away from ministry, since many MBI students needed more than a diploma. Whaley reported to his Curriculum Committee: "Increasingly the baccalaureate . . . [has] become the minimal credential for the ministers which are the vocational focus of our curriculum. During that same period youth have become. . . . less inclined to value a B.A. secured at the expense of an additional year."[1]

By stipulating and narrowing requirements for general educational courses, Day School officials were able to reduce general educational hours from a maximum of seventy-three (including thirteen offered at MBI) to forty-six. They also created an articulation arrangement with two local universities that allowed students to take the general education courses off-campus during their sophomore through senior years, concurrent with their MBI courses.

Educational leaders and faculty considered a four-year degree program as early as 1965, when they first offered a B.A. degree in five years. Occasional evaluations of the "three-two" and "two-three" matriculation arrangement took place, but the four-year degree only emerged as a major issue in 1981 when the Educational Branch completed a self-study review. In preparation for MBI's ten-year accreditation review by the AABC, members of the Self-Evaluation Committee questioned whether the educational programs were fulfilling the historical objectives. Eventually they recommended that school officials reexamine how effective the present programs were.

In 1982 the Dean of Education suggested evaluating a four-year degree. Meanwhile, the Academic Dean and the Curriculum Committee, responding to the self-study proposal, met in Elburn, Illinois, to evaluate the feasibility of a four-year plan. At Elburn II (January 1984) they considered how best to achieve learning outcomes for students. Elburn II ended with a "discrepancy" between desirable learning outcomes and existing outcomes. The five-year plan previously acceptable, now seemed inadequate. The question remained, "Which approach best suits the requirements of a degree program? Should MBI teach all general education courses, requiring more faculty and become in effect a Bible college? Should MBI

---

1. Howard Whaley, Memorandum to the Curriculum Committee, 6 February 1984, p. 1.

teach everything but general education, having students take those courses at a local college or university?

Gradually, the Curriculum Committee leaned toward the second model that would send students to a local institution for general education study. In April 1984 the faculty concurred, approving by an overwhelming margin, fifty-nine to one, a proposal to seek an "articulated" arrangement with local universities. In early 1985, the Board of Trustees also agreed, establishing a new four-year Bachelor of Arts degree to be issued by MBI.

The three-year diploma program continues and remains unchanged. However, now a student can consider a B.A. degree with only one additional year of training. (Students in the Missionary Technology-Aviation and Sacred Music departments still need five years for the Bachelor of Science degree.) The four-year program will allow MBI to integrate the general education received at secular institutions with the Christian world view and ministry orientation.

Dean of Education Kenneth Hanna regarded integration as a crucial need. "We have been requiring two years (for general education), but we have not integrated it with the courses here. In terms of the whole culture and the knowledge bank, we have not brought (such courses to confront) the Christian world view." With students in residence at MBI while taking some courses outside, "they will be concurrently exposed to a biblical world view and a non-biblical world view. By being exposed to a typical secular world view, the student will bring back to campus questions, perspectives, and issues we can discuss in classes. With this, integration is much more likely."

Academic Dean Whaley added that the school's mission, student resources, confidence of the Christian public, and the curriculum mandated the new program in order to continue "our claims to leadership in training full-time Christian workers."[2] The new program will allow "MBI to continue to specialize in its historic strength without diluting its faculty while at the same time delivering a respected four-year baccalaureate."[3]

Dean Whaley emphasized that the new program follows years of study of the historic mission of the school. The school will never become a liberal arts college, he added, since that "is not consistent with why Moody Bible Institute exists."[4]

"The educational program today refreshes our historic purpose," the Dean of Education explained.[5] "It is an updating to ensure that the historic objective —which is still valid—is fulfilled in a way that meets today's needs." Hanna described the new baccalaureate as a course adjustment to reach the correct destination. "You need to constantly adjust your course to keep on target, which for us is world evangelization. As long as that is the target, adjustments along the way are not a change or veering off course." With the new four-year baccalaureate, the

2. Mark Giebink, "Dean Whaley Explains B.A. Revision Factors," *Moody Student*, 3 May 1985, p. 1.
3. Whaley, Memorandum, p. 6.
4. Interview with Howard Whaley, 10 July 1985.
5. Interview with Kenneth Hanna, 9 July 1985.

education program of Moody Bible Institute appears to be right on target.

One day the Institute may produce video instructional programs. Education by videotape has become a more practical option as the number of video cassette recorders (VCRs) sold mushroomed in the 1980s. Lower costs and better quality have brought entertainment and education programs on video cassette tapes into increasing numbers of homes. In 1983, 4 million Americans had purchased VCRs. In 1985 an estimated 18 million American households will own these units, according to projections of the Electronics Industry Association.

Videotapes would allow the lay person to receive a Christian education in his home via television. Lessons could be recorded on the main campus and rented to Correspondence School students for home viewing. Video programs also would be prepared and shown to large groups at Evening Institutes and Correspondence School classes at various locations. Video programs recorded at the main campus could be distributed to Evening School campuses in seven states and to more than 50,000 students in correspondence courses around the country. MBI might supply local churches with programs on leadership training as well. These two options, classroom video supplements and home video lessons, may become realities in the 1990s. The Educational Branch hopes to produce and test-market video educational materials by the end of the 1980s.

MBI AND THE NATION'S CITIES

Historically, the school has had a continual, positive impact on the Chicago metropolis. Although MBI leaders regard the school's mission to be neither a social gospel or deep political activism, they desire to affect city leaders with Christian virtues and spiritual awareness. They pray often for the mayor and members of the city council. And, on appropriate occasions, the school takes an active stand. In 1978 MBI placed ads in the two major Chicago newspapers opposing a proposed march by a neo-Nazi group through Skokie, a suburb just northwest of MBI with a large Jewish population. MBI reaffirmed its support for the people of Israel and vowed to stand with the Jewish community against the "propaganda of hatred."

The school continues to influence the business community each Easter week with a series of Easter Meditations. Every day at noon, Moody professors present the Easter message in the auditorium of a major downtown bank, attracting office workers and business executives to a forty-minute service.

The students probably have the greatest influence on the city. When students arrive on campus in late August for the school year, local merchants are the first to know, and not merely because of an influx of youthful customers. Moody students are recognizable, they say, by attractive clothing, a friendly, caring attitude, and almost always smiles.

About one-third of the students work part-time in Chicago, and their witness is powerful. Students recognize that as employees, their primary task is to work, not to present the gospel. Nonetheless they have opportunities to share their faith. Employers are impressed by the students' integrity, according to Calvin Becker, Director of the Student Employment Service. "Employers can trust them with cash. They know students will be on time. We always have more requests for our students than we have students to go around." This positive reputation not only brings honor to their Lord but some unusual job opportunities. The Chicago Board of Elections has hired Moody students to collect voting data during past municipal elections. During the 1984 Presidential Election the News Election Service summoned students to assist in reporting results of the East Coast and Midwest voting.

Every three years the Student Employment Service hosts an Employers' Recognition Dinner to thank local employers of students. Local business leaders enjoy a complete meal and entertainment, while learning about the ministries of the school. No formal gospel message is presented, but the music focuses on truths of the Christian faith, and the employer sits with his student employee.

The power of this witness is unmistakable. A manager of a Chicago realty firm wrote after one dinner: "It was my pleasure to attend the Employers' Dinner last evening, and also to learn more about your school and its students. We couldn't be happier to have two Moody students . . . working for us. Both are industrious, very pleasant and dependable, . . . qualities that are difficult to find in young employees today."

Chicago Mayor Harold Washington lauded the school for its continued presence and impact in the city during a 1984 campus visit. The mayor described MBI as "a pillar and model for the entire community. . . . Chicago desperately needs the enduring compassion, humility and wisdom of your institution." He pledged the city's support in any expansion program on campus, adding, "We are thankful that you are here, that you are growing, and that you represent a vibrant voice of Christianity."[6]

Both the City Council and mayor of Chicago recognized MBI's impact on the city in early 1986 with a Council Resolution and a Mayoral Proclamation commending the school. The mayor proclaimed Founder's Week 1986, Feb. 3-9 "Moody Bible Institute Week in Chicago." In the proclamation, Mayor Washington noted the centennial anniversary and urged "all citizens of Chicago to remember and honor the work that Dwight Lyman Moody and all those associated with Moody Bible Institute have done on behalf of their neighborhood and the City of Chicago."

The school remains committed to evangelizing the city. President Sweeting clearly articulated that commitment in a convocation address to faculty and students in 1981:

> As spokes in a wheel lead to the hub, so all roads lead to the urban centers. The city is where the action is. . . .
> In his work, *The Meaning of the City*, the French social critic and commentator Jacques Ellul points out that the first biblically recorded cities were founded by men who rejected God. They were products of self-will and self-ambition. But

6. Dan DeSmyther, "Mayor Visits Campus," *Moody Student*, 18 May 1985, p. 1.

Ellul goes on to acknowledge, "Our task is therefore to represent Him [God] in the heart of the city."

. . . . The cities of the world are waiting to be stormed by God's faithful servants. They are places of challenge and opportunity. They are strategic centers of conflict. . . .

We believe that it is no accident that we are in the city these momentous days. With God's help and upholding, we intend to stay.[7]

Sweeting offered three reasons Moody Bible Institute must remain in the city. First, God established the school in the city, where MBI was "a school keyed to meet the spiritual needs of the city." Second, God has compassion for the city, and therefore MBI must also. He showed his concern for Nineveh, Ephesis, Corinth, and Rome by sending prophets and apostles there, Sweeting noted. Third, cities represent a unique opportunity for evangelism, with large populations and pace-setting leadership. Of course, MBI also embraces international and rural evangelism (see chapter 11), "but not at the expense of the unreached masses of the cities."

Moody Bible Institute continues to influence the country as well through its publishing, broadcasting, film, and continuing education programs. During the American bicentennial celebration in 1976, it actively advocated a return to the Christian principles upon which America was founded. Moody Press distributed copies of its colorful commemorative volume *America: God Shed His Grace on Thee* to all members of Congress as a way of reminding them about our country's religious heritage. During a Founder's Week meeting at Chicago Amphitheatre, President George Sweeting addressed a capacity crowd of more than 12,000, including local and national political leaders. He urged the American people toward personal and spiritual renewal on three fronts: 1) First and foremost, to Jesus Christ: to magnify righteousness and to decry sin as a devastating force; 2) To be the right kind of citizens, what Jesus called the salt and light of the earth; and 3) To build healthy, moral, and godly families.[8]

Representatives of the school, including President Sweeting and Dr. John MacArthur, Jr., trustee, will tour the country in 1986 to celebrate one hundred years of education at Moody Bible Institute. Along with the school's musical groups, they will reflect on the school's heritage, as exemplified in the MBI centennial motto: "Teaching the Word, Reaching the World." Crowds are expected to gather in sixteen cities, stretching from New York City to Seattle, to hear about God's goodness to the school D. L. Moody founded.

Campus Expansion

School officials anticipate an enrollment surge as MBI enters Century II. The student population has remained level at about 1,350 since 1979, but at least 1,700 students are expected to be taking courses on campus by 1990, due largely to the

7. George Sweeting, "The Challenge of the City" (pamphlet), pp. 11-13.
8. Wesley Hartzell, "Bicentennial Rally Stirs Chicago," *Moody Monthly*, April 1976, p. 49.

fourth-year residency resulting from the new B.A. program. Projections for 1995 indicate 2,000 students, including 300 in Graduate School.

The projected increase in enrollment, while welcomed by school administrators, presents a series of logistical hurdles. Housing, already tight, could not accommodate 1,700. Classroom space reaches total utilization at 1,400. Seeing this potential problem, members of the Self-Evaluative Study (for the AABC) in 1981 recommended two intermediate-size auditoriums seating a maximum of 500 students, and several large classrooms seating 60. Three years later the Academic Planning Committee reviewed enrollment projections and likely changes in academic programs; they concluded a new academic building was essential.

They proposed a new building that would be twice the size of Fitzwater Hall, the present main academic building. This would accommodate almost all the students in the Day School. The building would house a World Missions Center and Communications Center. As envisioned, the building would include an auditorium seating eight hundred students, a television studio, numerous classrooms, and faculty offices. The committee also recommended that the library be expanded and a new main auditorium be built.

School administrators have shared this need with private individuals and friends of the school, but have not disclosed plans to the general public at the time of this writing. Following a financial policy that requires significant support before beginning a building program, they anticipate announcing the project during Founder's Week 1986. Known as the Century II Project, the program has received approval of the board of trustees and the support of employees. In addition, officials noted that by the early 1990s a major residential building will become available for purchase as potential student housing.

Looking at the Century II Project, Dean of Education Hanna noted that the new academic programs and the need for facilities have appeared almost simultaneously with the centennial anniversary and concluded: "The new programs and the reaffirming of our [mission] coincide with the centennial not so much by design as by divine assistance."

In his report "Education and the Future at Moody Bible Institute," presented to the Board of Trustees, the Dean of Education predicted the school would be deeply committed to answering five challenges as the Twentieth Century concludes.[9] First, *urbanization* will dominate. Around the world, large cities will expand, attracting people from rural areas. MBI will need to evangelize these areas. "That means training people in the city of Chicago to reach the cities of the world." Second, *evangelism* remains the urgent task of the church. "Education may be our method, but evangelization of the world is our goal," Hanna writes. He called on the school to renew that vision in its second century. Third, the spread of *internationalism* requires continued training of cross-cultural ministers. Many American missionaries who rose up in the post-World War II era will soon retire. In some

---

9. Kenneth G. Hanna, "Education and the Future at Moody Bible Institute: A Fifteen Year Plan, 1984 to 1999," 31 January 1984, p. 4.

cases national leaders have replaced them. However, the church has expanded rapidly in many countries. "With over 2,200 alumni serving Christ internationally, MBI has a strategic opportunity," Hanna writes.

Expansion is the fourth challenge. Hanna expects the Day School to grow as many young people and their parents become aware of the educational program at MBI. The Moody Broadcasting Network, Pastors, and Sonlife (youth) conferences are among many ways potential students will hear about a quality, tuition-free Bible education. The new baccalaureate program also is expected to enlarge the student population. Finally *Chicago* will present a unique opportunity: "The city is ready for renewal. The population declined in the city and grew in the suburbs during the seventies. With the recent influx of immigrants, there is a new sense of need for evangelism. . . . MBI can and must make a difference in our home city."

Moody Bible Institute enters her second century of service with the promise of growth and a tradition of single-minded evangelical purpose. The late James M. Gray would have been pleased to see the adherence to doctrinal fundamentals that has continued for one hundred years. While president, Gray responded to the challenge of theological liberalism with a series of books upholding the fundamental evangelical position.

During the theological debate Gray wrote the words to the song "One with the Lord" to remind students and faculty of their common cause and need for unity against attacks by modernist theologians. The song, written in 1908, became closely associated with the school[10], and students probably sung the words many years before its first copyright in 1937.

"One with the Lord" remains the unofficial school song of Moody Bible Institute today. Freshmen memorize it, seniors affectionately parody it, and all graduates cherish it. The words of the final verse formed Gray's prayer that the school would remain true to its mission of education and evangelism. As MBI steps into Century II, that prayer seems to have become reality.

> God bless the school that D. L. Moody founded;
> Firm may she stand, though by foes of truth surrounded!
> Riches of grace bestowed may she never squander,
> Keeping true to God and man her record over yonder.

---

10. Interview with Gerald Raquet, 18 September 1985. MBI obtained the copyright in 1960.

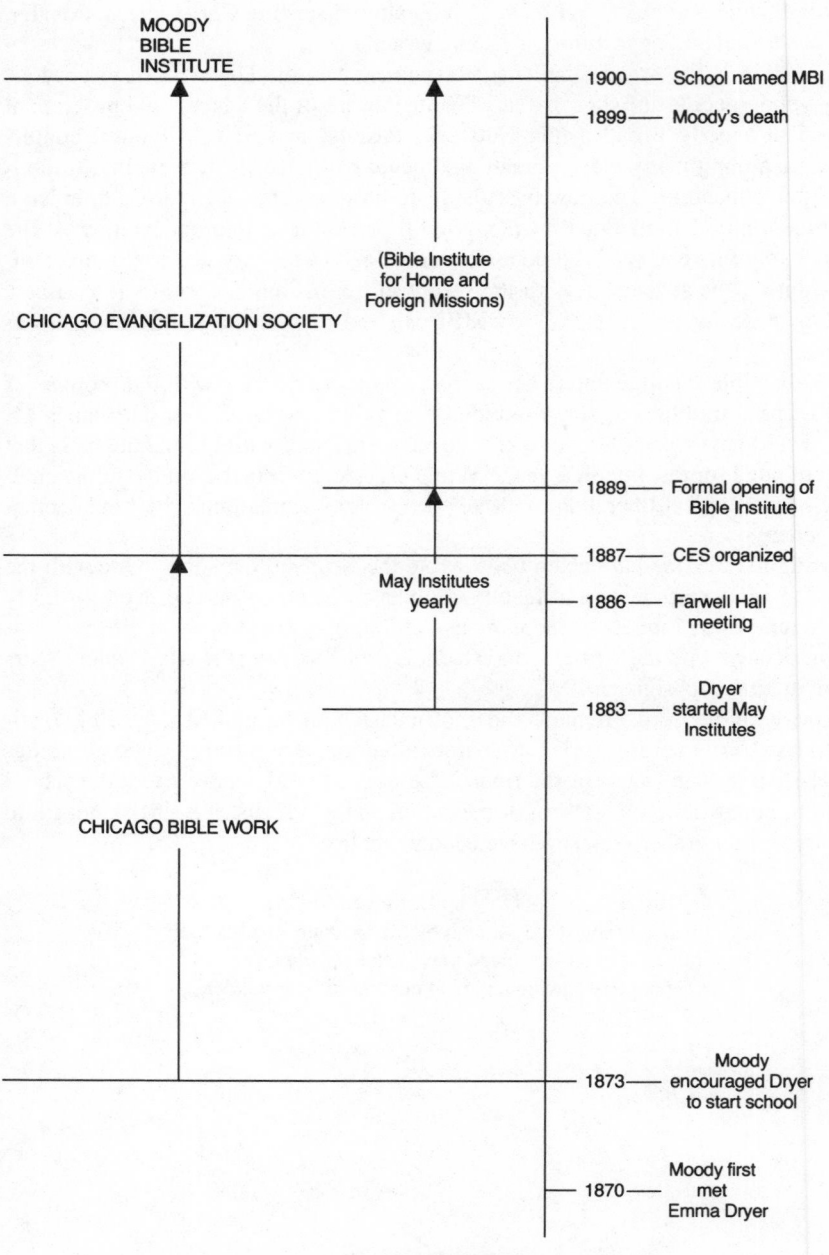

FIGURE 1
Time Line of Events Leading to the Origin of Moody Bible Institute

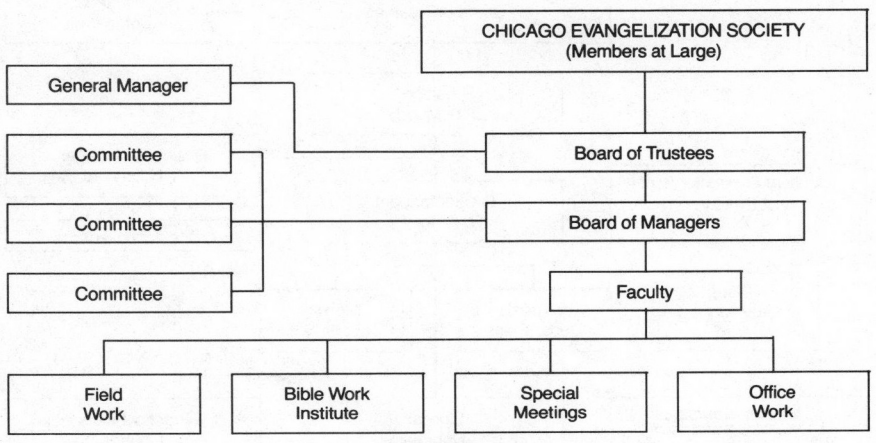

FIGURE 2
Original Organizational Plan of the Chicago Evangelization Society
(1887)
SOURCE: Original Constitution (see Appendix A).

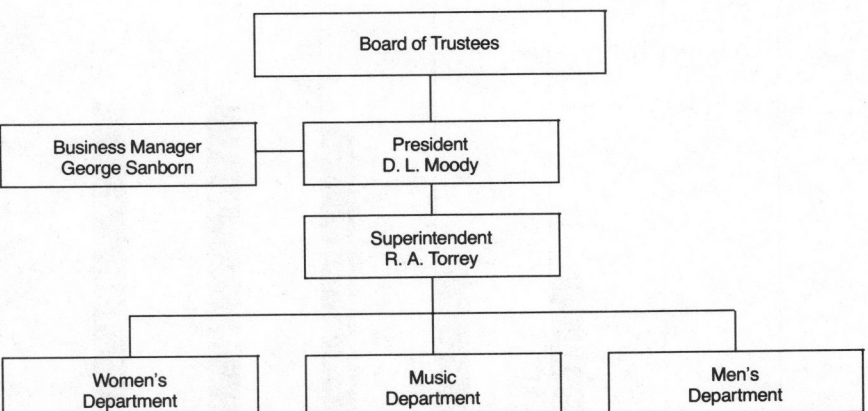

FIGURE 3
Organizational Plan of the Bible Institute for Home and Foreign
Missions of the Chicago Evangelization Society in 1889*
*Constructed from what appeared to be the actual function after the formal opening in 1889 as described in the first published brochures.

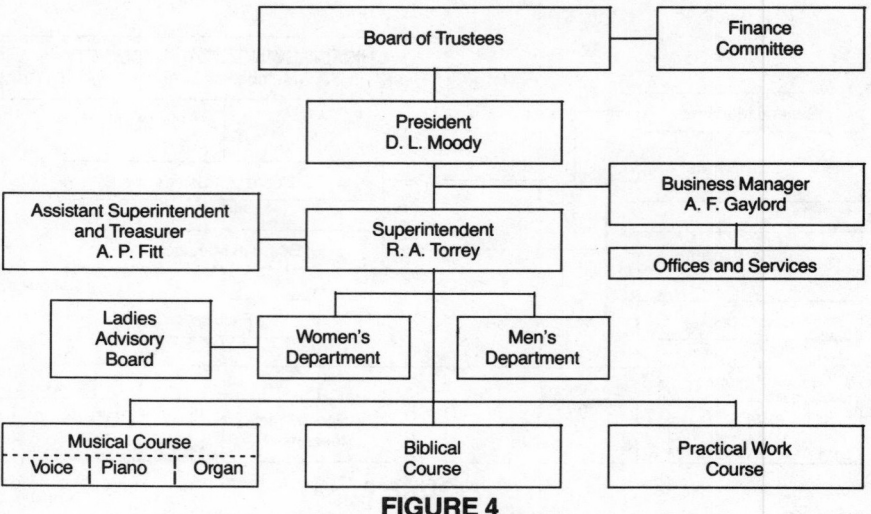

FIGURE 4
Organizational Plan of the Bible Institute for Home and Foreign
Missions of the Chicago Evangelization Society in 1895
SOURCE: School Catalog, 1895.

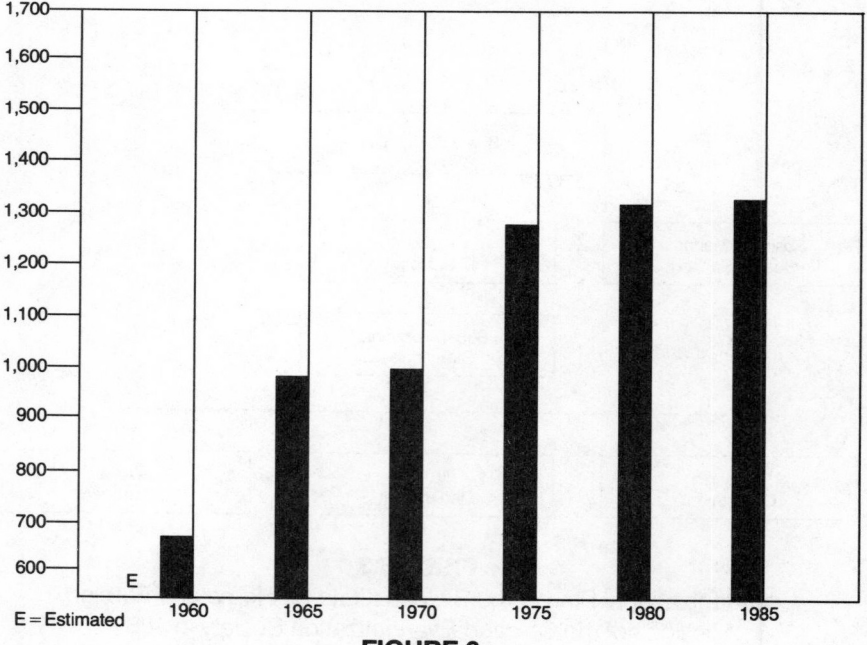

FIGURE 6
Enrollments in the Day School Program
SOURCE: Office of Enrollment Management

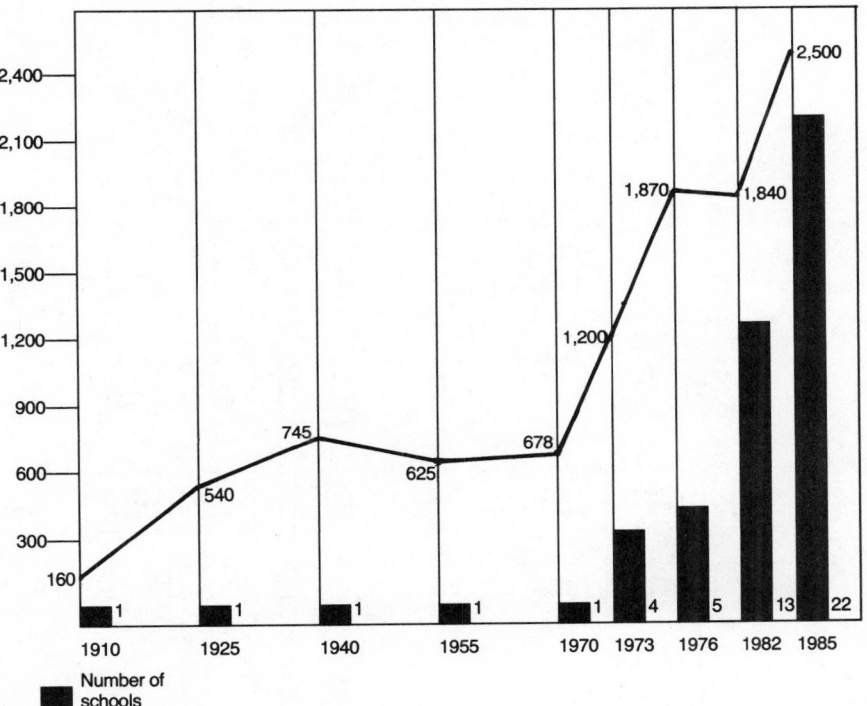

FIGURE 7
Enrollments and Number of Schools in Evening School Program
(Based on fall semester enrollments)
SOURCES: Office of the Evening School and
1984 Report of the Dean of Education

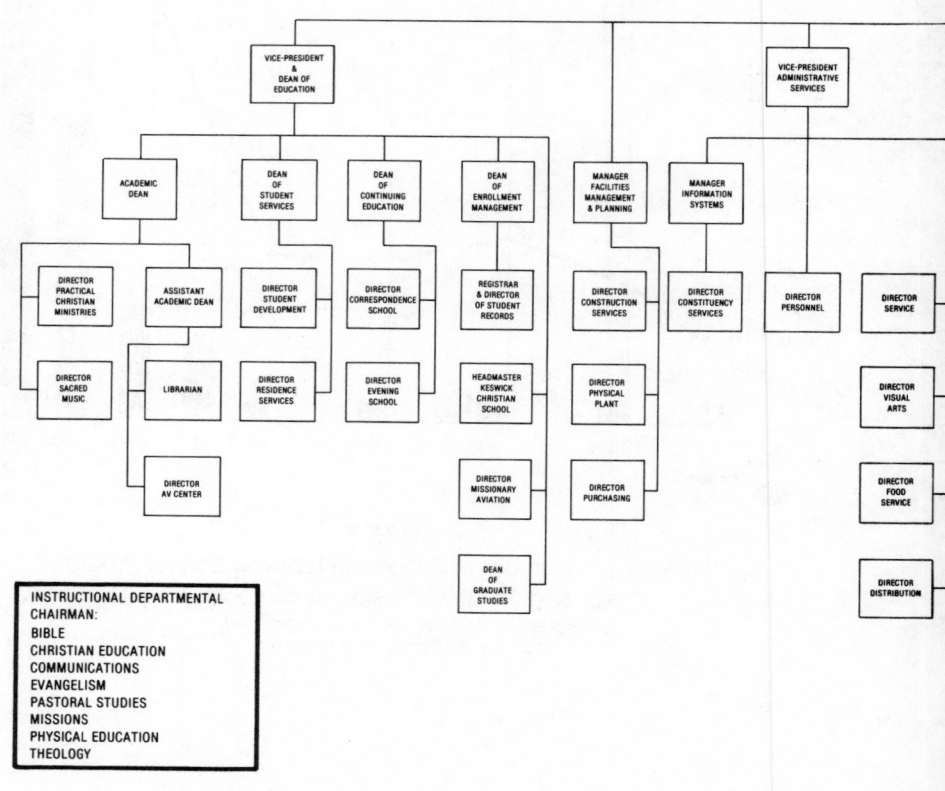

FIGURE 5
Organizational Plan of Moody Bible Institute in 1985

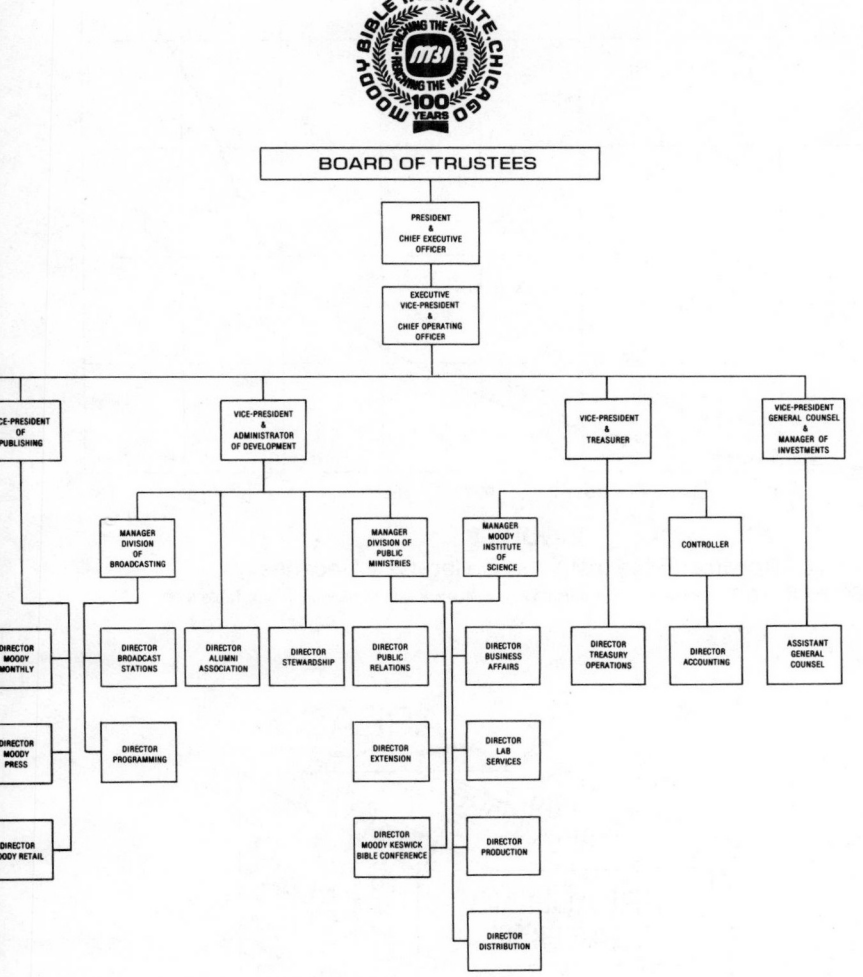

FIGURE 5
Organizational Plan of Moody Bible Institute in 1985

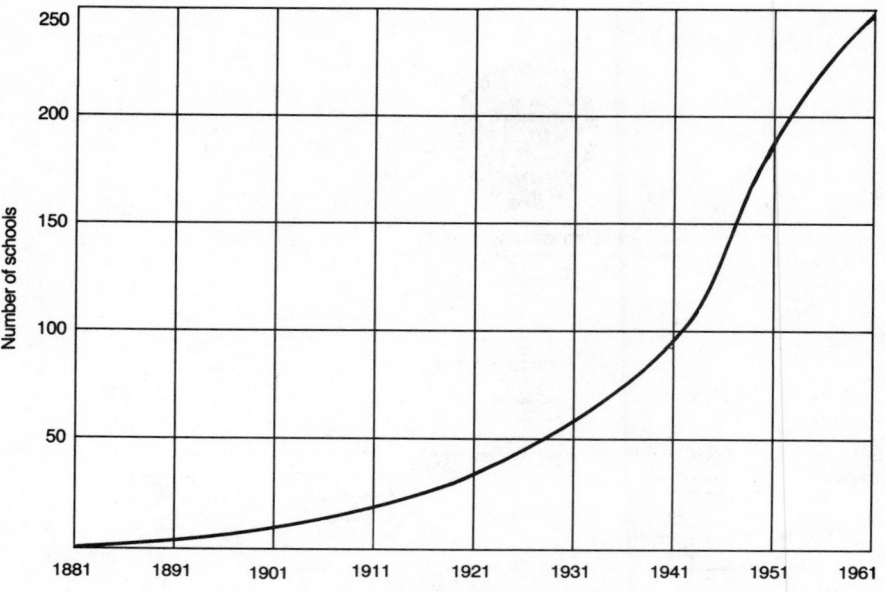

FIGURE 8
Growth of Bible Institutes-Colleges by Decades
SOURCE: S.A. Witmer, *The Bible College Story: Education with Dimension,* p. 40, Table I.

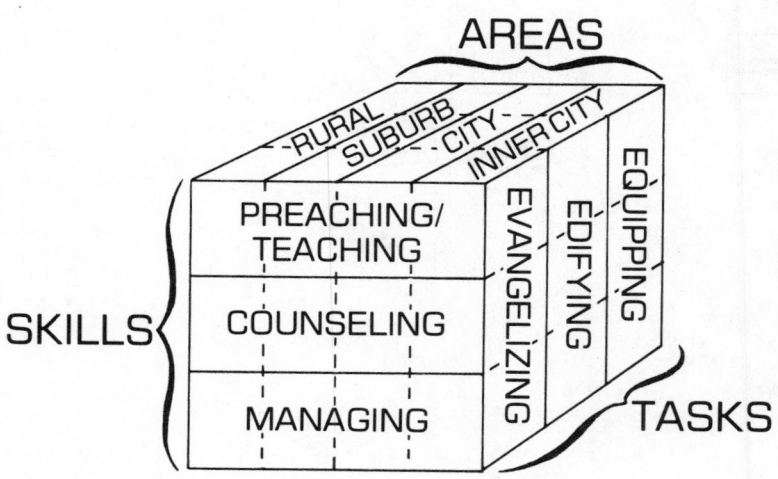

FIGURE 9
Moody Bible Institute Graduate School Education Model

Bibliography

BOOKS

Accrediting Association of Bible Colleges Manual. Wheaton, Ill.: Accrediting Association of Bible Colleges, 1964.

Appleby, David P. *History of Church Music*. Chicago: Moody, 1965.

Archibald, George Hamilton. *The Modern Sunday-School*. New York: Century, 1926.

Bailey, Albert E. *The Gospel in Hymns*. New York: Scribner, 1950.

Benson, Clarence H. *A Popular History of Christian Education*. Chicago: Moody, 1943.

———. *The Sunday School in Action*. Chicago: Bible Institute Colportage Association, 1932.

Best, John W. *Research in Education*. Englewood Cliffs, N.J.: Prentice-Hall, 1959.

The Bible. King James Version.

Blanchard, Frances C. *Life of Charles Albert Blanchard*. New York: Revell, 1932.

Bower, William Clayton, and Hayward, P. R. *Protestantism Faces Its Educational Task Together*. Appleton, Wis.: Nelson, 1949.

Brown, Arlo A. *A History of Religious Education in Recent Times*. New York: Abingdon, 1923.

Brown, Marianna. *Sunday School Movements in America*. New York: Revell, 1901.

Brown, Robert McAfee. *The Spirit of Protestantism*. New York: Oxford U., 1901.

Cairns, Earle E. *Christianity in the United States*. Chicago: Moody, 1964.

———. *Christianity Through the Centuries*. Grand Rapids: Zondervan, 1954.

Carnell, Edward John. *The Case for Orthodox Theology*. Philadelphia: Westminster, 1959.

Chapman, John Wilbur. *The Life and Work of Dwight L. Moody*. Philadelphia: Winston, 1900.

Clark, Francis Edward. *The Children and the Church*. Boston: Congregational Sunday School & Pub. Soc., 1882.

Codel, Martin, ed., *Radio and Its Future*. New York: Harper, 1930.

Cubberley, Ellwood P. *The History of Education*. Cambridge: Riverside, 1946.

Cully, K. B. *The Search for a Christian Education Since 1940*. Philadelphia: Westminster, 1965.

Daniels, W. H. *D. L. Moody and His Work*. Hartford: 1876.

————. *Moody: His Words, Work, and Workers*. New York: Nelson & Phillips, 1877.

Dargan, Edwin Charles. *A History of Preaching*. Vol. I, 1905; Vol. II, 1912. New York: Hodder & Stoughton.

Day, Richard Ellsworth. *Breakfast Table Autocrat*. Chicago: Moody, 1946.

————. *Bush Aglow*. Philadelphia: Judson, 1936.

Dennis, James S. *Foreign Missions After a Century*. New York: Revell, 1893.

DeRemer, Bernard R. *Moody Bible Institute: A Pictorial History*. Chicago: Moody, 1960.

DeWolf, L. Harold. *The Case for Theology in Liberal Perspective*. Philadelphia: Westminster, 1959.

Dwight, Henry Otis. *The Blue Book of Missions for 1907*. New York: Funk & Wagnalls, 1907.

————. *The Centennial History of the American Bible Society*. New York: Macmillan, 1916.

Dwight, Henry Otis; Tupper, H. A.; and Bliss, E. M. *The Encyclopedia of Missions*. New York: Funk & Wagnalls, 1904.

Eavey, Charles B. *History of Christian Education*. Chicago: Moody, 1964.

Edwards, Newton, and Richey, Herman G. *The School in the American Social Order*. Boston: Houghton Mifflin, 1947.

Elliott, Godfrey, ed., *Film and Education*. New York: Philosophical Library, 1948.

Elliott, Harrison S. *Can Religious Education Be Christian?* New York: Macmillan, 1940.

The Encyclopedia Americana. Vol. XIV. New York: Americana, 1947

Executive Committee of the International Sunday School Association. *Organized Sunday School Work in America*. Chicago: International Sunday School Assn., 1908.

Ferré, Nels F. S. *Searchlights on Contemporary Theology*. New York: Harper, 1961.

Fitt, A. P. *Moody Still Lives*. New York: Revell, 1936.

Flood, Robert G. and Jenkins, Jerry B. *Teaching the Word, Reaching the World*. Chicago: Moody Press, 1985.

Furniss, Norman F. *The Fundamentalist Controversy, 1918-1931*. New Haven: Yale U., 1954.

Gaebelein, Frank E. *Christian Education in a Democracy*. New York: Oxford U., 1951.

Garrison, W. E. *March of Faith*. New York: Harper, 1933.

Gasper, Louis. *The Fundamentalist Movement*. Paris: Mouton, 1963.

Gaustad, Edwin Scott. *Historical Atlas of Religions in America*. New York: Harper & Row, 1962.

Giraud, C.; Garrison, G. R.; Willis, E. E. *Television and Radio*. New York: Appleton-Century-Crofts, 1963.

Glover, Robert Hall. *The Progress of World-Wide Missions*. Reprint. New York: Harper, 1960.

Good, Carter V., ed., *Dictionary of Education*. New York: McGraw-Hill, 1959.

Grattan, Clinton Hartley. *American Ideas About Adult Education, 1710-1951*. New York: Teacher's College, Columbia U., 1959.

Hall, J. H. *Biography of Gospel Song and Hymn Writers*. New York: Revell, 1914.

Halverson, Marvin, and Cohen, Arthur, eds., *Handbook of Christian Theology*. New York: Meridian, 1958.

Harkness, Robert. *Reuben Archer Torrey, the Man, His Message*. Chicago: Bible Inst. Colportage Assn., 1929.

Hartshorne, Hugh; Stearns, Helen R.; and Uphaus, Willard. *Standards and Trends in Religious Education*. New Haven: Yale U., 1933.

Head, Sydney W. *Broadcasting in America*. Boston: Houghton Mifflin, 1956.

Hopkins, C. Howard. *History of the Y.M.C.A. in North America*. New York: Assn. Press, 1951.

Hordern, William. *The Case for a New Reformation Theology*. Philadelphia: Westminster, 1959.

––––––. *A Layman's Guide to Protestant Theology*. New York: Macmillan, 1957.

Jackson, Samuel Macauley, ed., *The New Schaff-Herzog Encyclopedia of Religious Knowledge*. New York: Funk & Wagnalls, 1908-1914, Vols. l-XIII.

Jones, Clarence. *Radio, the New Missionary*. Chicago: Moody, 1946.

Kane, Joseph N. *Famous First Facts*. New York: Wilson, 1964.

Kempfer, Homer. *National Home Study Blue Book and Directory of Approved Home Study Schools and Courses*. Washington, D.C.: National Home Study Council, 1955.

Knowles, Malcolm S. *The Adult Education Program in the United States*. New York: Holt, Rinehart & Winston, 1962.

Lankard, Frank Glenn. *A History of the American Sunday School Curriculum*. New York: Abingdon, 1927.

Lightner, Robert P. *Neo-evangelicalism*. Findlay, Ohio: Dunham, 1961.

Loveless, Wendell P. *Manual of Gospel Broadcasting*. Chicago: Moody, 1946.

McFarland, John T.; Winchester, B. S.; Fraser, R. D.; and Butcher, J. W., eds., *The Encyclopedia of Sunday Schools and Religious Education*. Vols. I, II, III. New York: Nelson, 1915.

McLoughlin, William Gerald. *Modern Revivalism*. New York: Ronald, 1959.

Mann, Chester A. *Dwight L. Moody, A Mighty Man of God*. Grand Rapids: Zondervan, 1937.

————. *The R. A. Torrey Year-Book*. New York: Revell, 1929.

Marquis, Albert. *Who's Who in America*. Vol. IX. Chicago: Marquis, 1916-1917.

Matthews, Basil. *Forward Through the Ages*. New York: Friendship, 1951.

Metcalf, Edith B. *Letters to Dorothy from the Bible Institute*. New York: Revell, 1893.

Moody, William R. *The Life of Dwight L. Moody*. New York: Revell, 1900.

Moyer, Elgin. *Who Was Who in Church History*. Chicago: Moody, 1962.

Murch, James DeForest. *Christian Education and the Local Church*. Cincinnati: Standard, 1943.

————. *Cooperation Without Compromise*. Grand Rapids: Eerdmans, 1956.

North American Protestant Foreign Mission Agencies. Missionary Research Lib., 1962.

Noss, John. *Man's Religions*. New York: Macmillan, 1956.

Olmstead, Clifton E. *History of Religion in the United States*. Englewood Cliffs, N.J.: Prentice-Hall, 1960.

Orr, James, ed., *The International Standard Bible Encyclopedia*. Grand Rapids: Eerdmans, 1955.

Pattison, T. Harwood. *The History of Christian Preaching*. Philadelphia: Amer. Baptist, 1903.

Person, Peter. *An Introduction to Christian Education*. Grand Rapids: Baker, 1958.

Pierce, Bessie Louise. *A History of Chicago*. Vol. III: *The Rise of a Modern City*. New York: Knopf, 1957.

Pollock, J. C. *Moody*. New York: Macmillan, 1963.

Price, J. M.; Carpenter, L. L.; and Chapman, J. H. *Introduction to Religious Education*. New York: Macmillan, 1932.

Report of the Ecumenical Conference on Foreign Missions. Vol. II. New York: Amer. Tract Soc., 1900.

Reynolds, William Jensen. *A Survey of Christian Hymnody*. New York: Holt, Rinehart & Winston, 1963.

Rice, Edwin Wilbur. *The Sunday-School Movement and the American Sunday School Union*. Philadelphia: Amer. Sunday-School Union, 1917.

Rice, Mohel, and Poole, Hazel. *Earned Degrees Conferred by Higher Educational Institutions, 1955-56*. Washington: U. S. Dept. of Health, Educ. & Welfare, 1957.

Robert Raikes: His Sunday Schools and His Friends. Philadelphia: Amer. Baptist, 1859.

Robinson, Haddon W. *A Study of the Audience for Religious Radio and Television Broadcasts in Seven Cities Throughout the United States*. Privately published, 1964.

Robinson, Margaret Blake. *A Reporter at Moody's*. Chicago: Bible Inst. Colportage Assn., 1900.

Rowe, Henry Kalloch. *The History of Religion in the United States*. New York: Macmillan, 1928.

Runyan, William M. *Dr. Gray at Moody Bible Institute.* New York: Oxford U., 1935.

Sellers, E. O. *Evangelism in Sermon and Song.* Chicago: Moody, 1941.

Sherrill, Lewis J. *The Rise of Christian Education.* New York: Macmillan, 1944.

Smith, H. Shelton; Handy, R. T.; and Loetscher, L. A. *American Christianity.* Vol. II. New York: Scribner, 1963.

Smith, Wilbur M. *An Annotated Bibliography of D. L. Moody.* Chicago: Moody, 1948.

————. *Will H. Houghton: A Watchman on the Wall.* Grand Rapids: Eerdmans, 1951.

Squires, Walter A. *Educational Movements of Today.* Philadelphia: Board of Chr. Educ. of the Presbyterian Church in the U.S.A., 1930.

Story, Robert C. *Earned Degrees Conferred by Higher Educational Institutions, 1950-51.* Washington: Office of Educ., 1955.

SVM Becomes the Commission on World Missions of the National Student Christian Confederation. New York: N.C.C.C.

Sweet, Louis M. *The Pastoral Ministry in Our Time.* New York: Revell, 1959.

Sweet, William Warren. *The American Churches.* Nashville: Abingdon-Cokesbury, 1948.

————. *The Story of Religion in America.* New York: Harper, 1942.

Taylor, Marvin J., ed., *Religious Education: A Comprehensive Survey of Backgrounds, Theory, Methods, Administration and Agencies.* Nashville: Abingdon, 1960.

Thiessen, John Caldwell. *A Survey of World Missions.* Rev. ed. Chicago: Moody, 1961.

Tolliver, Wayne. *Earned Degrees Conferred, 1960-61.* Washington: U. S. Dept. of Health, Educ. & Welfare, 1963.

Trumbull, H. Clay. *The Sunday-School: Its Origin, Mission, Methods, and Auxiliaries.* New York: Scribner, 1888.

Vieth, Paul H., ed., *The Church and Christian Education.* St. Louis: Bethany, 1947.

Vincent, John H. *The Modern Sunday-School.* New York: Hunt & Eaton, 1887.

Webber, F. R. *A History of Preaching in Britain and America.* Milwaukee: Northwestern, 1957.

White, Paul. *The Moody Church Story.* Chicago: Moody Church, n.d.

Willard, W. Wyeth. *Fire on the Prairie: The Story of Wheaton College.* Wheaton, Ill.: Van Kampen, 1950.

Williams, A. W. *Life and Work of Dwight L. Moody.* Chicago: Ziegler, 1900.

Witmer, S. A. *The Bible College Story: Education with Dimension.* New York: Channel, 1962.

————. *Report: Preparing Bible College Students for Ministries in Christian Education.* Fort Wayne: Accrediting Assn. of Bible Colleges, 1962.

Worship and Service Hymnal. Chicago: Hope, 1961.

ARTICLES AND PERIODICALS

Aldridge, L. M. "Moody Press Distributes 1,500,000 Bible Portions in Many Lands During Year," *Chicago Daily News* (27 June 1936).

Alumni News Bulletin, 1940-1948.

Archer, Jules. "The Bible Need No Longer Be Greek to You," *The Christian Herald* (November 1950).

Berg, Roland H. "First Pictures Ever Taken Inside the Beating Heart," *Look* magazine (October 1957).

Chicago Inter-Ocean (23 January 1886), p. 7.

Chicago Tribune (23 January 1886), p. 3.

The Christian Worker's Magazine. Vols. XI-XX. Chicago: Moody Bible Institute, 1910-1920.

Coder, S. Maxwell, "Introduction to the Supplement," *Moody Monthly* (February 1946), p. 398.

Correspondence School News. Vols. VII, XV. Chicago: Moody Bible Institute, 1956, 1964.

Culbertson, William. *Review of Cooperative Evangelism in Moody Monthly* (August 1958), pp. 54-55.

———. Review of *Moody: A Biographical Portrait in Moody Monthly* (May 1963), pp. 45, 48.

DeSmyther, Dan. "Mayor Visits Campus," *Moody Student,* (18 May 1985), p. 1.

Egemeier, C. V. "Our New Editor-in-Chief." *Church School Promoter,* III (August 1941), 54.

"E. L. 0. Re-defines Aims and Goals," *ELO Bulletin* (November 1964).

Ely, Donald P., ed., "Historical Perspectives," *A-V Communications Review* (January-February 1963).

Everest, F. Alton. "Acoustic Treatment for Small Projection Rooms," *American Cinematographer* (July 1953), pp. 324, 352.

———. "Acoustic Treatment of Three Small Studios," *Journal of the Audio Engineering Society* (July 1968).

———. "Challenges Before the American Scientific Affiliation," *Journal of the American Scientific Affiliation,* XVI (March 1964).

———. "The Efficient Use of Light in Macrocinematography," *Journal of the Society of Motion Picture Engineers,* LXXI (September 1962), 664-67.

———. "Parabolic Reflector for Sound Recording," *Tele-Tech and Electronic Industries* (March 1955), pp. 77, 122, 126, 128.

Everest, F. Alton, and Hargett, G. Keith. "Photography of Heart Valves with the Cardiac Pulse Duplicator," *Journal of the Biological Photographic Association,* XXV (November 1957), 169-74.

Everest, F. Alton, and Moon, Irwin. "A Film-Processing Machine of Flexible Characteristics," *Journal of the Society of Motion Picture Engineers,* LXVII (November 1958), 758-62.

Findlay, James. "Moody, 'Gapmen,' and the Gospel: The Early Days of Moody Bible Institute," *Church History,* XXXI (September 1962), 322-35.

Glebink, Mark. "Dean Whaley Explains B.A. Factors," *Moody Student,* (3 May 1985), p. 1.

Gray, James M. "A Forward Step by the Moody Bible Institute," *Moody Bible Institute Monthly* (June 1922), pp. 1063-64.

———. "The Layman's Bible Commentary," *The Institute Tie* (July 1907), p. 496.

———. "Our New Adventure in Music," *Moody Bible Institute Bulletin* (May 1930), p. 3.

———. "Radio," *Moody Bible Institute Monthly* (March 1926), p. 309.

———. "Religious Education Course," *Moody Bible Institute Monthly* (December 1923), p. 163.

Hamlin, Teunis. "The Evolution of Northfield," *Northfield Echoes,* Vol. III. East Northfield: E. S. Rostall, 1896.

Hart, Rollin Lynde. "The War in the Churches," *The World Book* (September 1923).

Houghton, Will. "Youth's Page," *The Moody Bible Institute Monthly* (September 1935), p. 21.

Hustad, Donald P. "Church Music—the Pastor's Responsibility," *Bibliotheca Sacra,* CXVIII (January 1961), 8-17.

———. "Developing a Biblical Philosophy of Church Music," *Bibliotheca Sacra,* CXVII (April 1960), 108-22.

———. "Gospel Songs Fading?" *Moody Memo* (May 1961).

———. "Music for Worship, Evangelism, and Christian Education," *Bibliotheca Sacra,* CXVIII (October 1960), 301-12.

———. "Problems in Psychology and Aesthetics in Music," *Bibliotheca Sacra,* CXVII (July 1960), 214-28.

"Idea Notebook," *Moody Monthly* (October 1953), pp. 49-52.

Institute Tie. Vols. I-X. Chicago: Moody Bible Institute, 1900-1910.

McCulley, Dale. "Colportage Was His Challenge," *Christian Life* (August 1947).

McKinley, Mary Jean. "History of Chorale Goes Back to '21," *Moody Student* (21 April 1949), p. 3.

Mavrodes, George I. "Give Adults a Chance to Learn," *Moody Monthly* (May 1957), pp. 15-17.

Millard, Joseph. "Now Science, Too, Joins the Church," *Redbook Magazine* (August 1950).

Moody Alumni News. Vols. I-VI, 1926-1932; I-XVI, 1949-66. Chicago: Moody Alumni Association.

Moody Bible Institute of Chicago Bulletin. Vols. I-XXIII. Chicago: Moody Bible Institute, 1915-1944.

Moody Bible Institute Monthly. Vols. XI-XXXVIII. Chicago: Moody Bible Institute, 1920-1938.

Moody Literature News. Chicago: Moody Bible Institute, 1951-1966.

Moody Monthly. Vols. XXXIX-LXVI. Chicago: Moody Bible Institute, 1938-1966.

"Moody Press Widens Activities in Trade Publishing," *Publishers Weekly* (April 1945).

Moody Student. Vols. I-XXXI. Chicago: Moody Bible Institute, 1918-1966.

Pen and Scissors (2 March 1889).

Pierson, A. T. "The Keswick Movement," *Northfield Echoes.* Vol. IV. East Northfield: Northfield Echoes, 1897.

————. "The Story of Northfield Conferences," *Northfield Echoes.* Vol. I. East Northfield: Rostall, 1894.

Ramm, Bernard. "Fundamentalism Defined," *United Evangelical Action* (October 1951).

Rausch, Rosemary. "Confined to Study Scripture," *Moody Monthly* (November 1983), p. 36.

Record of Christian Work, V (February 1886), 5-6.

"Revell: Seventy-five Years of Religious Book Publishing," *Publishers Weekly* (December 1944).

Reynolds, William J. "Twentieth Century Church Music," *Church Music in Dimension,* I (Winter 1964), 1.

Ridenour, Fritz. "Churches Ring the School Bells," *Moody Monthly* (September 1963), p. 30.

Scot, Darrin. "World's Biggest Little Studio," *American Cinematographer* (August 1961).

Siemens, David F., Jr. "The Mathematics of the Honeycomb," *The Mathematics Teacher* (April 1965), pp. 334-37.

Smith, Wilbur M. "In the Study," *Moody Monthly* (January 1952), p. 319.

Street, Harold B. "For Such a Time as This," *Good News Broadcaster* (May 1962).

Streyckmans, Felix B. "Sermons from Science," *The Kiwanis Magazine* (March 1951).

The Sunday School Times. Vols. XXVIII-XXIX. Philadelphia: Sunday School Times, 1886-1887.

Taylor, Kenneth. "Gold Behind the Ranges," *Christian Life* (June 1948).

Talbot, Gordon. "What Sunday Schools Say About Electives," *Moody Monthly* (December 1963), pp. 31-33.

Torrey, R. A. Letter to the editor, *Moody Monthly* (October 1923), pp. 51-52.

————. "Practical and Perplexing Questions," *The Institute Tie* (July 1907), pp. 488-89.

Wall, Gary L. "The Man On the Coil," *Moody Monthly* (March 1979), p. 111.

Woodson, Weldon D. "Those Inspiring Sermons from Science," *Business Screen* magazine (April 1961).

LETTERS, REPORTS, AND OTHER MATERIALS,
PUBLISHED AND UNPUBLISHED

American Scientific Affiliation Constitution.

Arnold, Glenn F. "A Comparative Study of Present Doctrinal Positions and Christian Conduct Codes of Selected Alumni of Moody Bible Institute: 1945-1971." Unpublished doctoral dissertation, New York U., 1977.

"A Story of God at Work," Whittier, Calif.: Moody Institute of Science, 1980. Moody Institute of Science 1983 Annual Report.

Blanchard, Charles A. Unpublished manuscript describing the events leading to the founding of Moody Bible Institute, February 1916.

Blackstone, William E. Letter to Dr. James M. Gray, 24 September 1915.

Beers, V. Gilbert. "The Work and Influence of D. L. Moody in the Field of Christian Education." Unpublished master's thesis, Northern Baptist Theological Seminary, 1953.

Boon, Harold W. "The Development of the Bible College or Institute in the United States and Canada Since 1880 and Its Relationship to the Field of Theological Education in America." Unpublished doctoral dissertation, School of Education, New York U., 1950.

Bosma, Kenneth. "Moody Bible Institute Alumni Survey, 1984," 19 November 1984.

Campbell, Wilbur Fred. "Dwight L. Moody and Religious Education." Unpublished master's thesis, Divinity School, Yale U., 1949.

Chicago Bible Work. Annual reports. Prepared by Emma Dryer, 1874, 1875, 1885-1886.

Chicago Evangelization Society. First annual report (1888).

Christian Booksellers Association. Bylaws.

Committee on Research, Division of Correspondence Study. *An Annotated Bibliography of Correspondence Study, 1896-1960*. National University Ext. Assn., 1960.

Cook, Harold R. "Factors Affecting the Accuracy of Our Missionary statistics." June 1964.

Dryer, Emma. Unpublished manuscript describing Emma Dryer's associations with D. L. Moody before and after the founding of the Chicago Evangelization Society, January 1916.

————. Letter to Mrs. Waite, 18 July 1924.

Ecumenical Conference on Foreign Missions. New York: Amer. Tract Soc., 1900. II, 424.

Evangelical Literature Overseas. Official financial statements, records, and manuals. Wheaton, Ill., 1953-1965.

Evangelical Teacher Training Association. Annual report, 1962-1963.

Evangelical Teacher Training Association. Bylaws.

Evangelical Teacher Training Association. "ETTA—What and Why?" n.d.

Everest, F. Alton. "Chronology of Sermons from Science." 27 February 1963.

Everest, F. Alton, and Moon, Irwin. "Proposal for a Christian Laboratory." December 1944.

Findlay, James. "D. L. Moody." Unpublished doctoral dissertation, Northwestern U., 1960.

Gaylord, A. F. Letter to L. W. Munhall, 14 July 1923.

Getz, Gene A. *Report of the Presidential Questionnaire.* 4 vols. Chicago: Moody Bible Institute Printing Plant, 1964.

Graves, Allen W. Personal letter, Southern Baptist Theological Seminary, 19 October 1965.

Heacock, Joe D. Personal letter, Southwestern Baptist Theological Seminary, 18 October 1965.

McBirnie, William S., Jr. "A Study of the Bible Institute Movement." Unpublished Doctoral dissertation, Southwestern Baptist Theological Seminary, 1952.

McCormick, N. F. Letter to D. L. Moody, 15 July 1887. Photostat in Moodyana file. Original in Cyrus H. McCormick Family Papers, Wisconsin State Historical Soc.

McIntyre, Betty. Report of Vocational Questionnaire. Alumni office, Moody Bible Institute, 1965.

Moody, Emma C. Letter to N. F. McCormick, 26 July 1887. Moodyana files.

Moody, D. L. Letter and telegram to N. F. McCormick, July 18 and 27, 1887. Moodyana files.

Moody Alumni Association. *Annual Reports.* 1951-1966.

Moody Bible Institute. *Annual Reports.* 1900-1905.

———. Annual reports for the Colportage Department (Moody Literature Mission). 1941-1966.

———. Annual reports of the Correspondence School. 1957-1966.

———. Annual reports for the Department of Radio. 1926-1966.

———. Annual reports of the Extension Department (Church Relations). 1928-1966.

———. Annual reports of the Missionary Technical Department. 1954-1966.

———. Annual reports for Moody Institute of Science. 1946-1966.

———. Annual reports for *Moody Monthly.* 1921-1966.

———. Annual reports for Moody Press. 1941-1966.

———. Annual reports for Practical Christian Work. 1927-1966.

———. Annual reports of the Publications Division. 1959-1965.

———. The Certificate of Incorporation and all Amendments thereto, to date, including Consolidation, and including Certificate of Change of Registered Agent and Registered Office, of the Moody Bible Institute of Chicago. Sealed by Charles F. Carpentier, July 2, 1958. (Photographic copy on file in the office of the executive vice-president, Moody Bible Institute. Original on file in the office of the Secretary of State, Springfield, Ill.)

———. Constitution of the Moody Chorale. n.d.

———. "An Evaluative Study of Objectives of Moody Bible Institute." Chicago, 1961.

————. Minutes of the Department of Christian Education. 1963-1964.

————. Minutes of the Department of Sacred Music. 1946-1966.

————. Minutes of the Executive Committee, 16 December 1925.

————. *Moody Monthly* advertising report. 1960.

————. Newspaper clipping file in Department of Sacred Music. 1951-1966.

————. Official records for Moody Press. 1941-1966.

Moody Bible Institute Registrar's Office. Annual reports. 1915-1966.

————. Official enrollment and graduation records. 1889-1966.

Moody Institute of Science. "Analysis of Some Aspects of the Results of the Sermons from Science Presentations." Los Angeles, 1963.

————. 1984 Annual Report.

————. "Television Policy for Moody Films." Los Angeles, 1964.

————. "Worldwide Photographic Project." Los Angeles, 1959.

Moody Monthly Reader Survey. Bala-Cynwyd, Pa.: Audience Analysts, Inc., 1965.

Moore, J. Kelva. Personal letter, New Orleans Baptist Theological Seminary. 22 October 1965.

Moore, W. F. Personal letter. 8 September 1965.

National Sunday School Association. Letter from Clate Risley, executive director. 10 January 1963.

————. "Textbook Survey Report." Wheaton, Ill., 1958-1959.

1980 Awards Program, New York: Society of Motion Picture and Television Engineers, 10 November 1980.

Olson, A. G. Letter to Wilbur W. Scafe. 7 September 1951.

Palmer, Joy E. "The Contributions of Clarence H. Benson to the Field of Christian Education." Unpublished master's thesis, Wheaton College, Wheaton, Ill., 1958.

Photographic file in Moodyana, Moody Bible Institute.

Price, Rebecca R. Personal letter, Fuller Theological Seminary. 6 December 1965.

Reed, Lenice. "The Bible Institute Movement in America." Unpublished master's thesis, Wheaton College, Wheaton, Ill., 1947.

Reynhout, H. "A Comparative Study of Bible Institute Curriculums." Unpublished master's thesis, Department of Education, U. Michigan, 1947. Published in mimeograph form by Providence Bible Institute.

Reynolds, William J. Personal letter. Aug. 11, 1965.

Rohrer, Norman B. Personal letter. 8 October 1965.

Scafe, Wilbur W. Letter written to A. G. Olson, n.d.

Skoda, George Paul. "The Teacher Training Movement." Unpublished master's thesis, Northen Baptist Theological Seminary, Chicago, 1937.

Smith, Wilbur M. Personal letters. October 25, 1965; January 9, 12, and 15, and April 16, 1968.

Stave, Douglas T. "Curricular Changes in Selected Bible Institutes and Bible Colleges." Unpublished doctoral dissertation, U. Oregon, 1962.

Talbot, Gordon Gray. "The Bible Institute Movement in the Christian and Missionary Alliance." Unpublished master's thesis, Wheaton College, Wheaton, Ill., 1956.

Van Dyke, Richard. "A Study to Evaluate the Current Evening School Program: Societal Factors." Unpublished paper, February 1983.

Warkentin, Elmo. "The History of 'Revitalizing the Sunday Schools of America' Through the National Sunday School Association." Unpublished master's thesis, Wheaton College, Wheaton, Ill., 1958.

Whaley, Howard. "The Effects of American Revivalism 1726-1826 on Missions." Unpublished master's thesis, Wheaton College, Wheaton, Ill., 1963.

PAMPHLETS

Bible Background to War. Chicago: Moody Bible Institute, n.d.

A Brief Story of the Bible Institute Colportage Association of Chicago. Chicago: Bible Inst. Colportage Assn., 1940.

Called of God into All the World. Chicago: Moody Bible Institute, n.d.

Catalog of Moody Films. Los Angeles: Moody Institute of Science, 1965.

Coder, S. Maxwell. *The Philosophy of Education of Moody Bible Institute.* Chicago: Moody Bible Institute, n.d.

Dedicatory Program: *Torrey-Gray Auditorium and William Howard Doane Memorial Building.* Chicago: Moody Bible Institute, n.d.

D. L. Moody Historical Exhibit. Chicago: Moody Bible Institute, 1946.

Doing Business for God. Chicago: Moody Bible Institute, n.d.

Dwight Lyman Moody: Messenger to Millions. Chicago: Moody Bible Institute, n.d.

An Encouraging Report from the Colportage Department of the Moody Bible Institute. Chicago: Moody Bible Institute, n.d.

ETTA: 50 Years Serving Christ thru Leadership Training, Wheaton, Ill.: Evangelical Teacher Training Association, 1980.

Facts of Faith. Chicago: Moody Bible Institute, n.d.

Fifty Years Ago. Chicago: Moody Bible Institute, n.d.

Fitt, A. P. *Preaching the Gospel in Print.* Chicago: Bible Inst. Colportage Assn., 1898.

God's Faithfulness. Wheaton, Ill.: Evangelical Teacher Training Assn., 1955.

His Business Was Souls. Chicago: Moody Bible Institute, n.d.

Historical Sketch of the Moody Bible Institute of Chicago. Chicago: Moody Bible Institute, 1924.

Houghton, Will H. *President's Report.* Chicago: Moody Bible Institute, 1937.

I Visited Moody Bible Institute. Chicago: Moody Bible Institute, n.d.

Inauguration of the Reverend William Culbertson, D.D. as President of Moody Bible Institute. Chicago: Moody Bible Institute, 1948.

Life of Moody. Chicago: Moody Bible Institute, n.d.

Missionary Aviation. Fullerton, California 1963.

The Missionary Technician. Chicago: Moody Bible Institute, n.d.

Moody Bible Institute. Music Program Schedules. 1951-1966.

The Moody Bible Institute of Chicago: What It Is and What It Does. Chicago: Moody Bible Institute, n.d.

Moody Press Books. Chicago: Moody Bible Institute, 1965-1966.

Moody Trains for a Ministry of Music. Chicago: Moody Bible Institute, n.d.

Moving Forward. Chicago: Moody Bible Institute, 1913.

Program for the 40th Founder's Week Conference. Chicago: Moody Bible Institute, 1946.

Redeeming the Time: The Story of Moody and Missions. Chicago: Moody Bible Institute, n.d.

Robinson, Paul F. *Questions and Answers About Missionary Technical Training.* Chicago: Moody Bible Institute, n.d.

Story of Scripture Press. Wheaton, Ill.: Scripture Press, 1956.

Tent Work in Chicago. Chicago: The Bible Institute, 1892.

A Testimony to God's Faithfulness. Chicago: Moody Bible Institute, n.d.

Twenty Fifth Anniversary Year. Chicago: Moody Bible Institute, 1911.

What Is the Evangelical Teacher Training Association? Wheaton, Ill.: Evangelical Teacher Training Assn., 1955.

Why Moody Bible Institute Trains Students in Jewish Missions. Chicago: Moody Bible Institute, n.d.

WMBI. Chicago: Moody Bible Institute, n.d.

WMBI Program Schedules. Chicago: Moody Bible Institute, 1926-1966.

WMBI Radio Dedication Souvenir. Chicago: Moody Bible Institute, 1928.

Wuest, Kenneth A. *The School and Its Students.* Chicago: Moody Bible Institute, 1938.

CATALOGS AND SCHEDULES

Annual Catalog: The Bible Institute for Home and Foreign Missions of the Chicago Evangelization Society, 1895-1899 (published annually).

Bible Institute. *Musical Department of the Bible Institute of the Chicago Evangelization Society* (a single-page brochure, printed sometime in 1889.).

Bible Work. Chicago: Chicago Bible Work, 1885.

Bible Work Institute of the Chicago Evangelization Society. Chicago: Chicago Evangelization Soc., 1887.

Calendar of the Bible Institute. "Summary for Ten Years — 1889-1899." Chicago: Bible Institute, 1899.

Calendar of the Bible Institute of the Chicago Evangelization Society. Chicago: Bible Institute, 1894.

Catalog of the Moody Bible Institute for Home and Foreign Missions, 1900-1903 (published annually).

Catalog of the Moody Bible Institute of Chicago, 1904-1966 (published annually).

Chicago Bible Work. Chicago: Chicago Bible Work, 1874.

Correspondence School Catalog of the Moody Bible Institute of Chicago, 1916-1966 (published annually).

Evening School Catalog of the Moody Bible Institute of Chicago, 1903-1966 (published annually).

Ladies' Department of the Bible Institute for Home and Foreign Missions of the Chicago Evangelization Society, 1889-1894 (published annually).

Men's Department of the Bible Institute for Home and Foreign Missions of the Chicago Evangelization Society, 1889-1894 (published annually).

Musical Department of the Bible Institute of the Chicago Evangelization Society. Chicago: Bible Institute (1890 or 1891).

Prospectus: Correspondence Department. Chicago: Moody Bible Institute, 1901-1902.

Term Announcements: Evening Department. Chicago: Moody Bible Institute, 1903-1904.

INTERVIEWS

Interviews were conducted with the following persons at Moody Bible Institute:

Wilfred Burton, director of the Music Department. Summer, 1965.

Wayne Christianson, executive editor of *Moody Monthly*. Summer 1965.

Robert Constable, Rollin Sherwood, and H. E. Stockburger. Fall 1964.

Victor Cory, president, Scripture Press. Summer 1963.

H. C. Crowell, retired executive vice-president. Summer 1965.

William Culbertson, president. Summer 1963.

Jay Fernlund, director of Correspondence School. Summer 1985.

Peter Gunther, director of Moody Literature Mission. Fall 1965.

Kenneth Hanna, Dean of Education, Summer 1985.

Donald P. Hustad, former director of the Music Department. Summer 1965.

Irwin Moon, manager of Moody Institute of Science. Fall 1964.

C. B. Nordland, manager of Public Relations Department. Summer 1965.

Gerald Raquet, chairman of Department of Sacred Music. Summer 1985.

Paul Robinson, director of the Missionary Technical Department. Summer 1963.

Kenneth Simmelink, chairman of Department of Missionary Aviation. Summer 1985.

J. Raymond Tallman, chairman of Department of Sacred Music. Summer 1985.

Kenneth Taylor, former director of Publications Division. Fall 1965.

Howard Whaley, Academic Dean. Summer 1985.

Appendix A

Official Documents

I. ORIGINAL CONSTITUTION OF THE CHIGAGO EVANGELIZATION SOCIETY
(Adopted February 5, 1887)

Actuated by a desire to promote the Gospel of our Lord Jesus Christ, we hereby agree to adopt for our united government the following Constitution:

ARTICLE I

NAME

This organization shall be called the "Chicago Evangelization Society."

ARTICLE II

OBJECT

The object of the "Chicago Evangelization Society" shall be to educate, direct and maintain Christian workers, as Bible readers, teachers and evangelists; who shall teach the Gospel in Chicago and its suburbs, especially in neglected fields. (Acts 10:43; 2 Tim. 3:16-17; 4:1-2.)

ARTICLE III

TRUSTEES AND MANAGERS

SECTION 1. The property and entire control of this Society shall be vested in a

Board of Trustees who shall be Christian men, members of good standing in Evangelical churches, who willingly give prayer, time, money, effort to advance it; and only such shall be qualified for office. (Jn. 14:15-21; Mark 16:15; 2 Cor. 5:10.)

SECTION 2. The Board of Trustees shall consist of seven persons who shall be named in the Charter, self-perpetuating. They shall possess all the powers of Trustees under and by virtue of the Law of the State of Illinois concerning corporations for other than pecuniary benefit. (Revised Statutes of Illinois; chapter 31, section 29-30) and shall have the management of all its concerns. They shall have power to remove their officers or members by a majority vote of the whole Board; to fill vacancies by a two-thirds vote of the whole Board; to appoint all officers; prescribe the duties of all officers not herein prescribed; construct by-laws for the government of the Work, and supervise its purposes and plans.

SECTION 3. For the purpose of more effectually advancing the "object" of this Society, the Board of Trustees shall have the power to create a Board of Managers — who shall be Christian men and women, as in Section 1, Article III — by electing nine persons, at least six of whom shall be women, who, together with the Board of Trustees, shall constitute a Board of Managers. The persons so elected to serve, shall hold their office as officers under Section 2 of this Article, until their successors are elected.

SECTION 4. To the Board of Managers shall be entrusted the operating work of this Society. They shall have power to organize Committees for the various departments of the work; to increase the members of a Committee by adding Christian men and women according to section 1, who are not members of the Board of Managers; and such other matters as may be delegated to them by the Trustees, to whom they shall report for approval all their actions when called upon to do so, and at the regular Quarterly and Annual Meetings of the Trustees.

SECTION 5. The Trustees shall elect from their number a President, Vice President, Recording Secretary and Treasurer.

They may also appoint a General Manager, whose duties shall be to make known the Work of the organization and its object to the public; to solicit aid for general expenses and endowment funds; and to act as Corresponding Secretary for the Society.

The Board of Managers may appoint a Faculty that shall plan and supervise the daily work, direct the studies, recitations and united meetings of the workers, and their general duties in this Society and in their respective fields. This Faculty shall be appointed by ballot.

SECTION 6. All officers shall begin the duties of their offices at a time specified by the Board of Trustees.

SECTION 7. An appointee may for misconduct or neglect of duty be dismissed, and his or her position declared vacant by a majority ballot of the whole Board of Trustees at a regularly appointed meeting of the Board. Information against an accused person shall be communicated in writing and due opportunity given for defense.

ARTICLE IV

The Workers

SECTION 1. The Workers selected for this Society shall be persons of good Christian character and ability; members of Evangelical churches, professing, in obedience to the Word of God, "to seek first the Kingdom of God and his righteousness," and "to sow the fruits of righteousness in peace," in their Christian fellowship, education and ministry. (Matt. 6:24-33; Jn. 14:15-27; Jas. 3:17-18.)

SECTION 2. These shall meet regularly, systematically to study the Holy Scriptures, the facts and truths of the Christian religion, the best ways for presenting the Gospel, and to pray for those persons in whose salvation and Christian growth they have become interested.

SECTION 3. And they shall diligently teach the Bible, declare its truths, and practice its Christian ministry in carrying out the object, principles and plans of this Society.

SECTION 4. The school for the training of Christian Workers shall be called the "Bible-Work Institute."

ARTICLE V

Membership

Any person in sympathy with the "object" of this Organization, who contributes annually to its support, may become a member of this Society by presenting to the Recording Secretary a written request for membership.

Notice of the Annual and Quarterly Meetings shall be sent to all such members.

ARTICLE VI

The Treasury

All accepted donations shall be used for the purpose which they are given and accepted. No property shall be mortgaged. No debts shall be contracted on the credit of this Society. (Rom. 18:8; 2 Cor. 8:21.)

ARTICLE VII

Meeting and Quorum

SECTION 1. This Society shall hold Quarterly meetings the second Wednesday of January, April, July and October.

The meeting in January shall be the annual meeting.

SECTION 2. At these meetings the Trustees shall receive reports from every department of the work, and a summary of these reports shall be kept on standing records.

SECTION 3. Special meetings may be appointed and called in the usual manner.

SECTION 4. Due notice of any meeting having been given, a majority of either Board shall constitute a Quorum.

ARTICLE VIII

AMENDMENT

For the more perfect promotion of the object of this Society, this Constitution may be altered or amended by a two-thirds vote of the whole Board of Trustees.

II. CERTIFICATE OF INCORPORATION OF THE CHICAGO EVANGELIZATION SOCIETY

STATE OF ILLINOIS
COOK COUNTY

TO HENRY D. DEMENT, SECRETARY OF STATE:

We the undersigned, Dwight L. Moody, Turlington W. Harvey, Elbridge G. Keith, Cyrus H. McCormick, Nathaniel S. Bouton, Robert Scott, and John V. Farwell, Citizens of the United States, propose to form a Corporation under an act of the General Assembly of the State of Illinois, entitled, "An Act concerning Corporations," approved April 18, 1872, and all acts amendatory thereof, and that for the purposes of such organization we hereby state as follows, to-wit:

1. The name of such Corporation is the Chicago Evangelization Society.

2. The object for which it is formed is to educate, direct and maintain Christian workers as Bible readers, Teachers and Evangelists who shall teach the Gospel in Chicago and its suburbs; especially in neglected fields.

3. The management of the aforesaid Society shall be vested in a Board of Seven Trustees.

4. The following persons are hereby selected as the Trustees to control and manage said Corporation for the first year of its corporate existence, viz: Dwight L. Moody, Turlington W. Harvey, Elbridge G. Keith, Cyrus H. McCormick, Nathaniel S. Bouton, Robert Scott and J. V. Farwell.

5. The location is in the City of Chicago in the County of Cook, State of Illinois.

Signed:

D. L. Moody	John V. Farwell
Turlington W. Harvey	Cyrus H. McCormick
Elbridge G. Keith	Nathaniel S. Bouton
Robert Scott	

STATE OF ILLINOIS
DEPARTMENT OF STATE
HENRY D. DEMENT, SECRETARY OF STATE

To all Whom these Presents shall Come — GREETING:

WHEREAS, a CERTIFICATE, duly signed and acknowledged, having been filed in the office of the Secretary of State, on the 12th day of February A.D., 1887 for the organization of the Chicago Evangelization Society under and in accordance with the provisions of "An Act Concerning Corporations," approved April 18, 1872, and in force July 1, 1872, a copy of which certificate is hereto attached:

NOW, THEREFORE, I, HENRY D. DEMENT, Secretary of State of the State of Illinois, by virtue of the powers and duties vested in me by law, do hereby certify the said Chicago Evangelization Society is a legally organized Corporation under the laws of this State.

IN TESTIMONY WHEREOF, I hereto set my hand and cause to be affixed the great seal of State.

DONE at the City of Springfield this 12th day of February in the year of our Lord one thousand eight hundred and eighty seven, and of the Independence of the United States the One Hundred and Eleventh.

Henry D. Dement
Secretary of State

III. BYLAWS OF THE MOODY BIBLE INSTITUTE OF CHICAGO[1]
DATED THE 30TH DAY OF APRIL A. D. 1985

ARTICLE I

NAME

The name of this corporation is THE MOODY BIBLE INSTITUTE OF CHICAGO.

ARTICLE II

OBJECT

The establishment of this Corporation is for the purpose of conducting and maintaining an educational organization to include a Bible Institute for the education and training of Christian workers, teachers, ministers, missionaries, musicians, and the general public, so they may competently and effectively proclaim the gospel of Jesus Christ, and to promote and further the belief and acceptance of the principles of the Christian Faith and the gospel of Jesus Christ as set forth in the Bible by use of all available means of education and instruction, including but not limited to:

(a) Conducting a Bible Institute for the study of the Bible and related subjects.
(b) Conducting a Bible correspondence school and other educational activities for the study and training of students in the Bible and related subjects.
(c) The operation, conducting, and maintaining of facilities for the instruction and training of students in Christian missionary aviation.
(d) The operation of one or more radio stations and related broadcasting ministries on a non-commercial educational basis to broadcast programs of an instructional and inspirational nature, including but not limited to programs pertaining to biblical truths and subjects and promoting a belief in the Bible and acceptance of its teachings.
(e) The publication and distribution of books and literature of an educational and religious nature relating to biblical truths and subjects and promoting a belief in the Bible and acceptance of its teachings.
(f) The production and distribution of films, presentations, and programs (including radio, television, or other media) based on scientific research and knowledge, of an instructional nature and pertaining to biblical truths as they relate to man and the universe in which he lives.

1. See also Certificate of Incorporation all Amendments thereto. Article X appears in excerpted form. (Sections 2-B are not shown.)

This Corporation shall have and exercise all powers necessary or convenient to effect any or all of the purposes for which it is organized.

ARTICLE III

DOCTRINAL STATEMENT

The following statement of faith represents the doctrinal position of The Moody Bible Institute of Chicago and shall be subscribed to annually by its Trustees, officers, faculty members, departmental managers, and directors:

ARTICLE I: God is a Person who has revealed Himself as a Trinity in unity, Father, Son and Holy Spirit—three Persons and yet but one God (Deut. 6:4; Matt. 28:19; I Cor. 8:6).

ARTICLE II: The Bible, including both the Old and the New Testaments, is a divine revelation, the original autographs of which were verbally inspired by the Holy Spirit (II Tim. 3:16; II Pet. 1:21).

ARTICLE III: Jesus Christ is the image of the invisible God, which is to say, He is Himself very God; He took upon Him our nature, being conceived by the Holy Ghost and born of the Virgin Mary; He died upon the cross as a substitutionary sacrifice for the sin of the world. He arose from the dead in the body in which He was crucified; He ascended into heaven in that body glorified, where He is now, our interceding High Priest; He will come again personally and visibly to set up His kingdom and to judge the quick and the dead (Col. 1:15; Phil. 2:5-8; Matt. 1:18-25; I Pet. 2:24-25; Luke 24; Heb. 4:14-16; Acts 1:9-11; I Thess. 4:16-18; Matt. 25:31-46; Rev. 11:15-17; 20:4-6, 11-15).

ARTICLE IV: Man was created in the image of God but fell into sin, and, in that sense, is lost; this is true of all men, and except a man be born again he cannot see the kingdom of God; salvation is by grace through faith in Christ who His own self bare our sins in His own body on the tree; the retribution of the wicked and unbelieving and the reward of the righteous are everlasting, and as the reward is conscious, so is the retribution (Gen. 1:26-27; Rom. 3:10, 23; John 3:3; Acts 13:38-39; 4:12; John 3:16; Matt. 25:46; II Cor. 5:1; II Thess. 1:7-10).

ARTICLE V: The Church is an elect company of believers baptized by the Holy Spirit into one body; its mission is to witness concerning its Head, Jesus Christ, preaching the gospel among all nations, it will be caught up to meet the Lord in the air when He appears to set up His kingdom (Acts 2:41; 15:13-17; Eph. 1:3-6; I Cor. 12:12-13; Matt. 28:19-20; Acts 1:6-8; I Thess. 4:16-18).

ARTICLE IV

NON-DISCRIMINATION POLICY

In operating and conducting the activities of The Moody Bible Institute of Chicago, it is the policy of the Institute to admit students of any race, color, national and ethnic origin to all the rights, privileges, programs and activities generally accorded and made available to students at the Institute; and in so doing, the Institute does not discriminate on the basis of race, color, national and ethnic origin in the administration of its educational policies, admissions policies, scholarship and loan programs, and athletic and other school-administered programs.

ARTICLE V

MEMBERSHIP

SECTION 1. Only persons who are evangelical Christians shall be eligible for membership in the Corporation.

SECTION 2. Members of this Corporation shall be:
  (a) Eligible persons who have heretofore and who may hereafter be elected to the Board of Trustees of this Corporation by two-thirds vote of the Trustees present so long as a majority of the entire Board of Trustees shall concur in the vote; provided however that unless a person so elected shall within thirty (30) days after his election to the Board of Trustees accept such office, he shall cease to be a Trustee and also a member of the Corporation. If a person shall be elected to and accept the office of Trustee, he shall continue to be a member of the Corporation only so long as he continues to be a Trustee.
  (b) In no event shall a member of the Corporation be a person who is not a member of the Board of Trustees of the Corporation.

ARTICLE VI

TRUSTEES

SECTION 1. General Powers and Duties
  The Board of Trustees of The Moody Bible Institute of Chicago shall control and manage the property, funds, business and affairs of the Corporation and further establish the policy and direction of the Corporation consistent with the corporate purposes as set forth in The Articles of Incorporation.

SECTION 2. Number and Qualifications

The Board of Trustees shall consist of not less than nine nor more than twenty-one persons, each of whom shall be a member of the Corporation. The Trustees shall be elected from eligible persons by the Board of Trustees of the Corporation and must be men giving evidence of conversion and consecration to Jesus Christ, whose doctrinal views of Christian truth are in accord with the doctrinal statement of the Corporation as set forth in Article III hereof, and who are willing to and shall sign such doctrinal statement annually.

SECTION 3. Trustees—Term of Office

Trustees shall be elected by two-thirds vote of the Board of Trustees for a term of three years, to be arranged so that as nearly as may be, the terms of one-third of the members of the Board shall expire each year. The election of new Trustees shall be held at the annual meeting of the Trustees, or any adjourned session thereof; or any other regular meeting of the Trustees, or any adjourned session thereof, at which time determination may also be made by two-thirds of the Board of Trustees as to the advisability of electing any Trustee or Trustees for a term of less than three years. Provision for election to a term of less than three years shall in no instance be made other than for the purpose of properly limiting the number of expiring terms to one-third in any given year during the succeeding three-year period.

SECTION 4. Filling Vacancies

Vacancies occurring in the Board of Trustees by death, resignation, or removal of a Trustee or Trustees, may be filled by election by a two-thirds vote of the remaining Trustees at any meeting of the Trustees, provided a written notice of intention to elect such Trustee or Trustees (naming him or them) shall have been delivered or mailed to each Trustee at least thirty days prior to the meeting.

SECTION 5. Removal from Office

Any Trustee may be removed from the office of Trustee by a two-thirds vote of the other Trustees present; provided, however, that this vote shall not be binding unless a number equal to at least a majority of the entire Board of Trustees shall concur in the vote, and provided further that no Trustee shall be removed at any meeting unless a written notice of intention to consider removal of such Trustee or Trustees (naming him or them) shall be delivered or mailed to each Trustee at least thirty days prior to the meeting.

ARTICLE VII

OFFICERS

Section 1. Officers

The officers of the Corporation shall be a Chairman and Vice-Chairman of the

Board of Trustees, a President, one or more Executive Vice-Presidents, one or more Vice-Presidents (the number thereof to be determined by the Board of Trustees), a Treasurer, a Secretary, and such Assistant Treasurers, Assistant Secretaries, or other officers as may be elected by the Board of Trustees. Officers whose authority and duties are not prescribed in these by-laws shall have the authority and perform the duties prescribed, from time to time, by the Board of Trustees. Any two or more offices may be held by the same person, except the offices of Chairman and Vice-Chairman of the Board of Trustees and President and Secretary.

SECTION 2. Qualifications and Duties

The officers of the Corporation and their respective qualifications and duties are as follows:

A. CHAIRMAN OF THE BOARD OF TRUSTEES. The Chairman of the Board of Trustees shall be elected from among the Trustees and shall be the senior officer of the Corporation and shall preside at meetings of the members of the Corporation and at meetings of the Trustees, and shall do and perform such other duties as may from time to time be assigned to him by the Board of Trustees.

B. VICE CHAIRMAN OF THE BOARD OF TRUSTEES. The Vice Chairman of the Board of Trustees shall be elected from among the Trustees and shall in the absence of the Chairman of the Board of Trustees, or his inability to act, perform all duties which would be performed by the Chairman of the Board of Trustees were he present or able to act.

C. PRESIDENT. The President shall be elected by the Trustees, and shall be a Trustee and shall be the Chief Executive Officer of the Corporation. Subject to the direction and control of the Board of Trustees, he shall be responsible for the spiritual leadership and doctrinal integrity of the Corporation, and shall be responsible for the conduct of the business and affairs of the Corporation; he shall see that the resolutions and directives of the Board of Trustees are carried into effect except in those instances in which the responsibility is assigned to some other person by the Board of Trustees, and, in general, he shall discharge all duties incident to the office of President and such other duties as may be prescribed by the Board of Trustees.

D. EXECUTIVE VICE PRESIDENT. The Executive Vice President shall be the Chief Operating Officer of the Corporation, subject to the direction and control of the President, and shall, if the President cannot be timely contacted or is unable due to physical or mental conditions to act, and until otherwise directed by the Board of Trustees, perform all duties which would be performed by the President were he present and able to act, and shall also perform such other duties as may be prescribed by the President or by the Board of Trustees.

E. VICE PRESIDENT, DEAN OF EDUCATION. The Vice President, Dean of Education, shall be the Chief Administrative Officer of the educational ministries of the Corporation, subject to the direction and control of the President, or at his direction, the Executive Vice President.

F. VICE-PRESIDENTS. The duties and functions of the other Vice-Presidents of the Corporation shall be assigned to them by the Board of Trustees and under the direction of the President, or at his direction, the Executive Vice President.

G. TREASURER. The Treasurer shall be the principal accounting and financial officer of the Corporation, subject to the direction and control of the President, or at his direction, the Executive Vice President. He shall: (a) have charge of and be responsible for the maintenance of adequate books of account for the Corporation; (b) have charge and custody of all funds and securities of the Corporation, and be responsible therefore, and for the receipt and disbursement thereof; and (c) perform all duties incident to the office of Treasurer.

H. ASSISTANT TREASURER. The Assistant Treasurer shall perform such duties as shall be assigned to him by the Treasurer and such other duties as may be assigned to him from time to time by the Board of Trustees and under the direction of the President, or at his direction, the Executive Vice President.

I. SECRETARY. The Secretary shall be elected from among the Trustees and shall keep the minutes of meetings of the members of the Corporation and meetings of the Board of Trustees, and attend to the giving and serving of all notices of the Corporation and of the Board of Trustees. He shall have the custody of the Corporate Seal and have charge of the books, documents, and papers properly belonging to his office, all of which shall at reasonable times be open to examination by any Trustee; and shall, subject to the control of the Board of Trustees, perform such other duties as commonly appertain to the office of Secretary.

J. FIRST ASSISTANT SECRETARY. The First Assistant Secretary shall be elected from among the Trustees, and shall, in the absence of the Secretary, or his inability to act, perform all duties which would be performed by the Secretary were he present and able to act.

K. OTHER ASSISTANT SECRETARIES. The duties with respect to the other Assistant Secretaries shall be specifically authorized and assigned from time to time by the Board of Trustees.

L. PRO TEM OFFICERS. In the event of the absence, inability or refusal to act of any of the officers of the Corporation, the Board of Trustees may appoint some one of their number to perform his or their respective duties

SECTION 3. When Elected, Term, Vacancies

Officers shall be elected by the Trustees at the annual meeting, or any regular meeting of the Board, or at any adjourned session thereof in such year.

Officers shall hold office for one year from the time they are respectively elected and qualify, and until their respective successors are elected and accept office; provided, however, that any and all officers shall be subject to removal at any time by an affirmative vote of a majority of the Trustees. Before taking office each elected officer shall subscribe to the doctrinal statement of the Institute.

If any vacancy occurs among the officers, the same may be filled for the unexpired portion of the term by election by the Trustees at any meeting of the Trustees. No officer or officers shall be elected or removed at any meeting of the Trustees other than an annual or regular meeting of the Trustees, unless a notice of intention to elect or remove such officer or officers shall be delivered or mailed to each Trustee at least one week prior to the meeting at which the election is held or the removal made.

ARTICLE VIII

Execution of Documents

The Board of Trustees shall by appropriate authorization or resolution, from time to time, direct and empower proper officers of the Corporation to sign, execute, acknowledge, and deliver, for and in the name of and on behalf of the Corporation, all such contracts, deeds, assignments, receipts, releases, and other documents, papers, or instruments as may be required or proper in the ordinary course of business of the Corporation.

ARTICLE IX

Committees

SECTION 1. Executive Committee

There shall be an Executive Committee of the Board of Trustees consisting of not less than three nor more than seven members of the Board of Trustees, who shall at the meeting of the Trustees at which officers of the Corporation are elected for the ensuing year, be elected by the affirmative vote of a majority of the entire Board of Trustees, for the same term for which officers are elected, subject to removal at any time by the affirmative vote of two-thirds of the Trustees.

During the intervals between meetings of the Board of Trustees, the Executive Committee shall possess and may exercise all the powers of the Board of Trustees in such manner as they may deem best for the interests of the Corporation, in all cases in which specific directions have not been given by the Trustees.

Any action of the Executive Committee shall be subject to revision and alteration by the Board of Trustees, provided that no rights of any third parties shall be affected by any such revision or alteration.

The presence of a majority of the members of the Executive Committee shall be necessary to constitute a quorum, and no action shall be taken except upon the affirmative vote of a majority of the Committee.

If a vacancy occurs in the Executive Committee, the same may be filled for the unexpired portion of the term by election by the Board of Trustees.

SECTION 2. Investment Committee

The Board of Trustees shall at the meeting of the Trustees, at which officers of the Corporation are elected for the ensuing year, elect an Investment Committee, consisting of not less than three nor more than seven members of the Board of Trustees for the same term for which officers are elected, subject to removal at any time by the affirmative vote of two-thirds of the Trustees, which Committee shall have charge of investing the funds of the Corporation which are available for investment, and from time to time changing such investments.

The Investment Committee shall make a report of all investments at the regular annual meeting of the Board of Trustees and at such other times as the Trustees may request. In case of a vacancy in the Investment Committee the same may be filled for the unexpired portion of the term by appointment by the Executive Committee of some member of the Board of Trustees.

SECTION 3. Audit Committee

The Board of Trustees shall at the meeting of the Trustees, at which officers are elected for the ensuing year, elect an Audit Committee, consisting of not less than three nor more than six members of the Board of Trustees for the same term for which officers are elected, subject to removal at any time by the affirmative vote of two-thirds of the Trustees. No salaried officer of the Institute shall serve as a member of the Audit Committee.

The Audit Committee shall determine on a regular basis that the Corporation's financial statements are reliable and are in accordance with generally accepted accounting principles, and to establish and monitor adequate financial controls and procedures; and shall evaluate both internal and independent audits performed, and report thereon to the Board of Trustees.

SECTION 4. Other Committees

From time to time the Board of Trustees may appoint any other committee or committees for any purpose or purposes, which committees shall have such powers as shall be specified in the resolution of appointment.

ARTICLE X

MEETING OF MEMBERS AND OF TRUSTEES

SECTION 1. Annual Meeting of Members of Corporation

The annual meeting of the members of the Corporation shall be held during the month of April in each year at its principal office, 820 North LaSalle Drive, Chicago, unless by action taken at the previous meeting of the members, or by consent of a majority of its members, some other time or place shall be designated. Notice stating the time and place fixed for said meeting shall be mailed to all members not less than ten (10) nor more than forty-five (45) days prior to the date of such meeting. . . .

ARTICLE XI

Power of Trustees to Borrow Money and Pledge Corporate Property Therefor

The Board of Trustees may from time to time authorize and direct designated officers of the Corporation to borrow money for and on behalf of the Corporation for its uses and purposes, in such amounts and on such terms as the Board of Trustees shall determine, and if required, pledge therefore personal or real property of the Corporation.

ARTICLE XII

Auditor

The Board of Trustees shall at its annual meeting, or may at any regular meeting, appoint a certified accountant, or firm of accountants, to audit the books of account of the Corporation, and to report concerning the same to the Board of Trustees.

ARTICLE XII

Corporate Seal

The Corporate Seal shall have inscribed thereon the names of the Corporation and the words, "SEAL, FOUNDED 1887, ILLINOIS," as per impression on this page.

ARTICLE XIV

Amendment of Bylaws

These bylaws, or any of them, may be modified, altered, amended, or repealed, or new bylaws adopted by the Board of Trustees at any regular or special meeting of the Board, by the affirmative vote of two-thirds of the Trustees then in office; provided that notice of the Board's intention to modify, alter, amend, or repeal the bylaws, or any of them, or to adopt new bylaws, shall have been mailed or delivered to each of the trustees at his last known place of residence by certified, return receipt mail at least one week prior to the meeting, but such notice may be waived by any Trustee.

ARTICLE XV

CHANGE OR AMENDMENT OF ARTICLES
OF INCORPORATION

The Articles of Incorporation of this Corporation may be changed or amended in the following manner:

The Board of Trustees shall adopt a resolution setting forth the proposed amendment and directing that it be submitted to a vote at a meeting of members having voting rights, which may be either an annual or a special meeting. Written or printed notice setting forth the proposed amendment or a summary of the changes to be effected thereby shall be given to each member entitled to vote at such meeting within the time and in the manner provided in The Illinois Not for Profit Act (chp. 32 I.R.S.) for the giving of notice of meetings of members. The proposed amendment shall be adopted upon receiving at least two-thirds of the votes entitled to be cast by members present or represented by proxy at such meeting.

Any number of amendments may be submitted and voted upon at any one meeting.

In the event of any change in the Articles of Incorporation of this Corporation, certificates thereof shall be filed in the office of the Secretary of State of the State of Illinois, and filed for record in the office of the Recorder of Deeds of Cook County, Illinois, as required by law.

Appendix B

The Board of Trustees

Appendix C

Significant Dates and Events

1837 — D. L. Moody is born on February 5.

1855 — D. L. Moody is converted on April 21.

1856 — D. L. Moody settles in Chicago.

1860 — D. L. Moody decides to devote his efforts entirely to Christian work.

1862 — D. L. Moody marries Emma C. Revell on August 28.

1864 — D. L. Moody opens his Illinois Street Church.

1864 — D. L. Moody becomes president of the Chicago YMCA.

1873 — D. L. Moody encourages Miss Emma Dryer to start a school for women.
— The Chicago Bible Work is organized.

1879 — D. L. Moody founds the Northfield Seminary, now called the Northfied School for Girls.

1880 — D. L. Moody starts the Northfield Conferences.

1881 — D. L. Moody founds the Northfield School for Boys.

1883 — Emma Dryer organizes the first May Institute.

1885 — First formal meeting with D. L. Moody in Farwell Hall to discuss city evangelism (in January).

1886 — Second formal meeting in Farwell Hall. D. L. Moody delivers his famous address encouraging the key evangelicals of the city to start a school to train "gap-men" (in January).

1887 — The Chicago Evangelization Society is organized on February 5 (the charter is dated February 12).

1889 — Formal opening of the Bible Institute, September 26.
— R. A. Torrey becomes superintendent of the Bible Institute and plans the first regular curriculum.

1889-1890 — Construction of three-story 153 Building; dedicated January 16, 1890.

1893 — Music Course organized.

1894 — The Bible Institute Colportage Association begins.

1895 — First formal catalog appears describing the program at the Institute.

1897 — Bible Institute extension ministry begins (became an official department of the Institute in 1906).

1899 — D. L. Moody dies on December 22.

1900 — A. P. Fitt becomes full-time secretary for the Institute.

— Name of the school is officially changed to Moody Bible Institute on March 21.

— The Institute begins publishing a monthly magazine, known originally as the *Institute Tie*.

1901 — February 5 set aside as Founder's Day.

— Henry Parsons Crowell elected to the board of trustees on April 24.

— Moody Correspondence School organized.

1903 — Moody Evening School begins.

1904 — James M. Gray becomes dean (the top administrator) at Moody Bible Institute, and H. P. Crowell becomes president of the board.

1911 — Dedication of first women's dormitory at 830 North LaSalle Street; now called Smith Hall.

1912 — Formal Missionary Course organized.

1914 — Sunday School Course organized.

1921 — Moody Chorale organized (called the Auditorium Choir until 1946).

1922 — Formal Pastors Course organized.

1923 — Jewish Missions Course organized (called Jewish Studies in 1967).

1924 — Religious Education Course organized (called the Christian Education Course in 1928).

1925 — James M. Gray officially becomes president of the Institute, although his deanship was considered the top position since 1904.

— General Course organized.

1926 — First Institute radio broadcasts over WMBI on July 28.

— Radio School of the Bible begins.

1927 — Missionary Medical Course organized.

1930 — Christian Education-Music Course organized.

1934 — Will H. Houghton becomes president on November 1.

1939 — New twelve-story Administration Building dedicated; renamed Crowell Hall on February 5, 1945.

— Dedicated the basement section of Torrey-Gray Auditorium.

1941 — Moody Press and Moody Literature Mission begin.

1943 — First Institute radio broadcast over FM.

1945 — Moody Institute of Science begins.

1948 — William Culbertson becomes president on February 4.

1949 — Missionary Technical Course begins.

1951 — Houghton Hall, new women's dormitory, dedicated on October 31.

1955 — Torrey-Gray Auditorium dedicated on February 1.

— Doane Memorial Music Building dedicated on February 1.

1962 — Fitzwater Hall, four-story academic building, dedicated on February 6.

1966 — Moody Bible Institute introduces a B.A. degree program.

1968-1969 — Culbertson Hall men's dormitory constructed.

1973 — National Pastor's Conference begins.

1978 — Moody Institute of Science film shown in Iron Curtain countries.

1982 — Moody Broadcasting Network begins twenty-four hour a day broadcast service.

1985 — Moody Graduate School opens.

1986 — MBI introduces four-year B.A. degree program.

Index